AGILE PROJECT DELIVERY

AGILE PROJECT DELIVERY

A Practical Approach for Corporate Environments Beyond Software Development

Aaron A. Blair

CANADIAN SCHOLARS

Toronto | Vancouver

Agile Project Delivery: A Practical Approach for Corporate Environments Beyond
  Software Development
Aaron A. Blair

First published in 2020 by
Canadian Scholars, an imprint of CSP Books Inc.
425 Adelaide Street West, Suite 200
Toronto, Ontario
M5V 3C1

www.canadianscholars.ca

Copyright © 2020 Aaron A. Blair and Canadian Scholars.

All rights reserved. No part of this publication may be reproduced, stored in a retrieval system, or transmitted, in any form or by any means, without the prior written permission of Canadian Scholars, under licence or terms from the appropriate reproduction rights organization, or as expressly permitted by law.

Every reasonable effort has been made to identify copyright holders. Canadian Scholars would be pleased to have any errors or omissions brought to its attention.

Library and Archives Canada Cataloguing in Publication

Title: Agile project delivery : a practical approach for corporate environments beyond software
  development / Aaron A. Blair.
Names: Blair, Aaron A., 1974- author.
Description: Includes bibliographical references.
Identifiers: Canadiana (print) 2020033896X | Canadiana (ebook) 20200339001 | ISBN
  9781773382142 (softcover) | ISBN 9781773382159 (PDF) | ISBN 9781773382166 (EPUB)
Subjects: LCSH: Agile project management. | LCSH: Success in business.
Classification: LCC HD69.P75 B53 2020 | DDC 658.4/06—dc23

Cover design by Rafael Chimicatti
Page layout by S4Carlisle Publishing Services
Screenshots of Jira, copyright to Atlassian, are reproduced with permission.

20 21 22 23 24   5 4 3 2 1

Printed and bound in Ontario, Canada

Canadä

For: Sarah, Nathan, and Miranda

Special thanks to my fellow Conestoga faculty and leadership for their insights, encouragement, and support and Atlassian for allowing their software to be featured in this text.

Special acknowledgement to June and Bob for their patience and feedback and whose support over the years have helped shape my writing and resilience.

Contents

Lists of Figures and Tables   xiii

Preface   xvii

About This Book   xix

PART I • WHAT IS AGILE?   1

Chapter 1 • Agile's Lean Foundations   3
    Chapter Overview   3
    What Is a Project?   3
    Lean Overview   4
    A Summary of the History of Agile   7
    The Birth of the Agile Manifesto   9
    The Similar Beginnings of Agile and the Project Management Institute   11
    When Is Agile Used?   13
    Summary   15
    Key Terms   15
    Discussion Questions   16
    Notes   16

Chapter 2 • Agile Overview   17
    Chapter Overview   17
    Agile Scrum Framework: Roles, Events, and Artifacts   17
    Agile = Iterative   18
    The Scrum Project Team   29
    Scrum Phases Overview   30
    Summary   39
    Key Terms   39
    Discussion Questions   41
    Notes   41

PART II • AGILE PROJECT INITIATION   43

Chapter 3 • Understanding Corporate Environments   45
    Chapter Overview   45
    The Composition of Corporations   45
    Agile Tools: Introduction   54
    Summary   62
    Key Terms   63
    Discussion Questions   64
    Notes   64

Chapter 4 • Capturing and Prioritizing User Stories through the Value Stream   65
    Chapter Overview   65
    What Is Value Stream Mapping?   65
    Creating Value Streams   67
    Combining Value Stream Mapping with Agile Principles   68
    User Stories   70
    User Stories Supporting Procurement Processes   75
    Agile Tools: User Stories   77
    Summary   89
    Key Terms   90
    Discussion Questions   91
    Notes   91

PART III • AGILE PROJECT PLANNING   93

Chapter 5 • Building the Agile Team   95
    Chapter Overview   95
    Agile at Scale   95
    Matrix-Managed versus Dedicated Teams   97
    Distributed versus Co-Located Teams   100
    Scrum Master as a Servant Leader   104
    Development Team Composition   105
    The Vendor Product Owner   106
    Agile Tools: Adding Users   106

Summary   112
Key Terms   113
Discussion Questions   114
Notes   114

Chapter 6 • User Story Estimation   117
Chapter Overview   117
Estimating Challenges   117
The Timeboxing Approach to Planning   118
Ideal Time versus Story Points   120
Planning Poker   121
Affinity Estimation   122
Large User Stories   124
Agile Contracting   125
Creating an Agile Budget   125
Agile Tools: Assigning Story Points to User Stories   127
Summary   134
Key Terms   135
Discussion Questions   136
Notes   137

Chapter 7 • Sprint Planning   139
Chapter Overview   139
The Planning Onion   139
Planning the Sprint   143
The Definition of Done   144
Product Backlog versus Sprint Backlog   145
Conducting the Sprint Planning Meeting   145
Agile Tools: Creating the Sprint Backlog   147
Summary   155
Key Terms   156
Discussion Questions   156
Notes   157

PART IV • EXECUTING AGILE PROJECTS   159

Chapter 8 • Scrum   161
    Chapter Overview   161
    Using Scrum in Agile   161
    The Self-Organizing Team   163
    Executing Agile Projects and Communication   167
    Scrum of Scrums   169
    Building Skilled Generalists in Virtual Teams   170
    Continuous Integration   170
    Integration Testing   171
    Use of Committees in Matrix-Managed Environments   172
    Agile Tools: Launching a Sprint and Modifying Tasks/Stories   174
    Summary   179
    Key Terms   180
    Discussion Questions   181
    Notes   181

Chapter 9 • Information Radiators   183
    Chapter Overview   183
    The Three Pillars of Scrum   183
    Kanban Board and Managing Work in Progress   185
    Burndown Charts and Burnup Charts   186
    Earned Value Management   192
    Niko-Niko Chart or Calendar   195
    Using Information Radiators to Detect Team Member Stress and
        Potential Burnout   197
    Agile Tools: Information Radiators   199
    Summary   200
    Key Terms   201
    Discussion Questions   202
    Notes   202

PART V • CLOSING THE SPRINT AND PREPARING FOR RELEASE   205

Chapter 10 • Reviewing Work   207
    Chapter Overview   207
    The Sprint Review   207
    Preparing for the Sprint Review   211
    The Sprint Review Meeting   211
    Agile Tools: Completing the Sprint   214
    Summary   216
    Key Terms   216
    Discussion Questions   217
    Notes   217

Chapter 11 • Closing the Sprint   219
    Chapter Overview   219
    The Sprint Retrospective and Incremental Improvement   219
    The Sprint Retrospective Meeting   222
    Risk Management   226
    Grooming the Backlog   229
    Agile Tools: Adding New Issue Types to the Backlog   229
    Summary   232
    Key Terms   233
    Discussion Questions   233
    Notes   234

Chapter 12 • Preparing for Release   235
    Chapter Overview   235
    The Controlled Environment   235
    The Service Management Framework   236
    Production Support   243
    Summary   247
    Key Terms   248
    Discussion Questions   249
    Notes   249

Appendix • A Summary of Tools and Techniques   251
   Agile Project Charter Template   251
   Stakeholder Log Template   251
   Value Stream Map Template   252
   Enterprise User Story Template   253
   Recommended Field Mappings for User Story Template   254
   Sample Agile Project Budget   254
   Definition of Done Checklist   255
   Terms of Reference Template   255
   Agile Earned Value Concepts and Formulae   256
   Sprint Retrospective Pre-Meeting Template   256
   User Story Scoring Based on Uncertainty and Dependency   256
   Common Service Management Deliverables for
      Release to Production   257
   Summary of Scrum Events and Activities   257

Glossary of Terms   259

Lists of Figures and Tables

FIGURES

Figure 1.1 • Kanban Board   5
Figure 1.2 • Mass-Production Supply Chain Overview   7
Figure 1.3 • Direct-Sales Model   8
Figure 1.4 • Agile and Its Family of Methodologies   10
Figure 1.5 • Agile/Lean Venn Diagram   12
Figure 1.6 • Agile Evolution Timeline   13
Figure 1.7 • Traditional Project Management Cycle   14
Figure 1.8 • Adaptive Project Approach   14
Figure 2.1 • Agile Values and Principles' Contribution to Roles, Events, and Artifacts   18
Figure 2.2 • Plan-Do-Check-Act Cycle   19
Figure 2.3 • Series of PDCA Iterations   19
Figure 2.4 • Iterative Sprint Cycles   20
Figure 2.5 • Nine- to Fourteen-Month Waterfall Project   21
Figure 2.6 • Agile Project Sequential Sprints   22
Figure 2.7 • Agile/Kanban Consistent Use of Resources and Flow of Work   23
Figure 2.8 • SDLC Phases and Activities   25
Figure 2.9 • SDLC Expansion in Phases Impacting Later Activities   25
Figure 2.10 • Initiation Phase Expanded   27
Figure 2.11 • Planning Phase Expanded   28
Figure 2.12 • Design Phase with Issues Found   28
Figure 2.13 • Scrum Phases Overview   30
Figure 2.14 • A Simplified View of a Kanban versus a Scrum Board   33
Figure 2.15 • Sprint Planning Cycle   34
Figure 3.1 • Hierarchical Organization   46
Figure 3.2 • Purchasing Unit Functions   47
Figure 3.3 • Product Owner Equivalents in Corporate Settings from the Chief Financial Officer to Staff Issuing Purchase Orders   48
Figure 4.1 • Common Value Stream Icons   66
Figure 4.2 • Value Stream Map Template   67
Figure 4.3 • Value Stream Example   68
Figure 4.4 • MoSCoW Requirements Distribution   70

Figure 4.5 • User Story Card   71
Figure 4.6 • Kano Model   74
Figure 4.7 • Enterprise User Story Template   76
Figure 5.1 • Matrix Management   98
Figure 5.2 • Matrix-Managed Resources Assigned to a Project   98
Figure 5.3 • Actual versus Estimated Resource Availability   99
Figure 5.4 • Distributed Agile Team   103
Figure 6.1 • Decreasing Uncertainty as a Project Progresses   118
Figure 6.2 • Cone of Uncertainty and Its Impact on Estimation Variability   119
Figure 6.3 • Timeboxing Planning Approach   119
Figure 6.4 • Planning Poker Example   122
Figure 6.5 • T-Shirt Sizing Example   123
Figure 6.6 • T-Shirt Sizing with Points   123
Figure 7.1 • The Planning Onion   140
Figure 7.2 • Sample of a Large Corporation's Project Portfolio   142
Figure 7.3 • Sprint Planning Meeting   146
Figure 8.1 • Types of Communication and Their Effectiveness   167
Figure 8.2 • Crystal Methods Based on Scale   168
Figure 8.3 • Testing Pyramid   171
Figure 8.4 • Integration Testing Issue Identification and Assignment Flow   172
Figure 9.1 • The Three Pillars of Scrum   184
Figure 9.2 • Kanban Board and Scrum Board   185
Figure 9.3 • Example of Five Whys   186
Figure 9.4 • Burndown Chart   187
Figure 9.5 • Burnup Chart   187
Figure 9.6 • Burnup Chart with Added Scope   187
Figure 9.7 • Ideal Engagement Burndown Chart   188
Figure 9.8 • Conforming Burndown Chart   189
Figure 9.9 • Underestimated Burndown Chart   189
Figure 9.10 • Overestimated Burndown Chart   190
Figure 9.11 • No Engagement Burndown Chart   190
Figure 9.12 • Cancelled Sprint   191
Figure 9.13 • Parking Lot Chart   192
Figure 9.14 • The Triple Constraint or Iron Triangle of Project Management   194
Figure 9.15 • Sample Niko-Niko Chart   195

Figure 9.16 • Waterfall versus Agile Work Peak Cycles   198
Figure 10.1 • Layered Feedback Example   208
Figure 10.2 • Mid-Course Corrections and the Zone of Success   212
Figure 11.1 • Learning Curve   220
Figure 11.2 • Incremental Improvement Impact to the Learning Curve   221
Figure 11.3 • Radical Change Impact to Efficiency   221
Figure 12.1 • ITIL Service Value System Cycle   236
Figure 12.2 • Agile, Lean, ITIL Venn Diagram   237
Figure 12.3 • ITIL Four-Dimensional Model   238
Figure 12.4 • IT Service Management Foundational Framework   239
Figure 12.5 • Service Management Processes Aligned to Service Questions   241
Figure 12.6 • Defect Share of Incidents   244
Figure 12.7 • Issue Management Cycle   244
Figure 12.8 • DevOps Cycle   247

TABLES

Table 3.1 • Agile Project Charter Template   49
Table 3.2 • Stakeholder Log Template   52
Table 4.1 • Recommended Field Mappings for User Story Template   89
Table 5.1 • Pre-Defined Business Resource Schedule   101
Table 6.1 • User Story Log   123
Table 6.2 • Sample Agile Project Budget   126
Table 7.1 • Definition of Done Checklist   144
Table 8.1 • Sample Terms of Reference   173
Table 11.1 • Sprint Retrospective Pre-Meeting Template   222
Table 11.2 • User Story Scoring Based on Uncertainty and Dependency   228
Table 12.1 • ITIL Service Management Processes Based on Categories   241
Table 12.2 • Common Service Management Deliverables for Release to Production   242
Table 12.3 • Summary of Scrum Events and Activities   243

Preface

Agile enables teams to collaborate and complete work. Agile also has great branding. After all, if you aren't agile, what are you? Agile's iterative nature was developed to improve software development. The approach has been largely successful.

As with any success story, other industries look to emulate. However, Agile hasn't always been easily implemented in organizations that do not have software development as a core competency. Healthcare, finance, and manufacturing all may use software, but they are sectors that don't typically create software; they purchase it.

Agile isn't one thing. It is not a singular approach to a particular business problem. Rather, Agile is a collection of methodologies and frameworks. However, the important thing to remember about Agile methods and frameworks is that they *are* methodologies. Regardless of which Agile methodology or framework is used, they all have their own roles, tools, and approaches to maximize success. Because Agile emerged to address a specific business challenge, Agile methodologies and frameworks on their own will not be able to be applied in the exact same manner to solve all business challenges. To be successful, adaptation to fit a specific business context is often necessary.

This text will focus on how different Agile approaches can be adapted for non-software development corporations by leveraging Lean concepts.

About This Book

This book is intended for project management students and professionals that are looking to learn about Agile methodologies. The text is designed to provide practical approaches to utilize Agile techniques in non-software development corporations that range in size and complexity. This text is not intended to inform readers how to change the culture of their organization into an Agile culture. Nor is this text intended to focus on project selection and portfolio management. Simply, this text provides readers with the necessary foundational Agile knowledge necessary to navigate a corporate environment and lead a team of people to achieve a common goal.

Bolded text are key terms that can be referenced at the end of each chapter as well as in a glossary of terms. Templates that appear throughout the text are summarized in the text appendix for quick reference.

PART I

WHAT IS AGILE?

In part I of this text, we introduce the Agile and explore Lean concepts. Part I provides an overview of Lean. Lean was a shift in supply chain approaches that utilized a pull method rather than the popularized push method of mass production. Pull methods enabled organizations to reduce waste and improve efficiency. Agile methodology reflects Lean thinking and moves away from predictive project management to adaptive project management. This shift in approach mirrors how Lean revolutionized the automotive sector.

In addition, part I provides an overview of Agile, its values, principles, roles, events, and artifacts. By the end of part I, readers will have an understanding of Agile, its evolution from Lean thinking, and the principles and values that guide how people interact and deliver results using Agile frameworks and methodologies.

1 Agile's Lean Foundations

CHAPTER OVERVIEW

In this chapter we review the history of Agile, which takes us back more than 60 years to the North American auto sector and its mass production assembly lines. This is where a Japanese engineer developed Lean for the Toyota Motor Corporation.

The goal of this chapter is for readers to become familiar with the history of Lean, its principles, and how it was applied to mass-production organizations. Readers will also learn how the Agile Manifesto was created, what its values and principles are, as well as the shared history the Agile Alliance has with the Project Management Institute.

By the end of the chapter, readers should be able to identify and define key terms associated with Lean and how they are applied to Agile and manufacturing organizations.

WHAT IS A PROJECT?

Because this text focuses on using Agile to complete project work, it is important to ensure readers have some context about projects in general. Projects refer to temporary work that has a beginning and an end. Projects are created to produce a unique product or service. Because the goal of projects is to produce a unique outcome, all projects inherently have risk. People are needed to complete project work and often represent the majority of a project cost and composition. Often, people who work on projects are assigned temporarily. They may be hired to work specifically on a project or taken from an operational role to fulfill a project resource need.

Projects have a certain value that they fulfill. They are investments by organizations. As a result, projects are constrained by time and budget to produce their outcome. For all projects, there may come a point where the cost outweighs the value or the project output is not timely enough for the organization to reap the full benefits.

Agile is one approach to organizing and completing project work. This text will focus on various Agile framework techniques to complete project work and will contrast it with other project approaches. Project concepts will be elaborated on throughout the text.

LEAN OVERVIEW

Before discussing using Agile approaches to complete project work, we must first review **Lean**. Lean is a **continuous improvement** framework that has been implemented globally across numerous sectors. Continuous improvement refers to an organization's ongoing effort to improve products, services, and/or processes. Continuous improvement can refer to incremental improvement over time as well as breakthrough improvement all at once. Continuous improvement seeks to improve efficiency and save organizational time and cost by eliminating waste and wasteful activities.

Lean was developed by Taiichi Ohno for Toyota in the 1950s. Lean was developed in response to Japan's unique consumer demands compared to those of the United States. Instead of attempting to emulate the mass-production processes of Henry Ford, Ohno developed Lean to be focused on customer value and eliminating waste by minimizing excess inventory.[1]

Mass production relies on a push methodology. The producer projects the amount of product they can sell and then produces it for sale to the market. To create consumer awareness, marketing and advertising budgets are used to reach and entice potential consumers.

In contrast to mass production, Lean uses a pull approach: build based on customer demand and build what the customer has requested, and nothing more.

Case Study 1.1 • Dell's Built-to-Order Model[2]

The pull method of production should be familiar to many computer consumers. To illustrate, Dell Technologies enables consumers to customize their computer via its e-commerce website. The computer is then built to the customer's specification and shipped within days. Dell maintains partial inventory but does not pre-build all its devices and ship or push its products to retail outlets for sale. Dell relies on the Lean pull methodology and builds based on a customer request.

A number of principles evolved to support Ohno's pull methodology:

- Maintain an unrelenting focus on providing customer value.
- Adopt a philosophy of continuous incremental improvement.
- Provide exactly what is needed at the right time, based on customer demand.
- Keep things moving—in a value-added and effective manner.
- Use techniques for reducing variation and eliminating waste.
- Value and respect people.
- Take the long-term view.[3]

As we progress through this text, we will revisit Lean principles and how they have influenced Agile methodologies.

Principles on their own do not enable an organization such as Toyota to produce vehicles. Practices are required to enable the work to be performed. To support the principle of keeping things moving, Ohno developed a practice known as **Kanban**. *Kanban* is a Japanese word for "card you can see." A Kanban board is a visual management tool that helps improve process flow and continuous improvement. Kanban boards are used to represent a process. People who support the process are represented on the Kanban board, where any activity or work item they perform can be made visible. For complex supply chains, this can result in a large and complex map that identifies a significant number of people and work items

	To-Do	In-Progress	Complete
Resource/Area	Note	Note	Note
Resource/Area	Note		Note
Resource/Area	Note		

Figure 1.1 • Kanban Board

that traverse numerous work stations. Agile frameworks that utilize Kanban often have a much more simplified view of a Kanban board.

The goal of the Kanban board is to minimize in-progress items. Visual management techniques are important in Lean methodologies. Both Kanban and visual management have significant influence on Agile, which will be covered at greater length throughout the text.

The practice of Kanban helps support another important Lean concept, which is the elimination of *muda*, a Japanese word for waste. Waste takes many forms, some more obvious than others. Excess inventory is an obvious form of waste. Defects that take additional time to fix or result in disposal of raw materials are also obvious forms of waste. But some forms of waste are less obvious. In the mass-production model, the process of shipping to retail outlets, return of unsold inventory, marketing, and advertising could be considered waste. This is because they do not directly contribute to customer value.

Case Study 1.2 • Dell's Direct-Sales Model[4]

To contrast the pull methodology with the push method of mass production, we return to Dell and its use of a direct-sales model. As mentioned previously, the company leverages a build-on-demand production approach through its e-commerce presence. As a result, Dell does not have to maintain retail outlets and does not have to ship inventory to be housed in these outlets. It only requires production facilities that ship directly to customers who have purchased its product. In addition, Dell does not have to reduce its profit margins through offering sales and customer incentives to reduce inventory because the company does not build unless a customer has ordered. Therefore, the only inventory Dell maintains are the parts necessary to build computers, not computers themselves.

However, it is also important to consider the waste Dell has eliminated for its customers. Customers do not need to travel to a store, compare configurations, or wait for sales. Customers can shop from the convenience of their home and, as a result, save travel time and costs. Because Dell has eliminated financial waste associated with mass production, it can also offer its customers competitive pricing.

Lean principles are at the heart of Dell's business model: achieve customer value through the elimination of waste and provide exactly what the customer wants, when the customer wants it, and nothing more.

Figures 1.2 and 1.3 illustrate the flow of product from a mass-production organization versus a direct-sales organization. Note where the customer is in each figure. In addition, note the different quantity of nodes and the potential differences in operating expenses as a result.

Lean has been utilized for more than 50 years and is implemented globally within some of the largest firms. Agile is often associated with a smaller scale. As this text is focused on the application of Agile in corporate settings, it will be necessary to draw on Lean concepts since many are at the core of the Agile frameworks.

A SUMMARY OF THE HISTORY OF AGILE

It is important to clarify that Agile is not a single methodology. Agile emerged in 2001 as a result of a collection of software developers recognizing an opportunity to deliver software projects more effectively. The group developed the "Manifesto

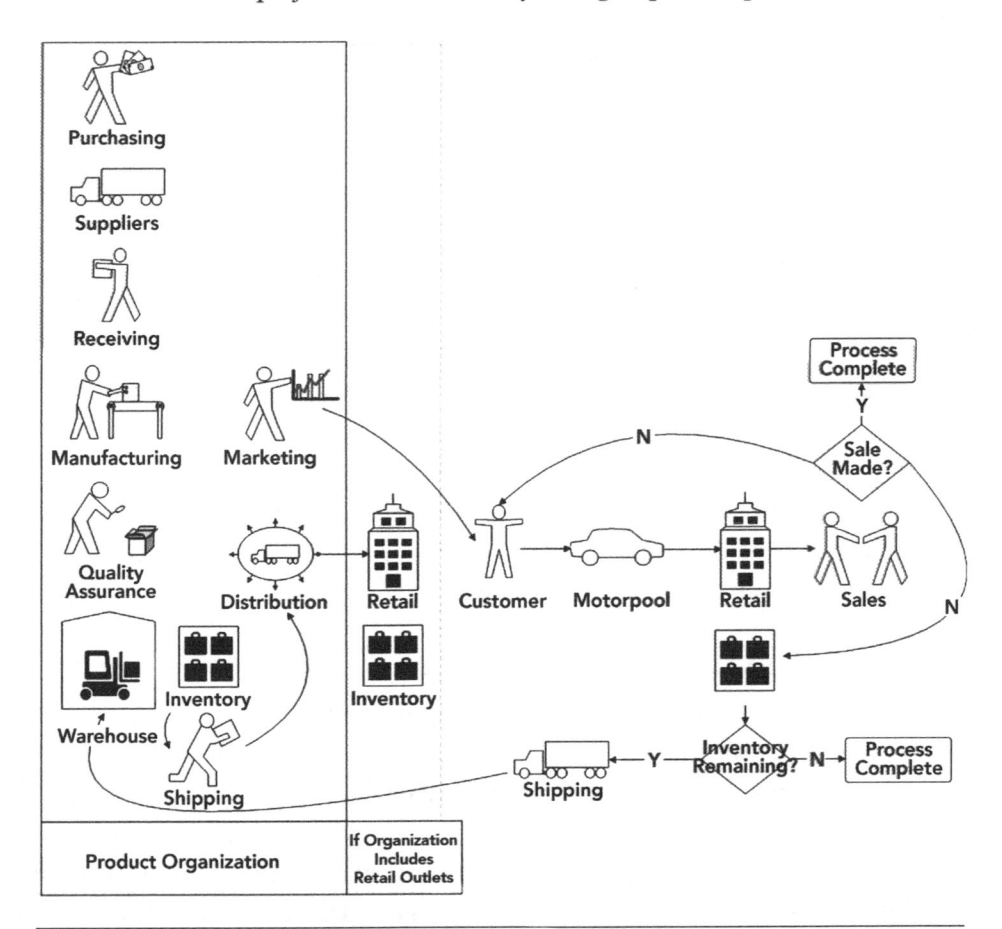

Figure 1.2 • Mass-Production Supply Chain Overview

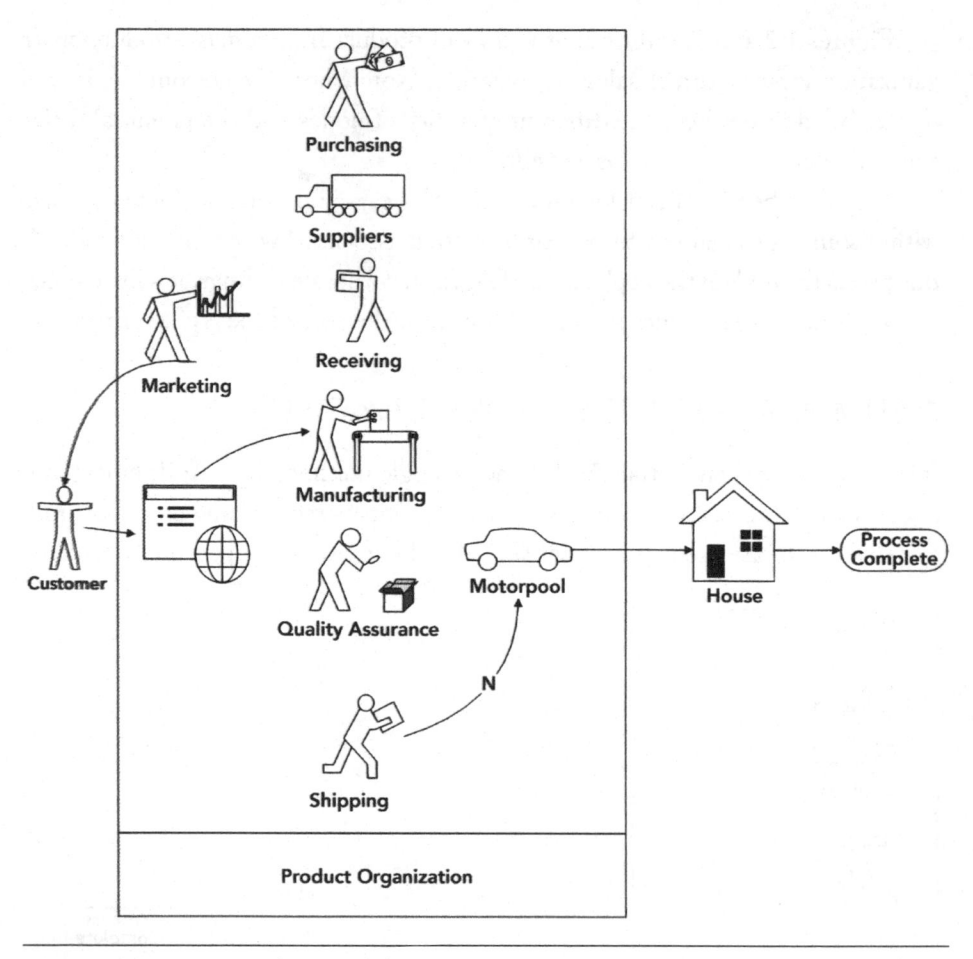

Figure 1.3 • Direct-Sales Model

for Agile Software Development," or the **Agile Manifesto**, which can be accessed freely from agilemanifesto.org. Their shared goal was to improve how software is developed, based on the following four values:

- *Individuals and interactions* over processes and tools
- *Working software* over comprehensive documentation
- *Customer collaboration* over contract negotiation
- *Responding to change* over following a plan[5]

Note: Although the Agile Manifesto places importance on the italicized items, it recognizes that the items following the italicized text are important and necessary. This means that documentation, processes and tools, negotiations, and plans are still valued by Agile. However, the italicized text should drive the work.

THE BIRTH OF THE AGILE MANIFESTO

Case Study 1.3 • Building Consensus for Consistency[6]

One weekend in February 2001, a group of 17 software developers gathered at a Utah ski resort to discuss their ever-changing and evolving industry. The software development industry was growing exponentially as technology became more accessible to the consumer. Telecom providers were provisioning high-speed internet capability to homes and businesses. This convergence of technology, capability, and access saw numerous industries looking to develop products through software development. The result was a fragmented approach and inconsistent model of delivery.

Of the 17 developers, representatives from Extreme Programming, Scrum, Dynamic Systems Development Method, Adaptive Software Development, Crystal, Feature-Driven Development, and Pragmatic Programming, along with other experts, shared their challenges with the waterfall-based software development lifecycle.

The outcome of the gathering was the Agile Alliance, which produced the Agile Manifesto. What made the Agile Manifesto so powerful is that it was achieved through co-design. Common themes were found, and a shared goal of improvement enabled a diverse group of experts to find a unified voice that would grow along with their industry over the next decade.

The history of the Agile Alliance provides important context. Agile is not the product of a single person who devised a comprehensive approach to solve a business problem, like Taiichi Ohno. Rather it is a collection of methodologies. The Agile Alliance is the result of experts collaborating and co-designing a solution to a problem that was affecting both outcomes and productivity in their field. Figure 1.4 helps illustrate the family of processes associated with Agile. Throughout the text, different methodologies' contributions to Agile will be referenced.

The Agile Manifesto subscribes to 12 principles, which expand on the four values:[7]

1. Our highest priority is to satisfy the customer through early and continuous delivery of valuable software.
2. Welcome changing requirements, even late in development. Agile processes harness change for the customer's competitive advantage.

3. Deliver working software frequently, from a couple of weeks to a couple of months, with a preference to the shorter timescale.
4. Business people and developers must work together daily throughout the project.
5. Build projects around motivated individuals. Give them the environment and support they need, and trust them to get the job done.
6. The most efficient and effective method of conveying information to and within a development team is face-to-face conversation.
7. Working software is the primary measure of progress.
8. Agile processes promote sustainable development. The sponsors, developers, and users should be able to maintain a constant pace indefinitely.
9. Continuous attention to technical excellence and good design enhances agility.
10. Simplicity—the art of maximizing the amount of work not done—is essential.
11. The best architectures, requirements, and designs emerge from self-organizing teams.
12. At regular intervals, the team reflects on how to become more effective, then tunes and adjusts its behaviour accordingly.

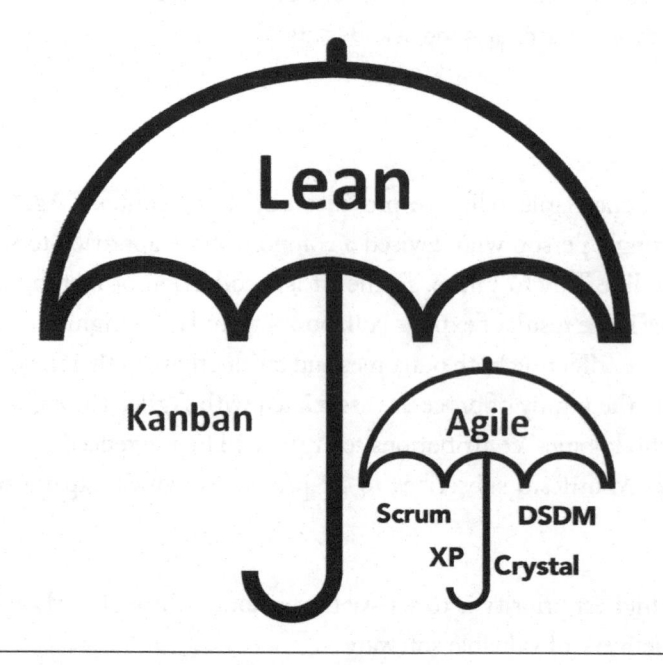

Figure 1.4 • Agile and Its Family of Methodologies

When looking at the Agile principles, it is easy to see where the Lean concepts overlap: both value the customer, people, and continuous improvement. Figure 1.5 overlays Lean and Agile principles using a Venn diagram.

The desire to achieve project consistency is not unique to Agile. Even though Agile and the **Project Management Institute**'s (**PMI**'s) waterfall approach to the **software development lifecycle (SDLC)** are often considered distinct and separate, they share a very similar history.

THE SIMILAR BEGINNINGS OF AGILE AND THE PROJECT MANAGEMENT INSTITUTE

> **Case Study 1.4 • The Dinner That Created an Institution**[8]
>
> PMI, often associated with waterfall project delivery models, shares a similar history with the Agile Alliance. In the 1960s, project management began to proliferate in industries such as aerospace, construction, defence, and manufacturing. A collection of experts met at the Georgia Institute of Technology over dinner to discuss the growth of their discipline and the need to ensure credibility through consistency. As a result of the gathering, Ned Engman, James Snyder, and Susan Gallagher founded PMI as a non-profit organization in 1969. PMI was incorporated in that same year.
>
> In 1975, PMI described its objectives as to "foster recognition of the need for professionalism in project management; provide a forum for the free exchange of project management problems, solutions and applications; coordinate industrial and academic research efforts; develop common terminology and techniques to improve communications; provide interface between users and suppliers of hardware and software systems; and to provide guidelines for instruction and career development in the field of project management."

Both the Agile Alliance and the Project Management Institute recognized a need to improve project consistency and delivery. The Agile Alliance emerged as software development grew as an industry, while PMI emerged as physical engineering industries grew.

The evolutions of project process improvement can be linked to evolutions of industries. Figure 1.6 illustrates how significant process improvements have

Agile

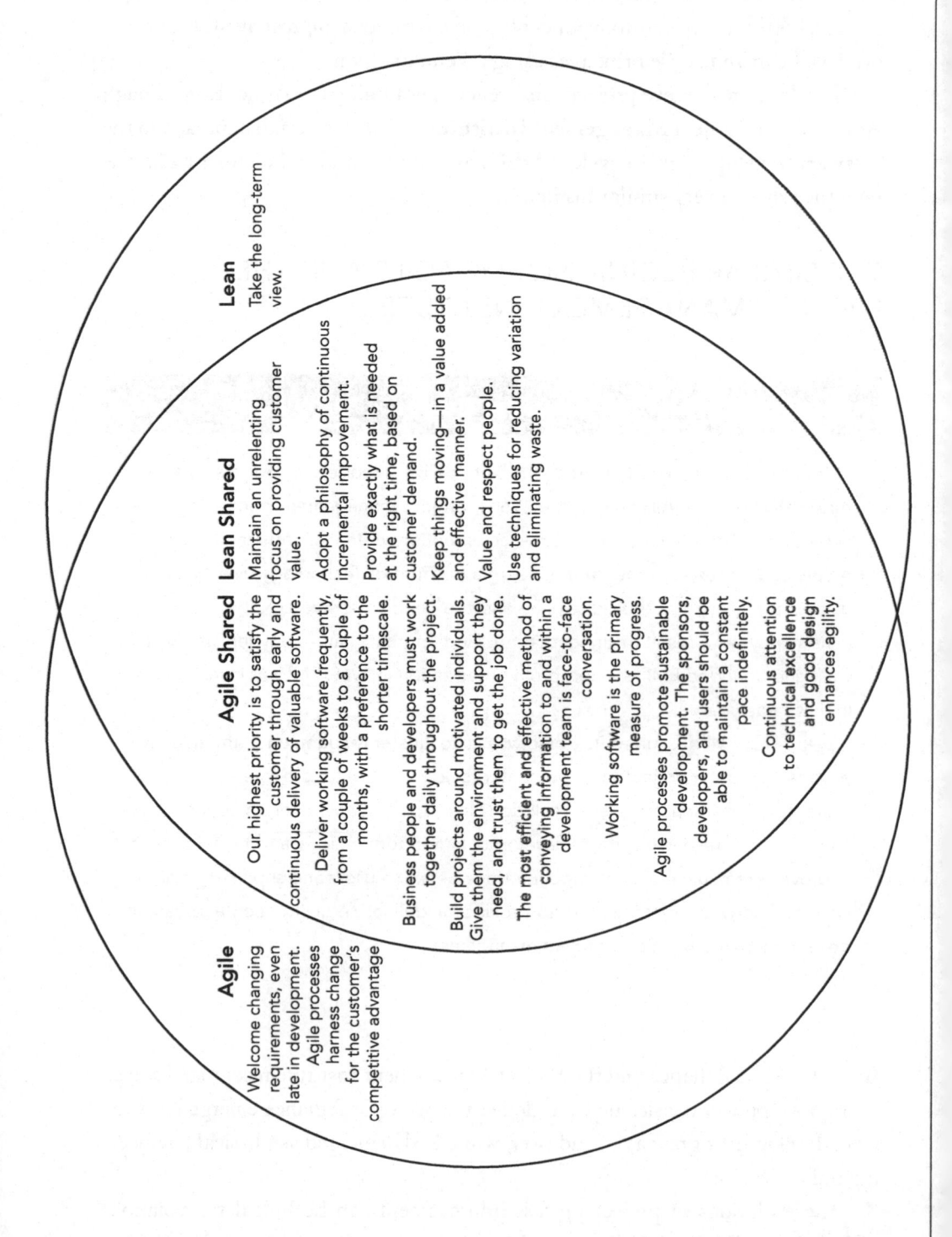

Welcome changing requirements, even late in development. Agile processes harness change for the customer's competitive advantage

Agile Shared

Our highest priority is to satisfy the customer through early and continuous delivery of valuable software.

Deliver working software frequently, from a couple of weeks to a couple of months, with a preference to the shorter timescale.

Business people and developers must work together daily throughout the project.

Build projects around motivated individuals. Give them the environment and support they need, and trust them to get the job done.

The most efficient and effective method of conveying information to and within a development team is face-to-face conversation.

Working software is the primary measure of progress.

Agile processes promote sustainable development. The sponsors, developers, and users should be able to maintain a constant pace indefinitely.

Continuous attention to technical excellence and good design enhances agility.

Lean Shared

Maintain an unrelenting focus on providing customer value.

Adopt a philosophy of continuous incremental improvement.

Provide exactly what is needed at the right time, based on customer demand.

Keep things moving—in a value added and effective manner.

Value and respect people.

Use techniques for reducing variation and eliminating waste.

Lean

Take the long-term view.

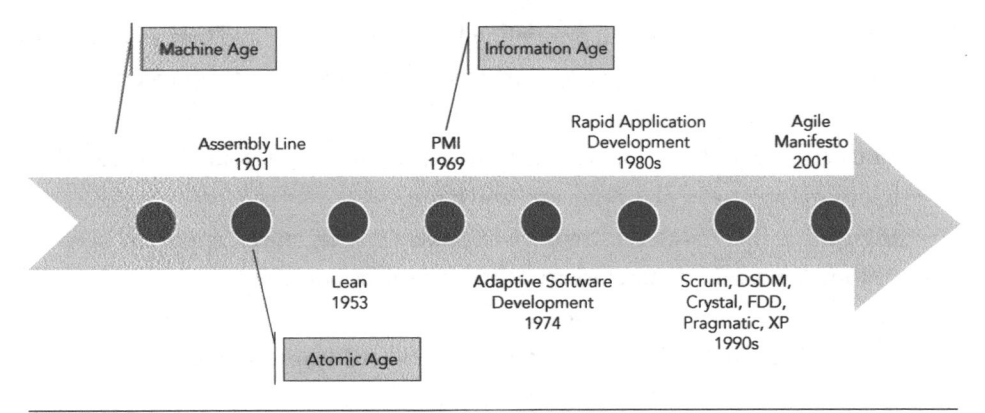

Figure 1.6 • Agile Evolution Timeline

accompanied eras that have seen significant changes to technology. Each era can be correlated to significant innovation:

- The machine age and the advent of the assembly line, telecommunications, and mass transportation
- The atomic age and the emergence of nuclear energy production and use of computer systems
- The information age and the emergence of the internet, software automation, and personal computing devices

The Agile Alliance and the Project Management Institute's desire for consistency reflects another Lean concept, the desire to eliminate *mura* or waste due to unevenness or variation. Both the PMI and the Agile Alliance saw that there was risk to their profession due to rapid growth and a lack of consistent approaches across industries.

WHEN IS AGILE USED?

Agile is an adaptive approach to project management. **Adaptive project management** refers to using iterations to incrementally progress toward a project outcome. It is best applied when requirements are unclear. Therefore, the need for prototyping and building upon experience is important. This will be explored at greater length in the next chapter. Waterfall project management is a predictive approach to project management. **Predictive project management** collects information, builds a plan based on known requirements and designs, and then aims to deliver

14　AGILE PROJECT DELIVERY

the project outcome based on a pre-defined scope, schedule, and budget created by the project team. Predictive project management works best for projects that are repeatable and well defined.

Both Agile and traditional project management follow a similar cycle. Both methodologies initiate, plan, execute, and close.

Figure 1.7 illustrates the traditional project management approach: a single progression from initiate to close to deliver a project outcome.

Agile follows the same progression; however, the cycles are completed in short intervals or iterations. This supports the continuous improvement philosophy of failing fast and adjusting based on learnings.

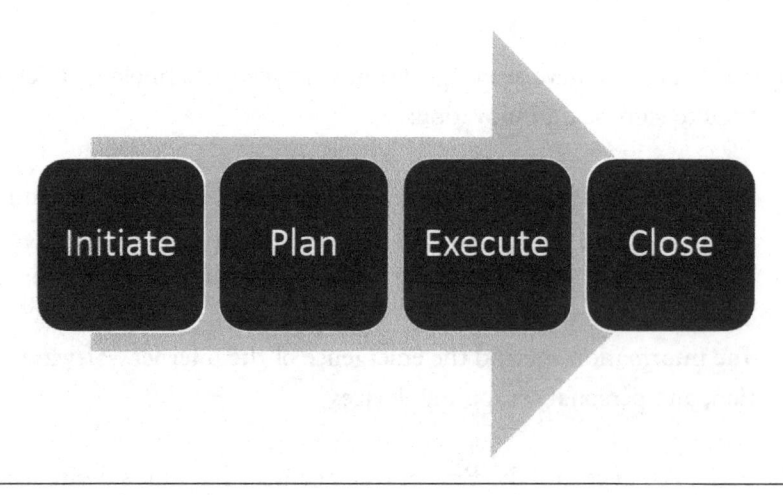

Figure 1.7 • Traditional Project Management Cycle

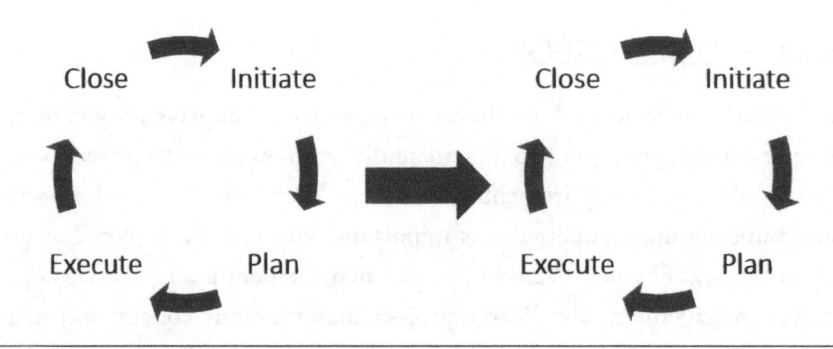

Figure 1.8 • Adaptive Project Approach

SUMMARY

- Taiichi Ohno developed the Lean continuous improvement framework to meet the needs of Toyota's consumer market.
- Unlike mass-production models, Lean is a customer-focused "pull model," which only builds what is needed, in order to minimize waste, or *muda*.
- The Agile methodology is based on the Lean continuous improvement framework.
- Agile and Lean share principles. When summarized, the methodologies' shared goal is to have a continuous flow of work that focuses on achieving value through the elimination of waste by empowering employees.
- The Agile methodology was created by a collection of developers who wanted to improve the consistency of software delivery projects.
- The Project Management Institute was created by a small group of subject-matter experts who wanted to improve the consistency of engineering projects.
- Waste due to unevenness or inconsistency is referred to as *mura* in the Lean framework.

KEY TERMS

adaptive project management: refers to using iterations to incrementally progress toward a project outcome

Agile Manifesto: a document created by 17 developers in 2001 that forms the basis of the Agile methodology values and principles

continuous improvement: an organization's ongoing effort to improve products, services, and/or processes. Continuous improvement can refer to incremental improvement over time as well as breakthrough improvement all at once.

Kanban: developed by Taiichi Ohno, *Kanban* is a Japanese term that means signal or "card you can see." Kanban is a visual management technique used to improve the flow of work and minimize work in progress.

Lean: a continuous improvement framework developed by Taiichi Ohno for the Toyota motor company

muda: a Japanese term for waste. This form of waste refers to activities that do not directly contribute to customer value.

mura: a Japanese term for waste. This form of waste refers to unevenness or inconsistency in outcome or result.

PMI: an acronym for the Project Management Institute

predictive project management: the process of collecting information and building a plan, budget, and schedule based on known requirements and designs

Project Management Institute: a non-profit organization that oversees a credentialling process for project management and publishes *A Guide to the Project Management Body of Knowledge (PMBOK)*. It was established in the late 1960s to help improve project delivery consistency in physical engineering sectors.
SDLC: an acronym for the software development lifecycle
software development lifecycle: a project management approach to deliver software projects. This process was commonly used prior to the Agile methodology and is still in use today. The software development lifecycle uses a waterfall approach.

DISCUSSION QUESTIONS

1. What is a framework? How is it different than a process?
2. How do values and principles influence the structure of work?
3. What does Lean's principle valuing people mean to you? How should it be incorporated into day-to-day work activities?
4. Why are frameworks needed? Why can't the work just get done?
5. What is the purpose of a visual management tool like Kanban? How does it enable work to be completed?

NOTES

1. C. Protzman, F. Whiton, and D. Protzman, *Implementing Lean* (Productivity Press, 2018).
2. D. Blanchard, "Commitment and Training Are Essential for a Lean Supply Chain: Manufacturers Are Now Looking beyond Their Four Walls for Opportunities to Drive Out Waste," *Industry Week* 4 (2012): 45.
3. Protzman et al., *Implementing Lean*.
4. S. Kumar and S. Craig, "Dell, Inc.'s Closed Loop Supply Chain for Computer Assembly Plants," *Information Knowledge Systems Management* 6, no. 3 (2007): 197–214.
5. K. Beck, M. Beedle, A. van Bennekum, A. Cockburn, W. Cunningham, M. Fowler, J. Grenning, J. Highsmith, A. Hunt, R. Jeffries, J. Kern, B. Marick, R. C. Martin, S. Mellor, K. Schwaber, J. Sutherland, and D. Thomas, *Manifesto for Agile Software Development* (2001), agilemanifesto.org.
6. Ibid.
7. Ibid.
8. S. Lenfle and C. Loch, "Lost Roots: How Project Management Came to Emphasize Control over Flexibility and Novelty," *California Management Review* 53, no. 1 (2010): 32–55.

2 Agile Overview

CHAPTER OVERVIEW

In chapter 2 we review approaches used in Agile. Like Lean, Agile is a philosophical and principled approach to work. Methodologies and frameworks have been developed to support Agile principles and values. This may seem incompatible with Agile's first principle, which values individuals and interactions over processes and tools. The result can be a misconception that Agile does not have or value processes and tools. This is simply not true. Agile values processes and tools, but these are only secondary to individuals and interactions. Therefore, any methodology or framework that supports Agile principles must be people-centred.

This text focuses team structure and interactions around Scrum methodology. Scrum is one of the more widely adopted Agile approaches. Scrum is also at the centre of common scaled Agile frameworks such as SAFe, LeSS, and DAD, which will be covered later in this text. Scrum has associated tools, artifacts, events, and roles. This chapter will provide an overview of each. In addition, this chapter will highlight the business problem that Agile was created to solve and contrast its approach to traditional project management, or the waterfall project management approach.

By the end of the chapter, readers should be familiar with the roles, phases, and events associated with the Scrum framework.

AGILE SCRUM FRAMEWORK: ROLES, EVENTS, AND ARTIFACTS

In chapter 1 we reviewed the Agile Manifesto values and principles. Of course, principles and values alone do not enable work to be completed. Agile values and principles provide the guideline for how people interact with one another in an Agile framework. Agile processes or events, the tools or artifacts that are used, and the different roles people play on a team are the key ingredients necessary for Agile values and principles to be converted into action.

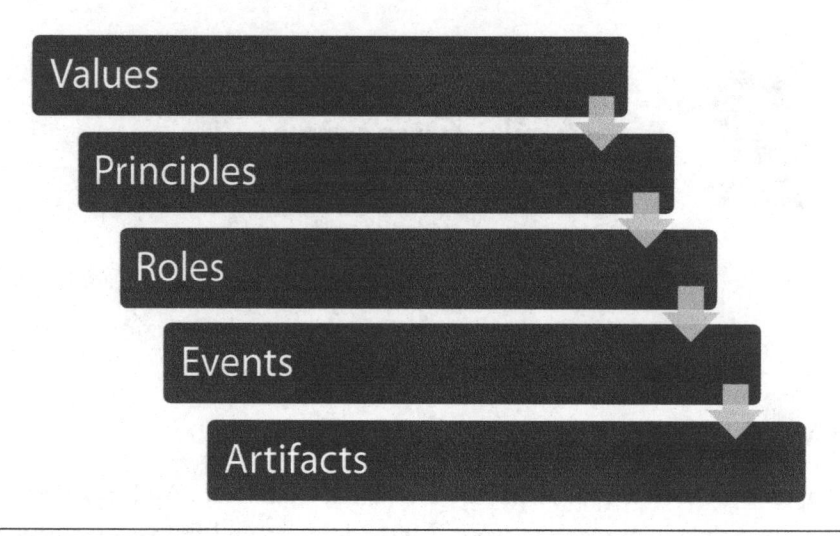

Figure 2.1 • Agile Values and Principles' Contribution to Roles, Events, and Artifacts

AGILE = ITERATIVE

Agile is an **iterative methodology**. Iterative methodologies are characterized by a series of short cycles that incrementally progress toward achieving a goal. In Agile, an **iteration** is a short cycle where work is performed. At the end of the cycle, a clearly demonstrable outcome should be completed. Iterative approaches to delivery differ from waterfall project-delivery approaches. **Waterfall methodologies** are more linear in nature. Each step in the delivery process is dependent on the previous one. If deliverables are not complete, this could delay the start of the next phase.

Iteration was not created by, or for, the Agile methodology. Iterative approaches can be attributed to Walter Shewhart, who in the 1930s developed the plan-do-study-act cycle. Shewhart developed plan-do-study-act in order to implement short projects quickly, with a goal of quality improvement. Plan-do-study-act is more commonly known as **plan-do-check-act** or **PDCA**.[1] PDCA is also associated with the Lean methodology known as *kaizen*. *Kaizen* is a Japanese term meaning "to make good." In application, the term refers to incremental, continuous improvement. Once waste, or *muda*, has been identified, the PDCA cycle begins. The following outlines the steps of a PDCA cycle:

- Planning for the change and the key steps needed
- Doing the change in a controlled or smaller-scale environment
- Checking or studying the change to determine if its effects meet the desired outcomes
- Acting on the change, implementing it on a larger scale

PDCAs are intended to be self-contained projects that can be executed quickly. Agile takes the PDCA and spreads it across a project as a sequence.

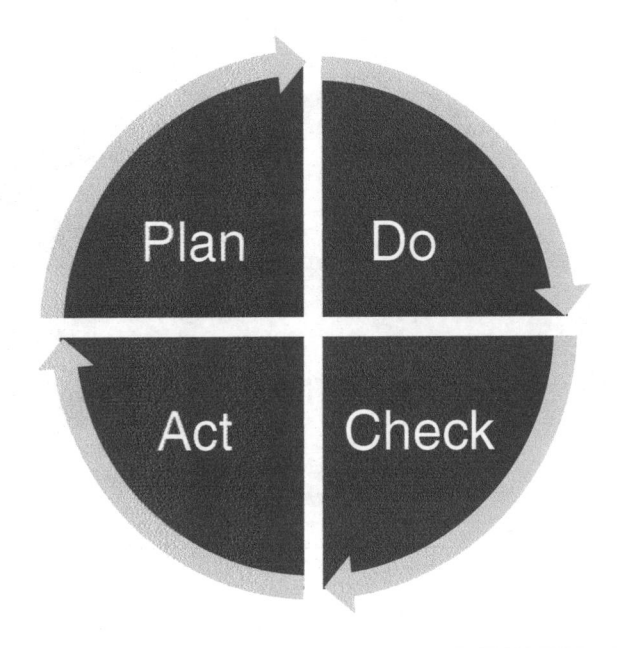

Figure 2.2 • Plan-Do-Check-Act Cycle[2]

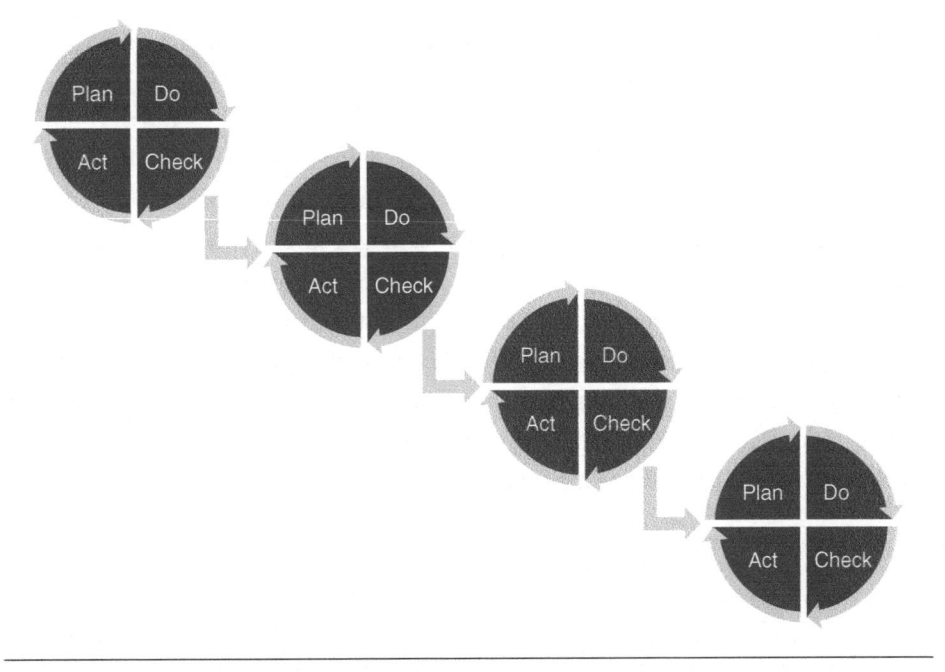

Figure 2.3 • Series of PDCA Iterations

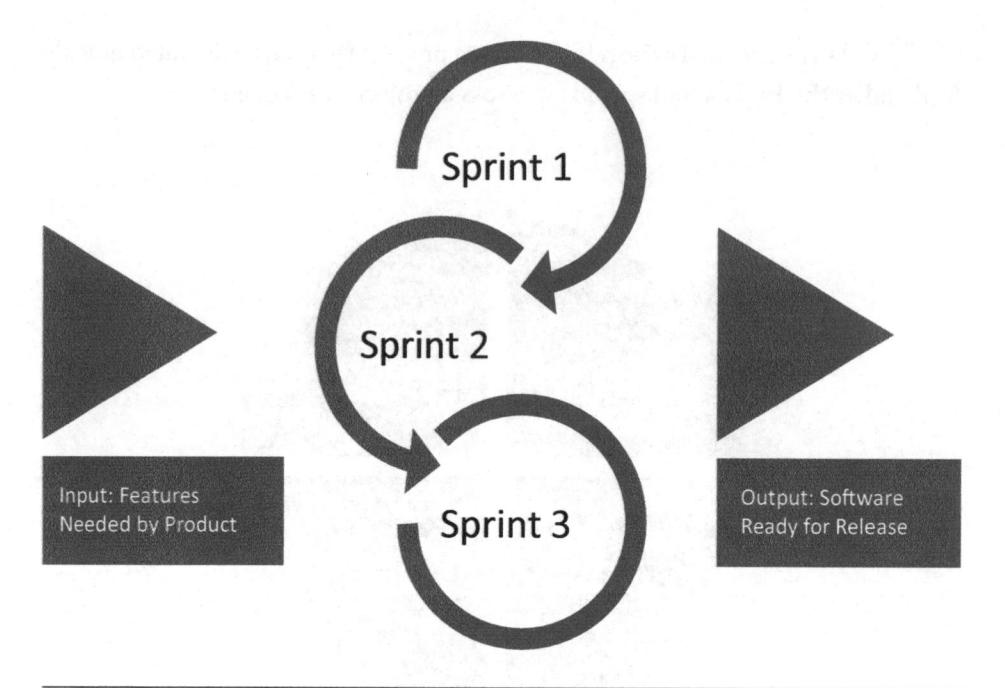

Figure 2.4 • Iterative Sprint Cycles

Utilizing iterations is common amongst Agile methodologies. Scrum places iterations in a series of timeboxed **sprints**. Sprints have a pre-determined duration during which a number of working software or product features are developed. At the end of a sprint, the features that have been developed should be demonstrable to the customer, stakeholders, product owners, and/or sponsors.[3]

Although the concept of a series of sequential sprints may sound very similar to waterfall—a sequential series of time-phased deliverables—the **key difference** is the position of the customer, product owner, sponsor, or stakeholder(s).

In figure 2.5, the customer or sponsor is engaged early in the planning and may sign off on estimates; however, once the project is moving through execution, the customer may not see the final product until it is ready for release. As a result, if the customer or stakeholders identify a need for change, there could be significant cost to go back to planning or design to accommodate the change. If the team had significantly misunderstood the customer requirements, much of the project work may have to be redone completely.

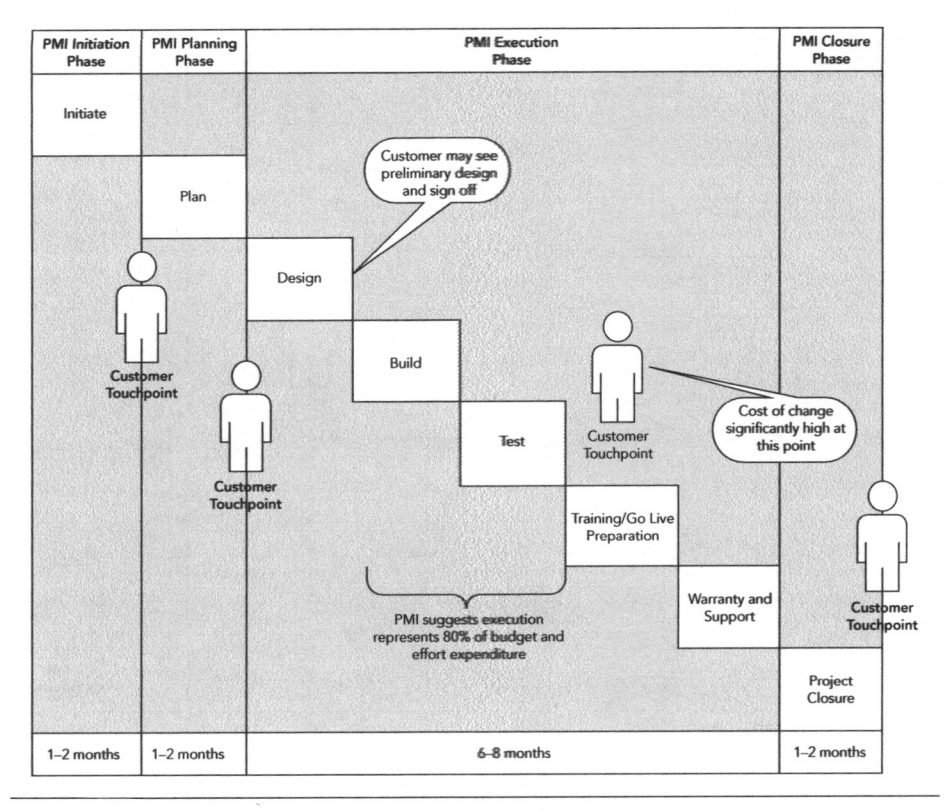

Figure 2.5 • Nine- to Fourteen-Month Waterfall Project

Case Study 2.1 • The Chaos of Project Delivery[4]

The Standish Group regularly publishes an annual report that highlights the health of the project management profession and its ability to deliver projects successfully. The report is known as the Chaos Report and has been administered since 1995. In the 2015 report project, the Standish Group provides project success indicators between the years 2011 and 2015. Sadly, the majority of projects during the period were over budget (56 percent) and late (60 percent). Of the projects reviewed averaged between 2011 and 2015, 38 percent were deemed successful, 43 percent were challenged, and 19 percent failed. However, when comparing Agile to waterfall, on average Agile projects were successful 39 percent of the time, compared to 11 percent for waterfall. Even more telling are size and complexity. Agile projects were considered successful only 18 percent of the time for large and complex projects, while waterfall projects were successful only 3 percent of the time. As project size and complexity decreased, success rates increased. However, Agile methods still took the lead, being deemed successful 58 percent of the time, while waterfall trailed at 44 percent.

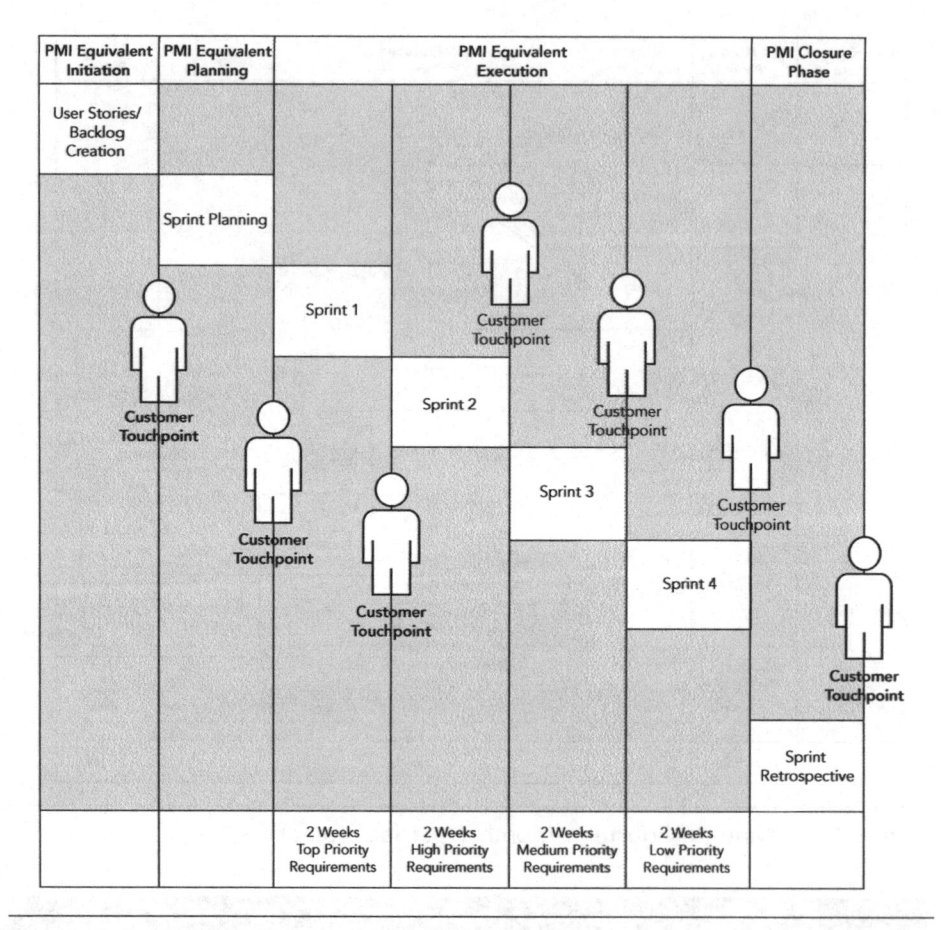

Figure 2.6 • Agile Project Sequential Sprints

In figure 2.6, we see the customer placed at the end of every sprint. They become part of the design process. If a customer requires changes, those changes can be added to the next sprint without additional resource cost (unless additional sprints are added). By prioritizing "must-have" requirements early, adding changes to the project comes at the sacrifice of "nice to have," or lower-priority, requirements. By the end of each sprint, there should be a usable product or set of features that the customer or stakeholders can review. Having a usable product or set of features at the end of each sprint enables organizations to bring products and solutions to market or production more quickly. This supports key Agile values and principles.

Agile values:

- *Working software* over comprehensive documentation
- *Responding to change* over following a plan

Agile principles:

1. Our highest priority is to satisfy the customer through early and continuous delivery of valuable software.
2. Welcome changing requirements, even late in development. Agile processes harness change for the customer's competitive advantage.
3. Deliver working software frequently, from a couple of weeks to a couple of months, with a preference to the shorter timescale.
7. Working software is the primary measure of progress.
8. Agile processes promote sustainable development. The sponsors, developers, and users should be able to maintain a constant pace indefinitely.

Changes are not viewed as disruptive in Agile because the goal is to have a consistent flow of work. This concept is borrowed from Lean principles:

- Keep things moving—in a value-added and effective manner.

In Lean, the Kanban board provides a visual method to help monitor a consistent flow of work. Agile used similar approaches to help ensure principle 8.

Figure 2.7 highlights Lean's third form of waste: **muri**. *Muri* is a Japanese term that refers to waste caused by overstressing people, equipment, and systems. Agile strives to achieve a consistent level of work during sprints. This differs from the waterfall approach, which backloads much of the effort in the execution phase.

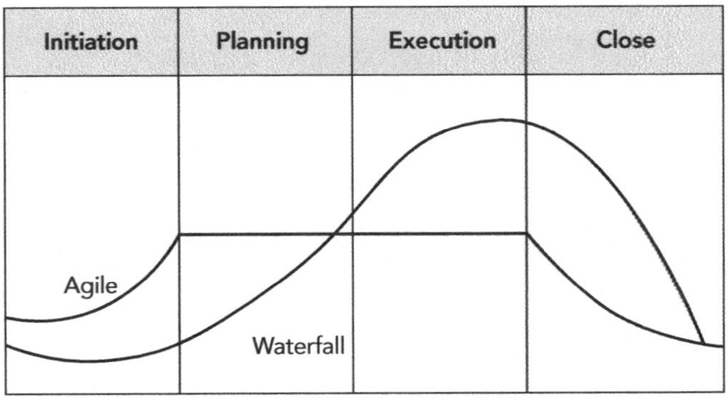

Figure 2.7 • Agile/Kanban Consistent Use of Resources and Flow of Work

Case Study 2.2 • The Marshmallow Challenge[5]

The marshmallow challenge is a team-building exercise in which three to four team members are given 20 pieces of spaghetti, one marshmallow, one yard of string, and one yard of tape. Teams are given 20 minutes to build the tallest freestanding structure that can support the marshmallow.

Tom Wujec provides excellent commentary on the exercise in his Ted Talk: Build a Tower, Build a Team. As part of his talk, Mr. Wujec reviews the marshmallow challenge performance of a variety of teams. Through his research, he finds there are two demographics that perform the best. Prior to getting to the top performers, Mr. Wujec reflects that most people struggle with the challenge, as they invest too much time discussing the problem until there is little time remaining to complete the task. Teams rush to complete, and as time is expiring, their ta-da moment of placing their marshmallow triumphantly on top of their tower quickly turns to an oh-no moment when their structure collapses under the weight of the gooey treat.

The two demographics that perform best in the experiment are engineers (thankfully) and kindergarteners. This revelation illustrates a couple of key reasons why Agile is successful. Kindergarteners perform well because—not having a lot of experience—they experiment, building on what works and discarding what doesn't. They receive instant feedback and build on that knowledge. Engineers perform better at the tasks because they are experts, highlighting the fact that resources with a high level of expertise are able to produce better products with minimal direction.

The final lesson from the marshmallow challenge reminds us that when work is novel, as the marshmallow challenge is for kindergarteners, experimentation and iteration work best.

The marshmallow challenge highlights one of the challenges associated with waterfall projects. As earlier phases expand, or take more time and effort than originally anticipated, pressure is added to later phases and activities. Figures 2.8 and 2.9 illustrate the impact of expanding phases and how they can compress subsequent phases.

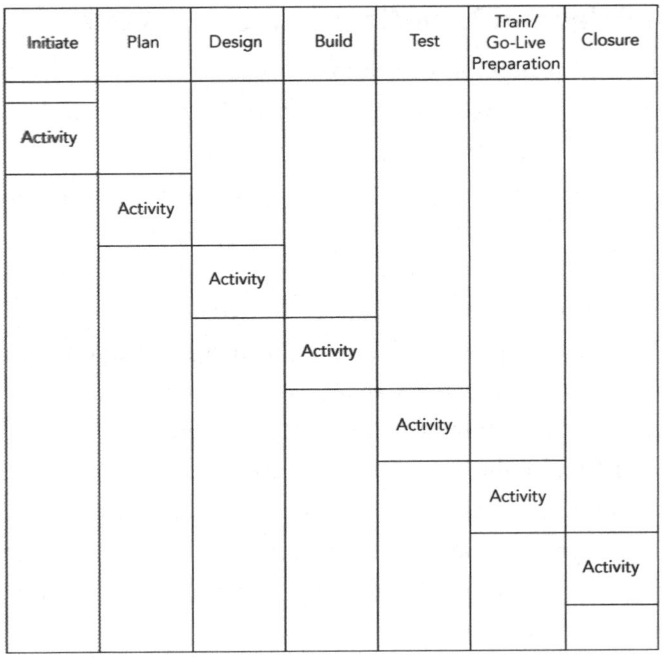

Figure 2.8 • SDLC Phases and Activities

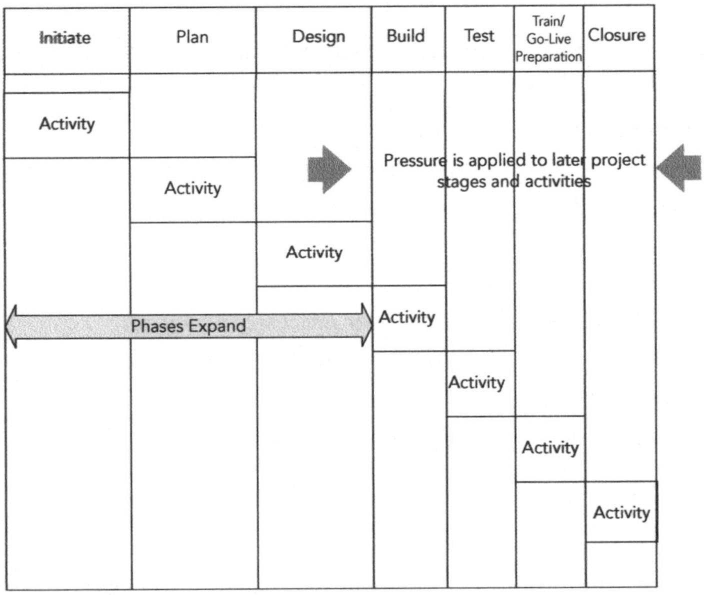

Figure 2.9 • SDLC Expansion in Phases Impacting Later Activities

Waterfall Roles and Their Contribution to Waste

Often in waterfall, phases and deliverables can cause silos between resource groups.

In figure 2.10, the project manager works with the sponsor to create a project charter. The project charter is a key input to planning.

Potential waste: The sponsor may not be familiar enough with the business problem or potential solutions to truly provide guidance.

In figure 2.11, the project charter has been handed off to the business analyst to review and create requirements for the project. The requirements are a key output to later activities that include test planning, budget estimation, schedule estimation, and design.

Potential waste: The business analyst is not the technical expert. Therefore, requirements may be captured that cannot be delivered.

Figure 2.12 highlights the developer or designer's review process. Consider the impact of finding issues during this project phase. Time and effort have been expended on the previous phases. The sponsor, or customer, has already agreed in principle to a set of conceptual requirements, timelines, and budget only to find their needs may not be fully met.

Potential waste: The customer being removed from the process creates fragmentation from what is desired to what is feasible. Time and money may be lost during these cycles if feasibility issues arise.

Lessons from Kindergarteners

As we learned from the kindergarteners who participated in the marshmallow challenge, when work is novel, experimentation or prototyping is more effective than spending too much time planning.

Consider Agile values that combat the potential wastes associated with figures 2.10, 2.11, and 2.12.

Agile values:

- *Individuals and interactions* over processes and tools
- *Working software* over comprehensive documentation
- *Customer collaboration* over contract negotiation
- *Responding to change* over following a plan

Agile principles:

1. Our highest priority is to satisfy the customer through early and continuous delivery of valuable software.
2. Welcome changing requirements, even late in development. Agile processes harness change for the customer's competitive advantage.

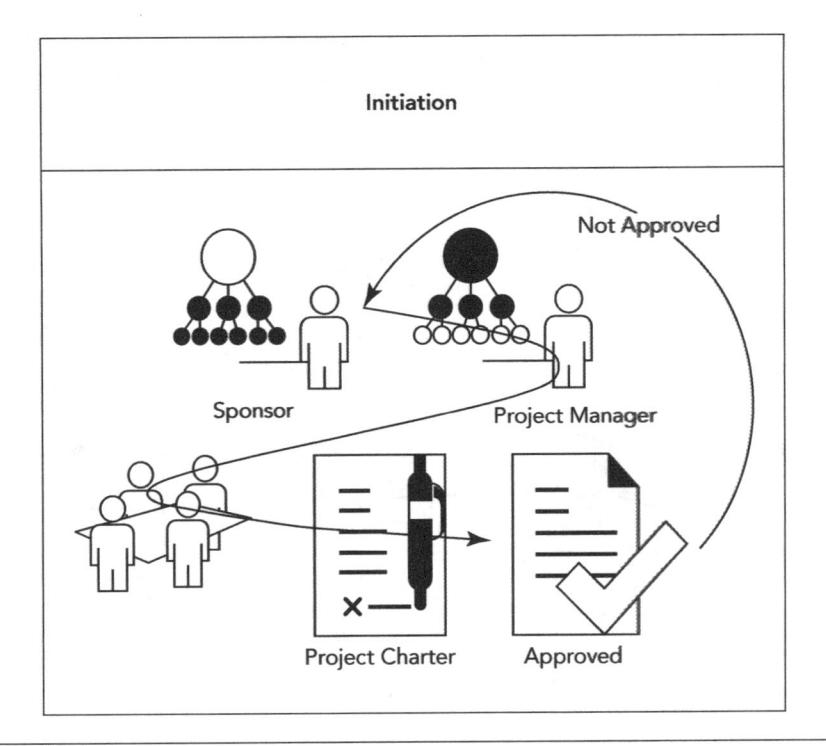

Figure 2.10 • Initiation Phase Expanded

3. Deliver working software frequently, from a couple of weeks to a couple of months, with a preference to the shorter timescale.
4. Business people and developers must work together daily throughout the project.
5. Build projects around motivated individuals. Give them the environment and support they need, and trust them to get the job done.
6. The most efficient and effective method of conveying information to and within a development team is face-to-face conversation.
7. Working software is the primary measure of progress.
8. Agile processes promote sustainable development. The sponsors, developers, and users should be able to maintain a constant pace indefinitely.
9. Continuous attention to technical excellence and good design enhances agility.
10. Simplicity—the art of maximizing the amount of work not done—is essential.
11. The best architectures, requirements, and designs emerge from self-organizing teams.
12. At regular intervals, the team reflects on how to become more effective, then tunes and adjusts its behaviour accordingly.

28 AGILE PROJECT DELIVERY

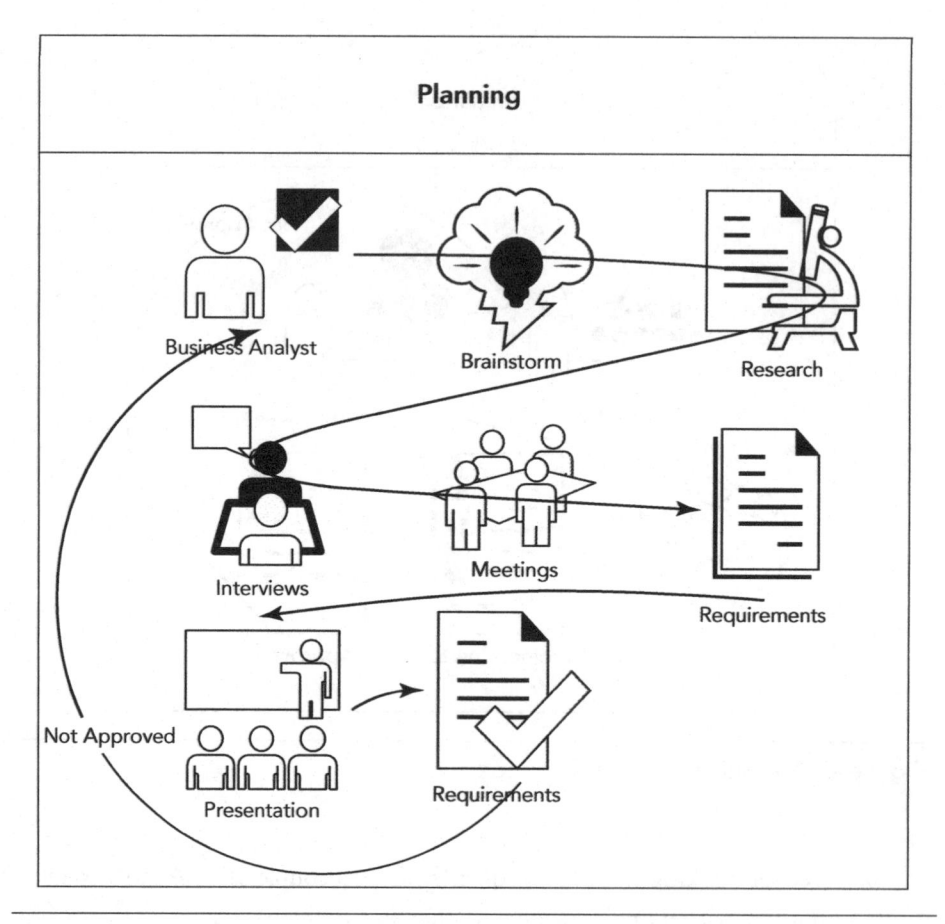

Figure 2.11 • Planning Phase Expanded

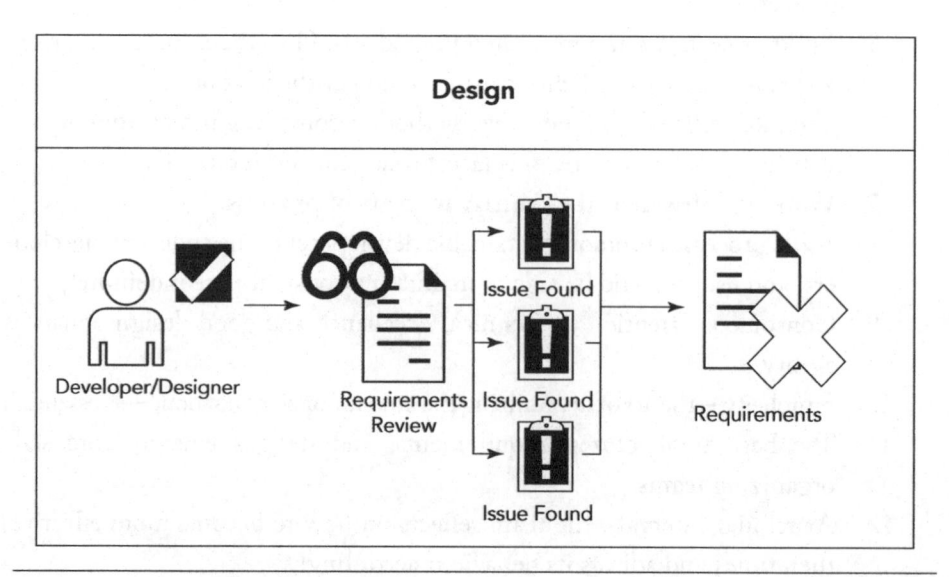

Figure 2.12 • Design Phase with Issues Found

Consider how Lean principles support the Agile values and principles, removing layers of hierarchy to create a flat and more customer-engaged project organization.

Having the customer and stakeholders be more involved across all phases of the project lifecycle aligns with Lean principles. If we consider our mass-production versus direct-sales models from chapter 1, you will notice both Agile and direct sales place the customer more directly in the process, eliminating layers of waste. Customers and stakeholders are in the best position to articulate their needs, and developers are in the best position to determine how they can fulfill those needs through their expertise.

Lean principles:

- Maintain an unrelenting focus on providing customer value.
- Adopt a philosophy of continuous incremental improvement.
- Provide exactly what is needed at the right time, based on customer demand.
- Keep things moving—in a value-added and effective manner.
- Use techniques for reducing variation and eliminating waste.
- Value and respect people.
- Take the long-term view.

THE SCRUM PROJECT TEAM

The Scrum project team comprises three key roles: the **product owner**, the **scrum master**, and the **development team**.[6]

The Product Owner

The product owner is responsible for defining **user stories** and prioritizing the team **backlog** to streamline the execution of the program priorities while maintaining the conceptual and technical integrity of features or components for the project.[7] Both user stories and backlog will be covered later in this chapter.

The Scrum Master

The scrum master is the facilitator of the Agile methodology. Scrum allows a team to self-organize. Scrum masters do not directly perform or manage the work. Instead they ensure that Agile principles are followed and coach and mentor the team to work in an Agile way. The scrum master is also responsible for removing obstacles that prevent the team from completing its work.[8]

The Development Team

The development team member's role is broad and may include the following:

- Estimation and planning
- Execution/delivery
- Management and status reporting
- Collaboration

Although the developer's role is associated with software development, it is not limited to this. The developer is responsible for anything that contributes to completing phase deliverables, which can include documentation, training, and so on.

The developer is considered an expert in their discipline and the best able to provide estimation, interpretation of a stated need, and completion of the work.[9]

SCRUM PHASES OVERVIEW

The Scrum framework utilizes a series of phases or steps that support the delivery of project outcomes. These steps often produce artifacts through a series of Scrum events.[10] Although phases may imply a linear relationship, it is important to

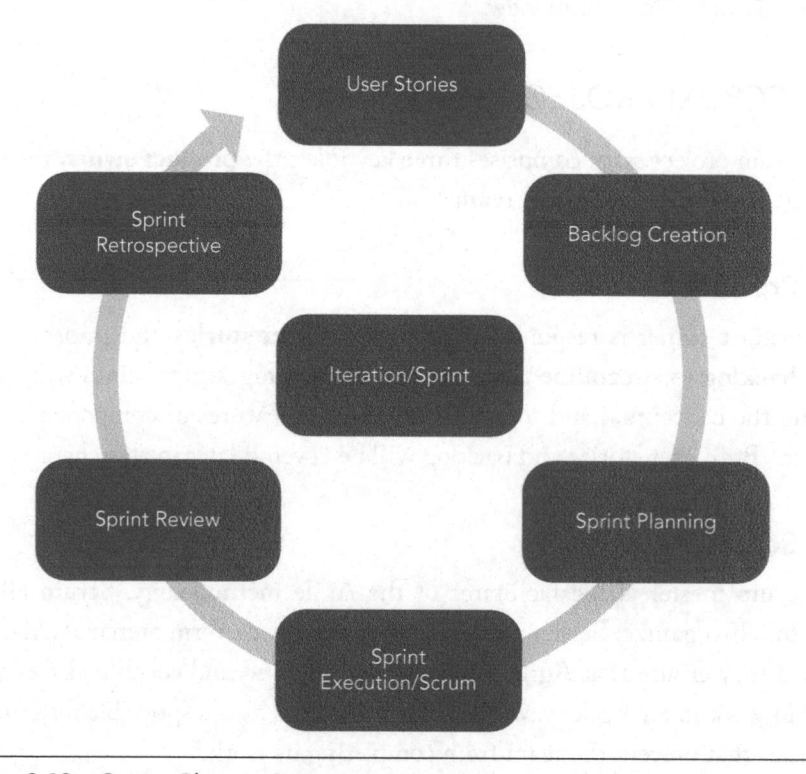

Figure 2.13 • Scrum Phases Overview

not confuse phases for project lifecycle steps, which are consistent with waterfall. There isn't an entire phase of a linear timeline devoted to user stories or creating backlog. Rather, each step in the Scrum framework occurs within a single iteration, like the PDCA cycle described earlier in this chapter. A number of iterations will occur within a project. In this section we provide a brief overview of each step or phase within an iteration or sprint. All phases will be covered at greater length throughout this text.

User Stories

User stories are short, simple descriptions of a feature or requirement told from the perspective of the person who will benefit from the new capability. This can be a **user** or **stakeholder** of the solution. User stories typically follow a simple template: As a < type of stakeholder >, I want < some goal > so that < some reason >.

User stories can vary, but they usually share some common characteristics:

- The product owner is responsible for generating them.
- They are meant to describe desired functionality and/or outcomes.
- They are not prescriptive like functional specifications or requirements.
- They are typically a sentence or two to help drive conversations about the desired outcome.
- They can be often expressed as "persona + need + purpose."

Once complete, user stories are placed in a backlog. User stories should provide enough information for a development team member to fulfill the user's or stakeholder's need or to solicit the needed input to satisfy the story. The expectation of a story is that it could generate a follow-up conversation between the development team member and the stakeholder.[11]

Backlog Creation[12]

The backlog is a key artifact. The backlog is a prioritized list of work, often in the form of user stories. The product owner is responsible for **backlog creation**, which includes the addition of user stories and setting user story priority. The backlog is a single repository or location where the user stories reside. The development team reviews the backlog and moves user stories through the development process. The backlog can vary in complexity, from a collection of sticky notes on a whiteboard to hundreds or thousands of items in an electronic repository. Spreadsheet software can also be used as a backlog tool. Some questions organizations should consider when deciding which backlog tools are most appropriate for their environment are as follows:

- How big is the backlog?
- How novel is the work?
- Is the team co-located and working the same hours?
- Is the team fully dedicated to the project?
- Are there offshore resources?

Relatively simple projects that have a fully dedicated and co-located team may not require a very complex or dynamic backlog. However, for larger and more complex corporate environments the backlog may need to be adapted to reflect an organization's needs. When backlogs are complex, more sophisticated tools are often needed to manage the complexity.

The Backlog as a Self-Organizing Tool
The backlog enables the development team to select user stories and begin work on them. The development team does not have to wait for another dependency to be completed. The only factors that need to be fulfilled before a user story can be removed from the backlog are as follows:

- It is in the right priority; that is, a development team member should not select a low-priority user story when there are alternative high-priority user stories pending.
- The development team member has enough work cycles to take on the user story.
- The development team member either understands the user story clearly enough to perform the work or has access to the right resources to have a clarifying conversation.

Once a user story has been selected, it is moved along a visual management tool. Boards are often used as visual management tools. There are a variety of visual management formats, but Scrum usually conforms to a modified Kanban board, depicted in chapter 1.

Like Lean, Agile uses a pull rather than push method of scheduling. This means that members of the development team select stories to work on and pull them from the backlog. In the waterfall approach, the schedule is estimated and then work is pushed, much like the mass-production model. By displaying work or tasks on a board, a development team member can move a user story card across each progress category and select new items to work on without waiting for updates to be made to a project schedule or receiving an assignment from a project manager.

Backlog Creation Summarized
- Input: user stories → Output: backlog
- The backlog is a prioritized list of new features or user stories
- Can be used in both Scrum and Kanban approaches
- Enables teams to self-organize and take ownership
- Eliminates up-front documentation cycles prior to development occurring
- In essence, a large to-do list of user stories or requirements

Sprint Planning

Sprint planning, one of the four Scrum events, is a collaborative approach between team members to determine the work to be completed during a current sprint.

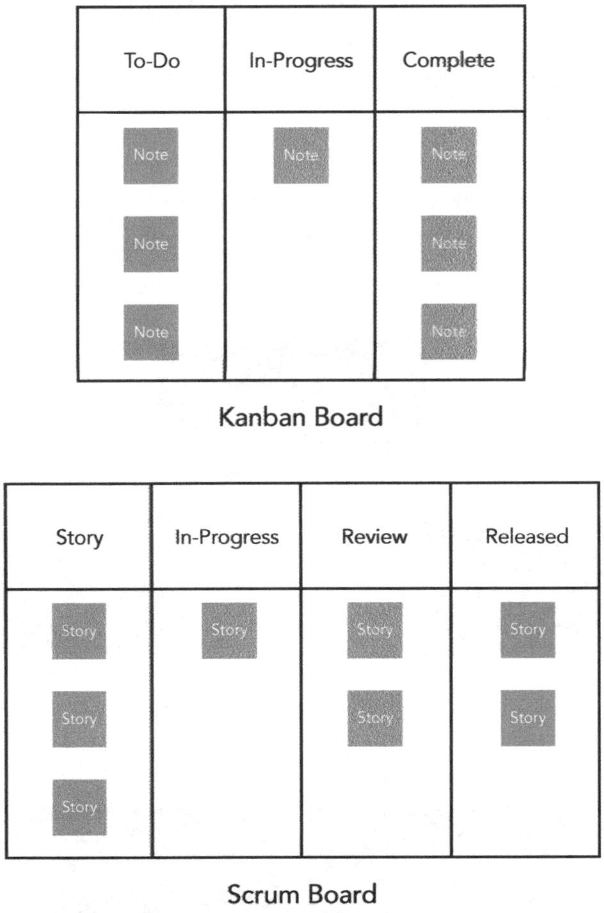

Figure 2.14 • A Simplified View of a Kanban versus a Scrum Board

The Sprint Planning Process

This process includes identifying the work that needs to be completed, who will complete the work and what their approach will be, and finally, the outcome of their work, or final product.

> *Inputs*—The backlog and previous work performance are analyzed to understand sprint capacity.
>
> *What*—The product owner describes the sprint goal and which backlog items contribute to achieving the sprint goal.
>
> *Who*—The product owner defines the goal based on desired outcomes. The development team needs to understand the goal and the backlog items that contribute to achieving the goal. Without these two roles, sprints cannot be planned.
>
> *How*—The development team plans the work required to deliver the goal. Negotiation occurs between the development team and the product owner.
>
> *Output*—Backlog items are added to the sprint. The team shares a collective understanding of the sprint's goal. Tools are updated to reflect the sprint commitments.

Each sprint should have a clear goal. The backlog is the key input to identifying the key features or outcomes that will contribute to that goal. The sprint goal, along with select user stories from the backlog, will help create the **sprint**

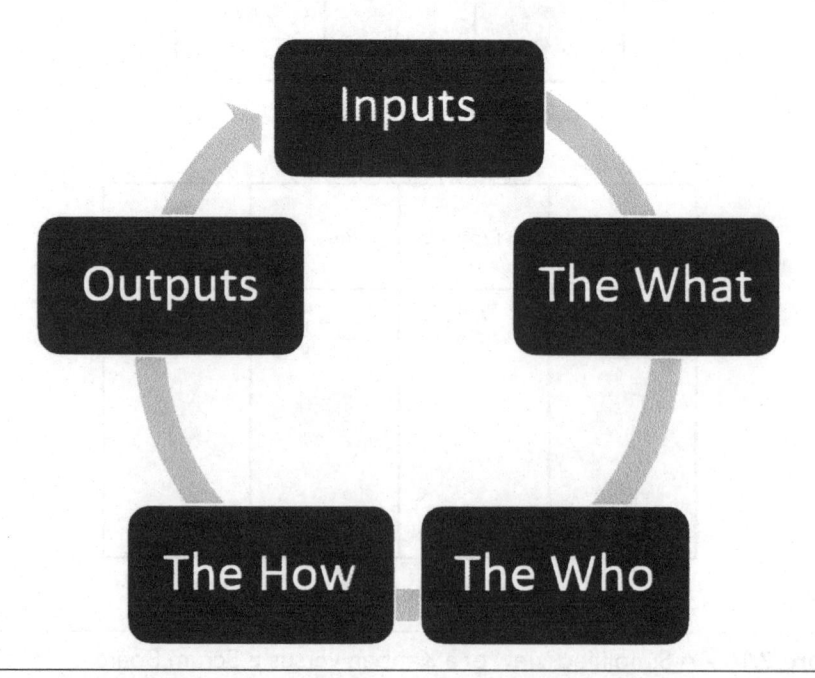

Figure 2.15 • Sprint Planning Cycle

backlog. The sprint backlog contains those backlog items that are to be completed specifically during that sprint.[13]

The sprint backlog enables the team to estimate each user story to ensure they can be completed within the sprint timebox. The majority of user stories should be able to be completed within a day. For user stories that exceed a day, further decomposition may be required to break the user story into smaller stories. The sprint planning session enables the development team to obtain clarification from the product owner for those user stories that are unclear.

Sprint planning duration is directly correlated to the duration of a sprint. For every week of a sprint, two hours should be allocated to planning. Therefore, if a sprint is four weeks, the sprint planning session should be eight hours.[14]

Sprint planning has two key components:

1. Set a sprint goal and identify the user stories that will fulfill that goal.
2. Estimate user stories and break into subtasks.

The sprint backlog progress can be tracked by using a **burndown chart**. A burndown chart is a visual reporting tool that is used to track and communicate progress to project stakeholders. Burndown charts help the scrum master to visually identify issues that impact the team's ability to achieve the sprint goal. The burndown chart will be covered in greater detail in part IV of the text.

Sprint Planning Summarized
- Inputs: duration of sprint, backlog → Outputs: sprint schedule and expected deliverables during the cycle
- A sprint is a defined period of time when work will be completed. Best practice is one to two weeks for each sprint.
- Usually there will be multiple sprints planned in an Agile project.
- Sprints are done in collaboration with the whole Scrum team.
- The product owner and scrum master set the planning session focus and agenda in advance.
- The sprint planning process must answer the what, how, who, inputs, and outputs of the sprint goal.

Sprint Execution/Scrum

During the sprint execution/scrum phase of the project, the development team completes the work. Visual management tools such as a Kanban or scrum board are reviewed collectively in what is called a **scrum**. A scrum is one of the four Scrum events and is a set time when all team members meet to review the board.

The scrum is facilitated by the scrum master. It typically occurs daily and is meant to be short in duration.[15]

Common questions for a scrum session include the following:

- What did you do yesterday?
- What will you do today?
- Are there any impediments in your way?

Scrum will be covered in more detail in part IV of the text.

Scrum is one specific method of managing a sprint or iteration; however, it isn't the only one. Scrum requires the team—including the development team, the scrum master, and product owner—to be present. For other methodologies, such as Kanban, team roles aren't always as defined. However, the need for regular interaction amongst team members is consistent across Agile.

The daily meeting should be available to all project stakeholders; however, the only participants are the development team. Allowing other stakeholders to attend a scrum meeting supports transparency as well as an opportunity to disseminate key information. During the scrum, the scrum board and sprint backlog are updated. This enables burndown charts to be updated as well. The scrum event enables a daily, real-time update of the sprint progress and whether it is on track to achieve the sprint goal.

Sprint Execution/Scrum Summarized
- Inputs: sprint planning, backlog → Outputs: deliverables, tracking tool updates
- The sprint is where the majority of the project work is completed.
- During the sprint the team meets regularly. This can be done in a variety of formats:
    - Daily stand-ups
    - Team huddles
    - Scrum
- During meetings, the daily questions are asked and the tools are updated.
- Sessions are facilitated by the scrum master to ensure Agile philosophies are adhered to.

Sprint Review

The **sprint review** is a Scrum event that is set up at the end of a sprint. The sprint review includes project stakeholders, and its goal is to showcase the work that has been completed during the sprint. Recall the marshmallow challenge; this is similar to the prototyping that kindergartners perform. The sprint review confirms what works and what needs to be modified. The sprint review also ensures that the customer or stakeholder is integrated more directly into the project delivery cycle to minimize the risk of the team misinterpreting the customer's or stakeholder's needs.[16]

The sprint review should only review features or outcomes that have been completed. In Scrum, "completed" means that the user story meets the following criteria:

- Developed
- Inspected
- Documented

These are also referred to as the "definition of done" criteria, which are covered in part III of the text. Team members who can support the definition of done criteria should be part of the development team. User stories that do not meet the definition of done criteria are added to a future sprint.[17]

The sprint review must be done with those who can approve the work. For the most part the product owner would be sufficient. However, in non-software and corporate settings it may be appropriate to have a customer or stakeholder delegate present. It is an opportunity for the development team to solicit feedback as well as obtain confirmation that the interpretation of the completed user stories have met the customer's or stakeholder's expectation. Agreement that the completed work meets expectations acts as customer approval that the user story is complete.

When there isn't agreement, the sprint review process enables the development team to seek clarification and incorporate changes into the next sprint. By performing the sprint review at the end of every sprint, product owners, customers, or stakeholders are able to see their feedback incorporated in short cycles. This helps build confidence and awareness amongst stakeholders.

Sprint Review Summarized
- Inputs: completed user stories → Outputs: customer/stakeholder agreement or change
- A user story is only complete when it meets the definition of done criteria:
    ◦ Developed
    ◦ Inspected
    ◦ Documented
- Development team seeks input and welcomes change

Sprint Retrospective

The **sprint retrospective** is a Scrum event where the team reflects on the previous sprint and discusses what can be done to improve future sprints.

The sprint retrospective is facilitated by the scrum master and should include all Scrum team members. For non-software corporate environments, the sprint retrospective could be open to additional customer or stakeholder delegates who may offer additional insights that may not be initially realized by the working team. The sprint retrospective is a continuous improvement technique that supports the final Agile principle:

12. At regular intervals, the team reflects on how to become more effective, then tunes and adjusts its behaviour accordingly.

It also builds on the following Lean principle:

- Adopt a philosophy of continuous incremental improvement.

In addition, the sprint retrospective supports the Lean philosophy of identifying and eliminating the three forms of waste: *muda*, *mura*, and *muri*. The sprint retrospective should be action-oriented. It is not a forum to justify *why* inefficiencies exist but rather *how* inefficiencies can be eliminated.

The sprint retrospective should, at a minimum, cover three primary questions:

1. What went well during the sprint?
2. What would we like to change?
3. How can we implement that change?

Data collected from the sprint, such as the following, should help guide the sprint retrospective:

- Percentage of the sprint backlog completed
- Team composition and relationships
- Processes and tools
- Customer/stakeholder feedback from sprint review
- Productivity

The sprint retrospective is often conducted at the end of a sprint; however, there may be opportunities to perform a sprint retrospective at other times. The goal of the sprint retrospective is to achieve continuous improvement. The opportunity for improvement is not limited to the end of a sprint cycle. Therefore, the use of a sprint retrospective should not be limited.[18]

Sprint Retrospective Summarized
- Inputs: backlog, sprint deliverables → Output: improved approach, knowledge transfer
- Facilitated by the scrum master
- Team reflects on the completed sprint and determines what changes could be made during the next sprint to increase efficiency
- Goal of retrospective is continuous improvement, never blame

SUMMARY

- The Agile framework is iterative, which enables the customer or stakeholder to have multiple engagement points throughout the development cycle.
- Agile is effective when work is novel or there is not a high degree of experience within the organization or team.
- The Agile project organization includes the product owner, scrum master, and development team.
- Agile project phases include the creation of user stories and backlog, sprint planning, sprint execution, sprint review, and sprint retrospective.
- The entire team must participate fully in each phase but should be open to additional project stakeholders.
- Visual management tools such as scrum boards and burndown charts are used to track sprint progress.
- Sprints are pre-determined timeboxed durations that act as commitments to deliver functionality or outcomes. The number of sprints will identify the total duration of a project.

KEY TERMS

backlog: a prioritized list of user stories

backlog creation: a phase in the Agile project lifecycle where the Agile project team works on creating a backlog for the project

burndown chart: a chart that shows the amount of work left to complete versus the time remaining

development team: a project team member who directly contributes to the completion of deliverables

event: significant Scrum activity. There are four common Scrum events: sprint planning, scrum or the daily stand-up, sprint review, and sprint retrospective.

iteration: a short cycle where work is performed

iterative methodology: usually characterized by a number of iteration cycles to produce an outcome. Agile is an iterative methodology.

kaizen: a Japanese term meaning "to make good." Used in conjunction with a continuous improvement action.

muri: a Japanese term that refers to waste caused by overstressing people, equipment, and systems

plan-do-check-act (PDCA)/plan-do-study-act (PDSA): an iterative process developed by Walter Shewhart to implement short projects quickly to help improve quality

product owner: an Agile team member who is responsible for defining user stories and prioritizing the team backlog. The product owner organizationally owns the product and outcome of the Agile project.

scrum: one of the four Scrum events, a timeboxed activity conducted at a set time when all team members meet to review sprint progress. The scrum is facilitated by the scrum master. It typically occurs daily and is meant to be short in duration.

scrum master: the facilitator of the Agile methodology. The scrum master does not directly perform or manage the work; they ensure that Agile principles are followed and coach and mentor the team to work in an Agile way.

sprint: a pre-determined timebox where a number of working features are developed

sprint backlog: the backlog items to be completed specifically during a sprint

sprint planning: one of the four Scrum events, a phase of the Agile project lifecycle. It is a collaborative activity between Agile team members to determine the work to be completed during the upcoming sprint.

sprint retrospective: one of the four Scrum events, an activity in which the team reflects on the previous sprint and discusses what can be done to improve future sprints

sprint review: one of the four Scrum events, a meeting to review the user stories the development team has completed. The audience of a sprint review is typically the customer or stakeholders.

stakeholder: any person impacted by the project outcome. Stakeholders can be part of the project team, internal or external to an organization.

user: any person who will directly interact with the project outcome

user story: a short, simple description of a feature or requirement told from the perspective of the person who will benefit from the new capability. Also a phase of the Agile project lifecycle.

waterfall methodologies: project management approach that is more linear in nature than iterative approaches. Each step in the delivery process is dependent on the previous. If deliverables are not complete it could delay the start of the next phase.

DISCUSSION QUESTIONS

1. Pick an Agile project phase and compare it to a PMI phase. What are the similarities and differences?
2. Consider an online product you use regularly (for example, online banking, shopping, food delivery) and create three user stories for what you require from your chosen service.
3. What are the three forms of waste associated with Lean principles? How are they different from each other?
4. Both waterfall and Agile have sequential activities yet they are often considered opposing frameworks. Why? Is this characterization accurate?
5. Agile is often put in context of software development. Can it be applied to other types of projects or activities? Explain.

NOTES

1. B. Karloff and F. Lovingsson, "PDCA (Plan, Do, Check and Act)," in *The A to Z of Management Concepts and Models* (London, UK: Thorogood, 2005), 245–246.
2. Ibid.
3. K. Rubin, *Essential Scrum: A Practical Guide to the Most Popular Agile Process* (Boston, MA: Addison-Wesley Professional, 2012).
4. Standish Group International, *Chaos Report 2015* (2015).
5. TED, "Build a Tower, Build a Team: Tom Wujec," YouTube. April 22, 2010, video, 7:22, https://www.youtube.com/watch?v=H0_yKBitO8M.
6. Rubin, *Essential Scrum*.
7. Ibid.
8. Ibid.
9. Ibid.

10. S. Ockerman and S. Reindl, *Mastering Professional Scrum: Coaches' Notes for Busting Myths, Solving Challenges, and Growing Agility* (Boston, MA: Addison-Wesley Professional, 2019).
11. Rubin, *Essential Scrum*.
12. Ibid.
13. Ockerman and Reindl, *Mastering Professional Scrum*.
14. Ibid.
15. Ibid.
16. Ibid.
17. Ibid.
18. Ibid.

PART II

AGILE PROJECT INITIATION

In part II of the text we turn our focus to utilizing various techniques employed by Agile-inspired frameworks. The focus will be how to use these techniques to help navigate non-software development corporate settings. As part of that focus we explore how Lean principles can aid in the initiation of a project utilizing Agile techniques. Agile philosophies were developed for small, dedicated, and localized teams; however, the principles can be scaled to meet large and complex environments. Frameworks such as Scaled Agile Framework (SAFe), Large-Scale Scrum (LeSS), and Disciplined Agile Delivery (DAD) have been developed to help organizations implement Agile at an enterprise level. Part II will begin by exploring adaptations that can be made to project delivery during a project's early stages.

By the end of part II, readers will be able to describe how to decompose organizational units. In addition, readers will become familiar with the role of Lean principles in current state discovery. Finally, readers will learn how interactions with stakeholders can help create and rank user stories for the development team.

3 Understanding Corporate Environments

CHAPTER OVERVIEW

In chapter 3 we review the organizational composition of corporate environments. This chapter identifies how roles differ in corporations and how they can be adapted to an Agile framework. In addition, in chapter 3, a case study is introduced that will be followed for the remainder of the text to help readers apply the adapted approaches, using various techniques from Agile frameworks, to corporate settings. Finally, this chapter will introduce a software tool that can be used to organize large projects that are managed using Agile philosophies. Like the case study, the software tool and how it can be used during different phases of a project will be referenced throughout the text.

By the end of chapter 3, readers should be familiar with how corporate environments create challenges for Agile values and principles, how the challenges can be mitigated using Lean concepts, and how to initiate an Agile project in a corporate setting.

THE COMPOSITION OF CORPORATIONS

The Agile Manifesto was established to enable small and focused teams to deliver software more effectively. Scrum best practices suggest that the ideal team has six team members, plus or minus three.[1] Growth beyond nine team members begins to take away from the agility of the team. In addition, Scrum teams are relatively flat. A **flat organization** has few or no levels of management between staff. Teams are autonomous and can make decisions for the organization without first seeking approval from various levels. In Scrum, for example, the development team decides how best to achieve a user story and the product owner answers questions and identifies priorities. Scrum masters ensure the process is being followed, but there aren't levels of management that "sign off" on documents before work can begin. Recall the Agile values:

- *Working software* over comprehensive documents
- *Customer collaboration* over contract negotiations

These values support a flat organizational structure.

Most corporations are not flat. They are hierarchical. A **hierarchical organization** has multiple layers of management. Workers are organized under each layer. Layers, or verticals, usually specialize at performing a function for the organization. Often large and complex organizations have divisions, departments, units, and functions to support operations. Figure 3.1 illustrates an example of levels that can exist in a large and complex organization. Hierarchical verticals can create organizational **silos**. Silos refer to closed management systems that do not interact or operate with other silos, or divisions, within an organization.

Within an organizational unit there can be multiple functions. Figure 3.2 highlights the different functions a unit can perform. For example, a purchasing unit can be responsible for fulfilling a tendering function, such as issuing requests for proposals, requests for quotes, and requests for information. The purchasing unit can also be responsible for other functions, such as creating a product catalogue, issuing purchase orders and invoices, or managing vendors. Each function can comprise sub-processes and process owners.

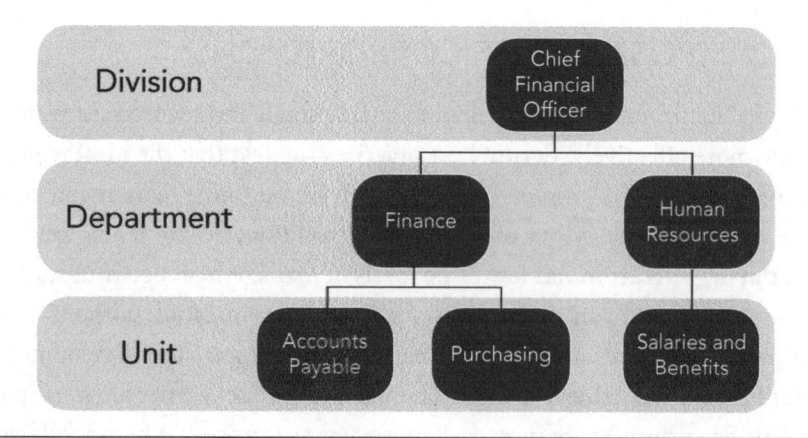

Figure 3.1 • Hierarchical Organization

Figure 3.2 • Purchasing Unit Functions

Non-Software Producing Large and Complex Organizations' Impact to the Product Owner Role

Many corporations—such as those whose core business model is financial services, manufacturing, retail, or healthcare—do not produce software. Despite not producing software, corporations may depend heavily on the use of software for their operations.

Corporations can have hundreds of units that employ thousands of employees who perform thousands of discrete operational functions. As a result, these organizations may not have a role consistent with the product owner.

To adapt Agile frameworks to meet the needs of these organizations, a shift from product owner to other forms of ownership may be required. Although corporations may not have product owners, they may have equivalent or similar roles, such as service owners, service managers, and process owners. These roles are often aligned with the hierarchical organizational structure of divisions, departments, and units.

When adapting Agile frameworks to meet the needs of a corporation, it is important to know the different roles each owner would play as a team member in a project using Agile philosophies.

Service owner—Responsible for the vision and mission of a project; agrees with the project success criteria; reviews and approves completed work

Service manager—Supports the creation of the vision and mission; facilitates the creation of measurable success criteria of a project; reviews and approves completed work

Functional manager—Supports the creation of the measurable success criteria of a project; supplies resources and subject matter experts to support the project; reviews and approves completed work

Process owner—Responsible for defining the measurable success criteria of a project; participates in user story creation; reviews and approves completed work

To adapt Agile frameworks to align with corporate needs, an authoring document may be required. Corporate projects can often represent significant investments, especially for those projects that span the corporate enterprise. To gain access to project funds and ensure there is alignment between corporate strategy

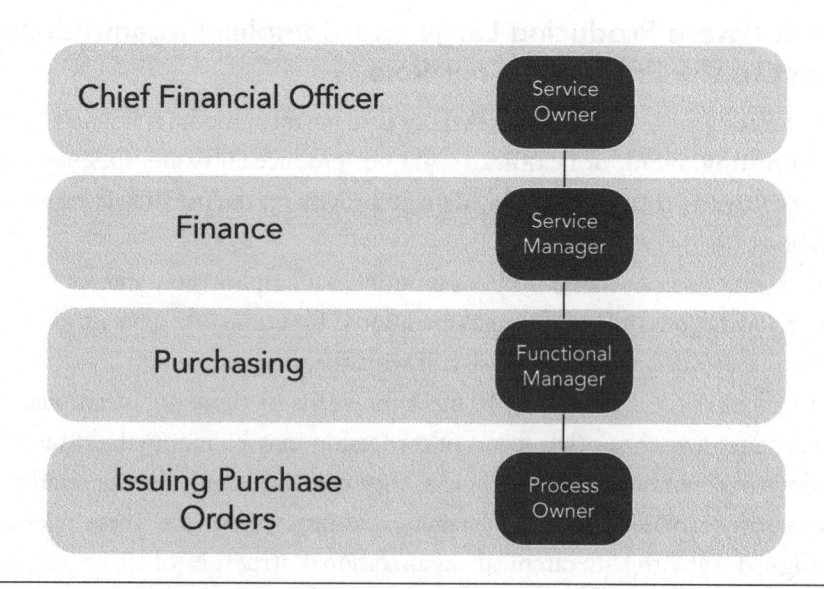

Figure 3.3 • Product Owner Equivalents in Corporate Settings from the Chief Financial Officer to Staff Issuing Purchase Orders

Table 3.1 • Agile Project Charter Template

Project Name	Name of the Project
Project Vision	Describes why the project exists *Example for a healthcare organization:* • To improve the delivery of care services by harnessing the power of technology
Project Mission	Describes what will be done to achieve the project's mission *Example for a healthcare organization:* • To leverage best practices from similar organizations to guide decision-making and implementation
Project Success Criteria	Describes the factors that will contribute to project success *Example for a healthcare organization:* • A reduction in medication errors • A reduction in wait times • Improved bed turnaround when unoccupied

and project goals, the project vision, mission, and success criteria are documented in an **Agile project charter**. Like a traditional waterfall project charter, the Agile project charter authorizes the project work. However, an Agile project charter only provides high-level guidance to a project team. It helps focus the work and provides a shared purpose for the Agile project team.

In large corporations it is often difficult for leaders to quantify the depth and breadth of their organization. Layers of management are necessary to ensure operational efficiency. This is why a single project sponsor, or senior leader, cannot substitute for the product owner; they are too far removed from the organizational processes and services being performed. The senior leader still plays a significant role in a project using Agile frameworks by helping with the mission, vision, and success measures of the project as well as approving funding and resources. However, through **organizational decomposition**, the project is able to identify both the end-user or customer and the service owner or process owner. The latter roles are a better substitute for a product owner than senior leadership. Organizational decomposition is the process of breaking down an organization into discrete functions and processes.

Once a functional representation of the organization is discovered, a process view of the organization can be facilitated. Organizational decomposition supports the Lean principle *genchi genbutsu*, a Japanese term for "go and see (or confirm)."[2]

Case Study 3.1 • Project Initiation for a Large Healthcare Project

An acute-care hospital had hired Imran as a project manager to help lead the hospital's digital transformation activities. Imran had significant experience in a variety of sectors including digital health. One of the key learnings Imran had acquired from previous healthcare projects is the need to have key stakeholders participate throughout the entire project. Much of healthcare involves face-to-face interactions, and Imran knew he would need in-person access to his stakeholders and resources. In addition, Imran's digital health experience had taught him that while technology implementation is a key deliverable, success often hinged on understanding roles, people, and their processes. Imran knew he would need to use Lean in combination with project management practices to be successful.

Imran's first order of business was to understand the project vision and mission and what success would look like in the eyes of the executive team. He met with his sponsors to collect this information and document it in an Agile project charter. As part of his sponsor interactions, Imran also began to document the functions that would be impacted by the project. He documented a first tier of functions and leveraged his sponsors to provide leader names in each of the boxes. The Agile project charter became the basis for his initial meetings with functional leaders.

Imran met with each functional leader to introduce himself and the project. Imran focused on the project vision, mission, and benefits. He couldn't provide details at such an early stage in the project. His goal was to confirm the functional ownership of each box in the hierarchy as well as any sub-functions within the organization and their owners.

Imran's initial hierarchy only contained the high-level organization:

Finance	People and Organizational Efficiency	Health Information Management	Quality and Strategic Planning

After meeting with each functional leader within the organization, Imran's map became much more complete:

Chapter 3 • Understanding Corporate Environments

Quality and Strategic Planning
- Patient Flow and Bed Allocations
- Hospital Scorecards
- Housekeeping and Portering
- Food and Nutrition
- Incidents
- Facilities

Health Information Management
- Chart Tracking
- Patient Locating
- Patient Kiosk
- Provider Table (Physicians)
- Patient Record Distribution
- Data Repository
- Registration
- Switchboard
- Coding/Abstracting
- Corrections and Record Reprinting
- Privacy
- Scanning Patient Records
- Patient Scheduling

People and Organizational Efficiency
- Labour Relations
- Recruiting
- Staff Scheduling
- Benefits
- Occ Health and Safety (WSIB)
- Workload Mgmt

Finance
- General Ledger
- Materials Mgmt
- Case Costing
- Budget/Forecast
- Capital Planning
- Payroll
- Accounts Payable/Receivables
- Physician Billing
- Patient A/R
- Supply Chain
- Contracts/Legal
- Business Intelligence

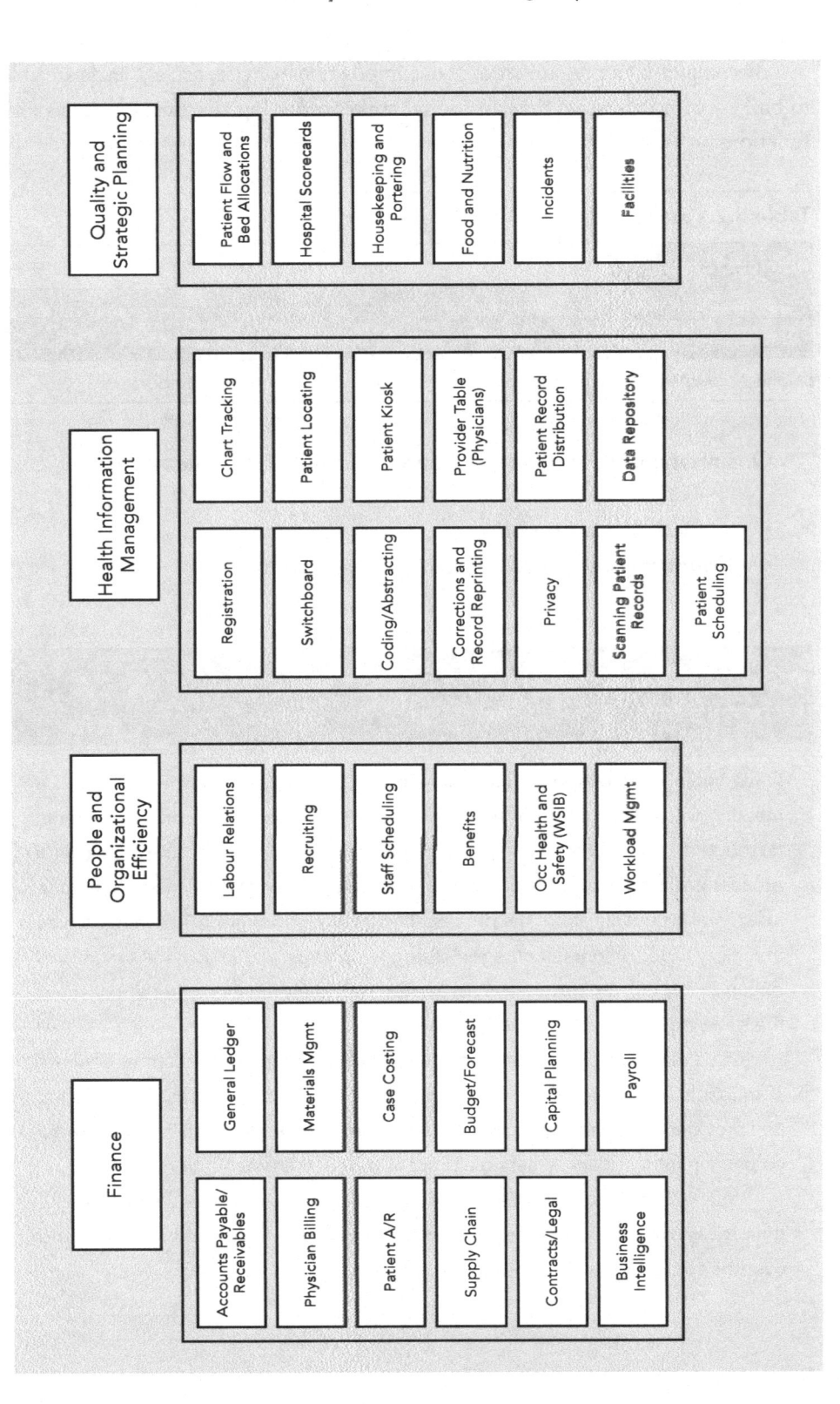

By completing an organizational decomposition exercise, project leads are able to build a comprehensive organizational **stakeholder log** that includes roles and functions.

Table 3.2 • Stakeholder Log Template

Project Name	Name of the project		
Stakeholder Name	Stakeholder Department	Processes Supported	Processes Owned
John Accounting	Finance	Payroll	Reporting

Organizational decomposition supports the following Agile values:

- *Individuals and interactions* over processes and tools
- *Customer collaboration* over contract negotiation

Case Study 3.2 • Creating the Process View of a Complex Organization

Once Imran had created a functional view of the organization, he scheduled a meeting with all members of the functional organization. In the meeting, Imran distributed sticky notes to participants and asked each member to write down a process performed by their organization and a member of their team that is the most knowledgeable about the process. Each member was given 10 minutes to use the sticky notes. Imran encouraged dialogue amongst participants. As members began to capture the processes associated with their functions, Imran collected the sticky notes and placed them on the wall.

Once complete, Imran reviewed the details with the entire team to confirm. Through the confirmation process, team members asked questions of each other and provided commentary. Additional sticky notes were added and moved based on participant feedback, creating a process view of the organization.

Imran utilized his participants' feedback to identify and secure commitment of the process owners in a current state mapping exercise that would be conducted over the coming weeks.

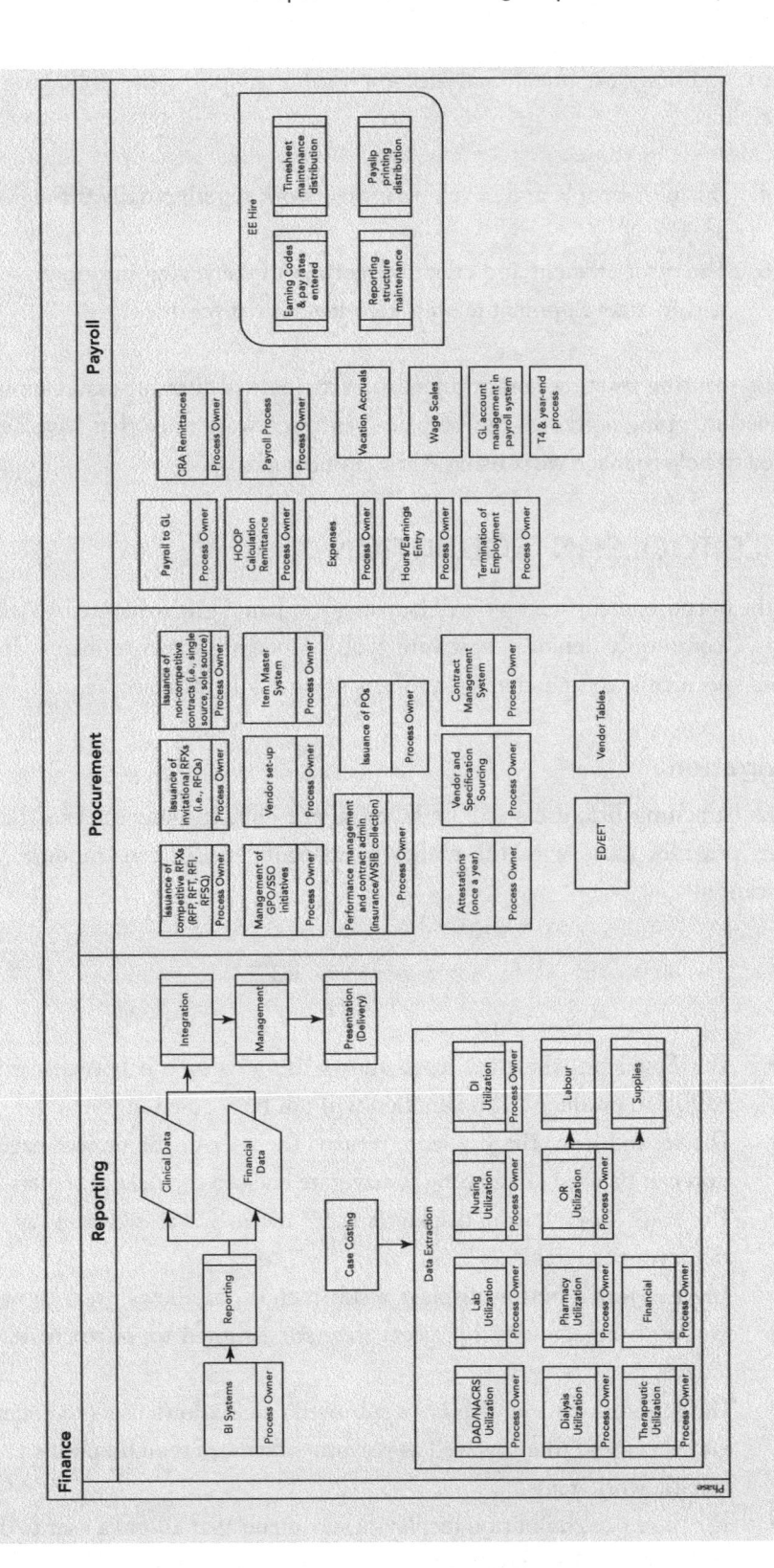

Chapter 3 • Understanding Corporate Environments   53

In addition, organizational decomposition supports the following Agile principles:

4. Business people and developers must work together daily throughout the project.
6. The most efficient and effective method of conveying information to and within a development team is face-to-face conversation.

By securing resource commitment to participate in current state mapping, the planned mapping activities can be placed into software tools that have been designed to help manage work using Agile frameworks.

AGILE TOOLS: INTRODUCTION

For the purpose of this text we will be using the **Jira** Agile software by Atlassian. Jira is a commonly deployed software tool in enterprise environments. It is designed specifically to help manage projects using Agile frameworks.

Navigation

When launching Jira, users will be taken to the default home screen. The home screen provides users with the ability to navigate to different modules of the application.

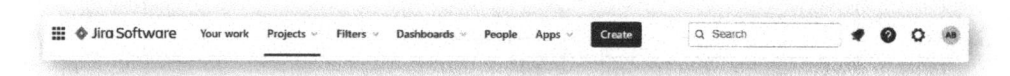

- The first icon, the tiled icon, allows users to switch between different Atlassian products. This function will not be covered in the text.
- The second icon, the Jira icon, returns the user to the project page. This icon can be used at any time to navigate back to the default screen.
- The `Your work` button displays a user's recently accessed items as well as any favourited items.
- The `Projects` button displays a sub-menu that allows users to navigate to recent projects or all projects they are assigned to, or to create a new project.
- The `Filters` button displays a sub-menu that allows users to create custom views and filters as well as perform advanced search options to locate specific work items.
- The `Dashboards` button displays a sub-menu that allows a user to display and create project dashboards that the user has access to.

- The `People` button displays the people and teams a user works with and allows users to add new team members and create new teams.
- The `Apps` button allows users to see and manage applications that have been installed on a Jira site.
- The `Create` button opens a window for users to create new issues for a project.
- The Search function allows users to search issues, projects, boards, filters, and queries.
- The bell icon displays any recent notifications about work progress.
- The question mark icon allows the user to access Atlassian support documents, interact with others in the Jira community, as well as view the general terms of service.
- The gear icon opens a system settings window.
- The final icon opens the account settings window. Note that the icon's appearance will differ depending on the user.

Your Work

The Your work pane can be used to view recent items, assignments, and favourites.

- The Worked on tab shows items that are assigned to a user and are in progress.
- The Viewed tab shows recently viewed items.
- The Assigned to me tab shows all work items assigned to the user.
- The Starred tab shows items that the user has favourited.

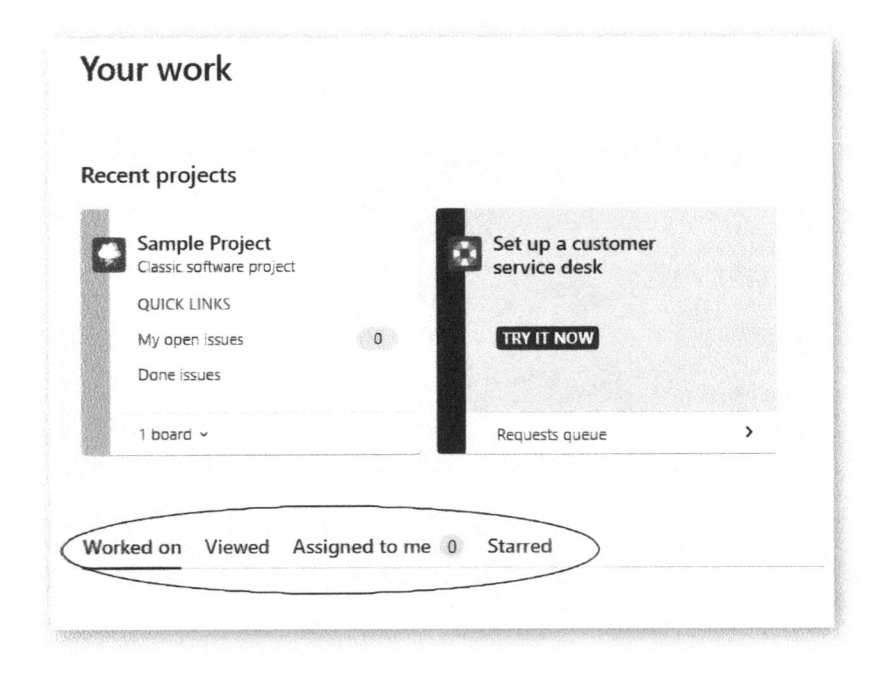

Projects

The Projects menu item takes the user to a list of all of their projects.

- Selecting a project will open the project work space, which will be covered later in the text.
- From the projects window, new projects can be created by selecting the top-right button, `Create project`.
- The three dots, or ellipsis, opens a menu to allow users to adjust project settings or delete the project.

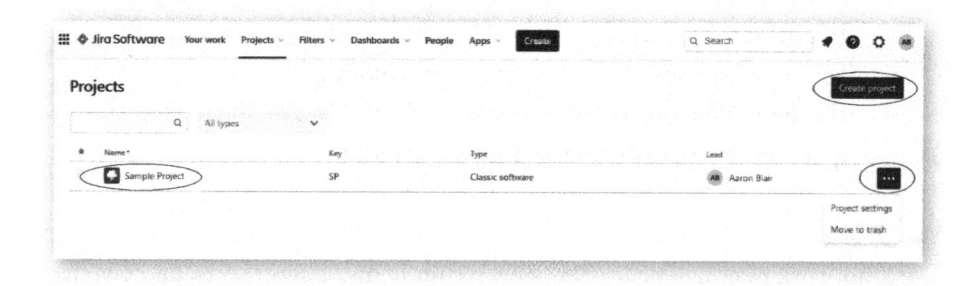

Filters

The Filters navigation allows users to navigate pre-defined searches as well as access more advanced search filter functions.

To see all existing filters, select the `View all filters` option from the Filters pull-down menu.

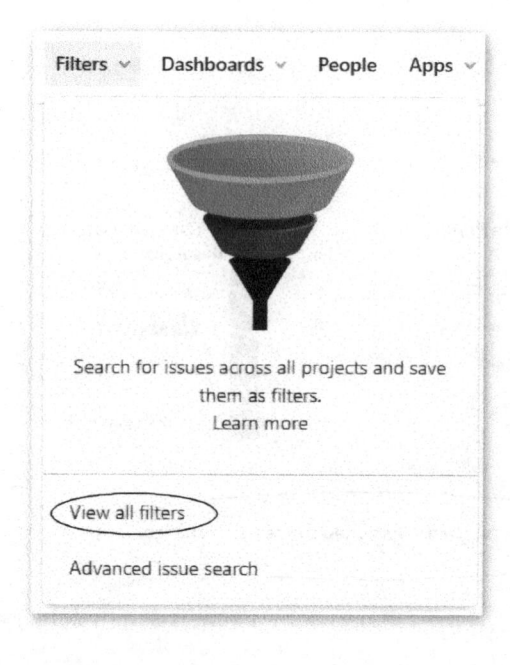

The Filters menu item allows users to see the results of pre-defined searches as well as create new filters.

- The star icon allows users to favourite a filter.
- The Name column displays a hyperlink of the filter name. Selecting the hyperlink will bring users to the filter results screen.
- The `Create filter` button takes users to the filter home screen, where users can create new filters.
- The ellipsis allows users to manage subscriptions and notifications as well as modify, copy, or delete the selected filter.

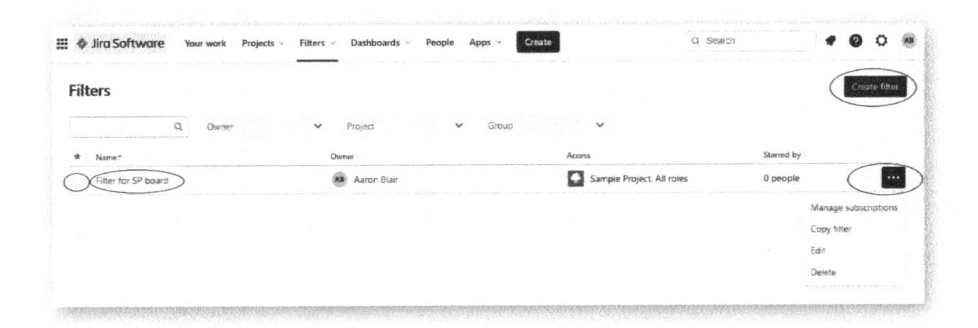

The Advanced menu item in the Filters drop-down menu will open the Advanced filter creation pane. Users can create complex filters and searches from the Advanced filter pane. Advanced filters can be saved and favourited for future use.

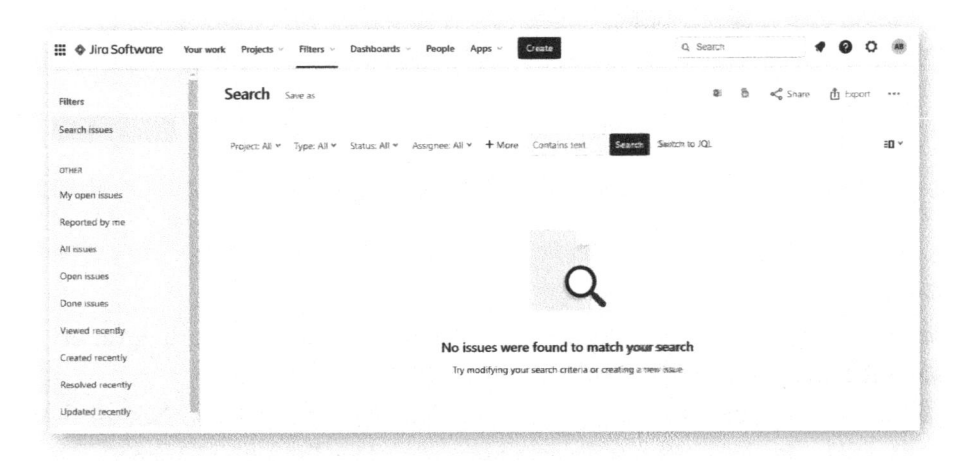

Dashboards
The Dashboards menu item takes users to a dashboard that provides an at-a-glance view of the assigned project, tasks, and activity.

- The star icon allows users to favourite a dashboard.
- The Name column displays a hyperlink of the dashboard name. Selecting the hyperlink will bring users to the selected dashboard screen.
- The Create dashboard button will open the dashboard creation window.
- The ellipsis allows users to copy the selected dashboard to be used for additional projects.

People

The People menu item takes users to the people screen, where users can create new teams, manage users, and search for available resources.

Settings

The cog menu option opens a sub-menu that allows users to perform a variety of administrative functions.

Jira settings allows advanced configuration of the Jira system. Not all functions will be available to users, as they are reserved for Jira administrators.

- The User management menu option allows users to add, invite, and configure users and permissions.
- The Billing menu option allows users to configure organizational payment information.

Chapter 3 • Understanding Corporate Environments   59

- The System menu option allows advanced configuration options.
- The Products menu option allows products to be added, such as Portfolio.
- The Projects menu option allows users to configure project attributes.
- The Issues menu option allows users to configure issue attributes.
- The Apps menu option allows users to add new apps to the Jira instance.

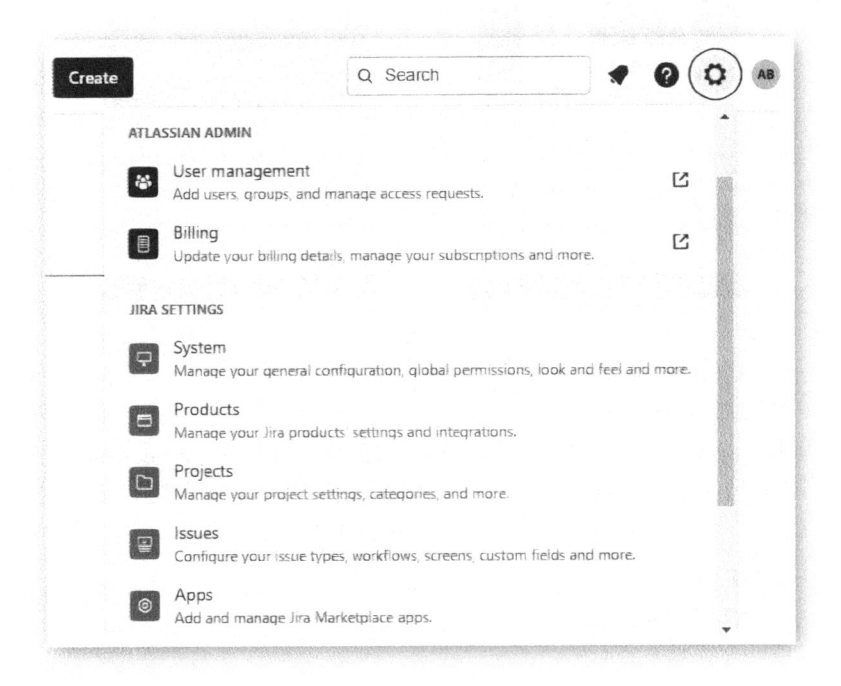

Creating a Project

Projects can be created within Agile. Once an Agile project charter is approved, it authorizes the lead to create a project. The following outlines the steps to create an Agile project in Jira:

- From the navigation bar, select `Projects`.
- Select `Create project`.
- Choose the `Select classic` button.

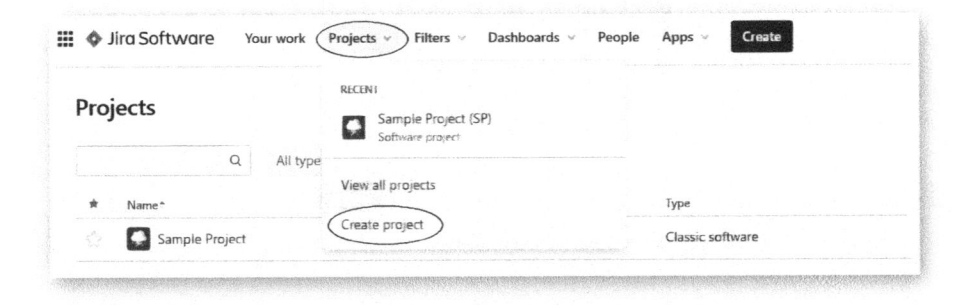

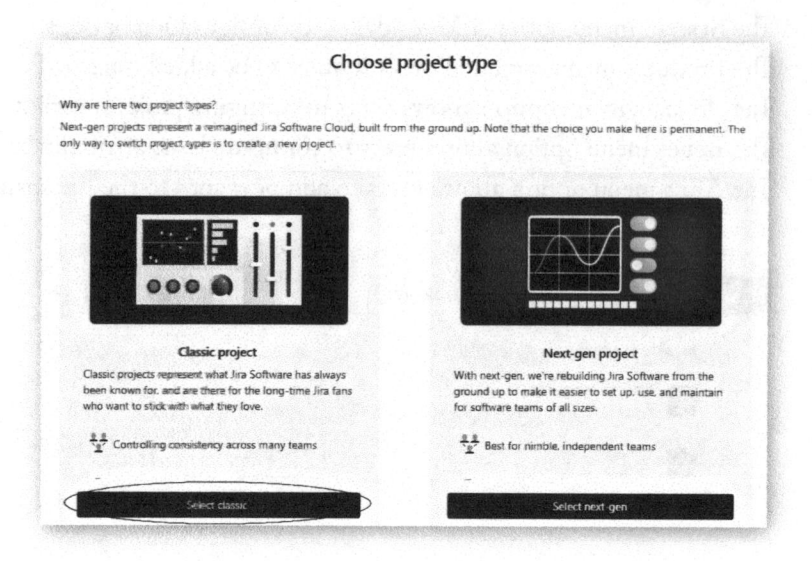

- Enter the project name.
- The project key will be auto-generated based on the project name entered.
- Use the Scrum template. Scrum is usually the default. However, if Scrum does not appear as the template, select the Change template button and select Scrum.
- Select Create.

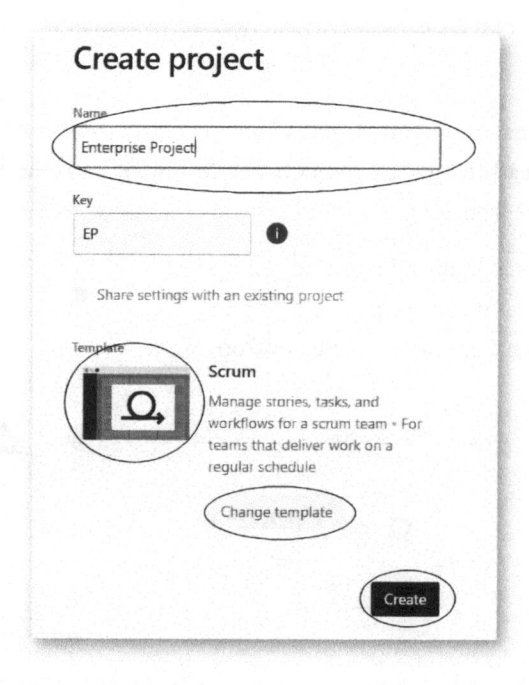

The project will be created. The user will be taken to the project details page with Active sprints as the default selection.

- Select `Project settings`. The user will be taken to the project details screen.

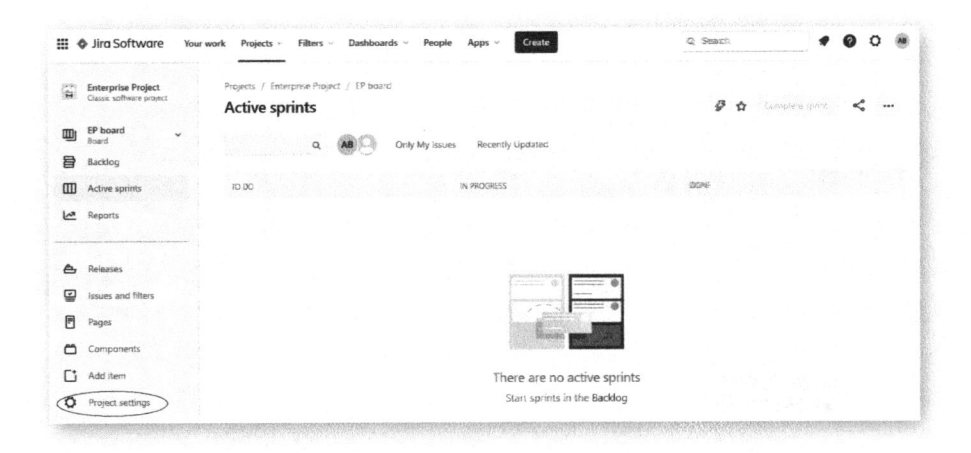

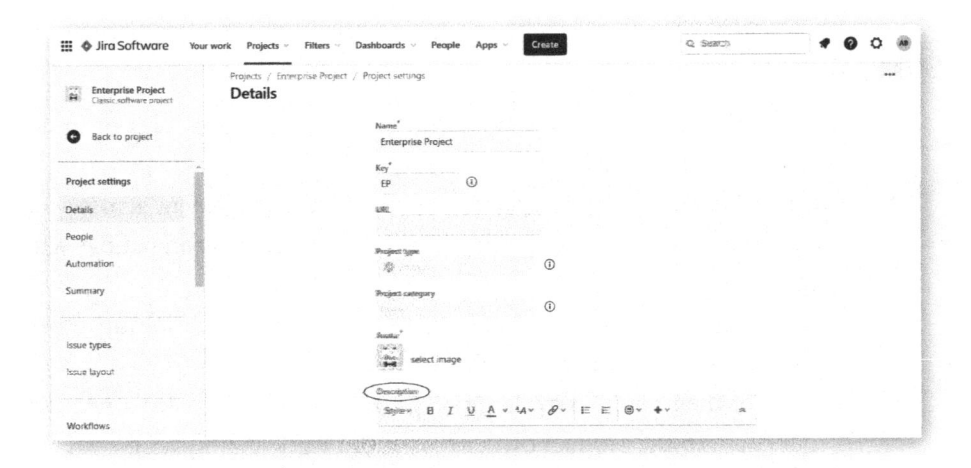

- Enter the Agile project charter information in the Description section. A URL can be added. Project type is defaulted to Software since Scrum is being used as the template.
- Select `Save details`. The project has been created and updated with the Agile project charter information.

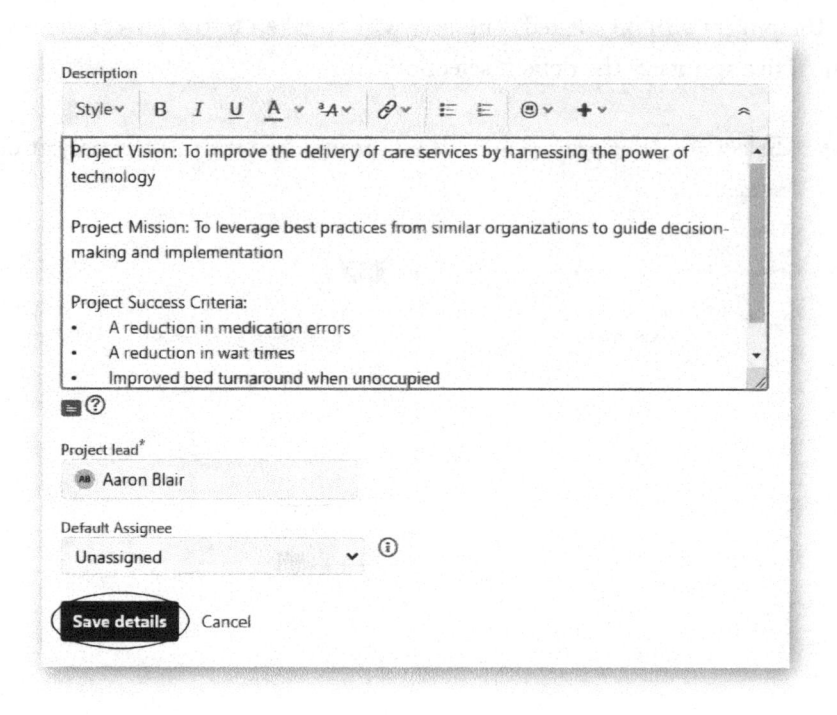

SUMMARY

- Agile methodology was developed for small teams (of six, plus or minus three) in flat organizational structures.
- Large and complex organizations have layers of management across a variety of functions, which, on the surface, may seem incompatible with Agile.
- Silos can form in large and complex organizations, inhibiting cross-departmental communication and collaboration.
- Because of their complexity, large organizations may not have a role that is equivalent to the product owner role in the Agile methodology.
- To adapt Agile to large and complex organizations, breaking divisions into discrete functions and processes is necessary, as this enables key Agile principles such as customer collaboration.
- Large and complex organizations can identify service owners, service managers, and process owners. These roles can function as the product owner to support Agile methodologies.
- Organizational decomposition approaches are used to facilitate breaking large organizational functions into discrete processes with process owners.

- A large number of interconnected Agile teams will often be working on large enterprise projects.
- To manage the size and complexity of enterprise Agile projects, software tools are often necessary.
- Organizational decomposition will form the foundation of collaboration and face-to-face interaction throughout an enterprise Agile project.

KEY TERMS

Agile project charter: a document that authorizes an Agile project's existence, the work, and allocation of resources. An Agile project charter only provides high-level guidance to a project team, such as the project vision, mission, and success criteria. It helps focus the work and provides a shared purpose for the Agile project team.

flat organization: an organization with few or no levels of management between staff

functional manager: responsible for a collection of processes within an organization. In Agile, a functional manager supports the creation of the measurable success criteria and supplies resources for the project.

genchi genbutsu: a Japanese term for "go and see (or confirm)"

hierarchical organization: an organization with multiple layers of management. Workers are organized under each layer. Each layer usually specializes in performing a specific function for an organization such as finance, marketing, etc.

Jira: a specialized software tool designed for managing Agile projects

organizational decomposition: a process that facilitates breaking organizations into discrete functions and processes. Organizational decomposition enables a project to get closer to the end-user or customer as well as the service owner or process owner.

process owner: an individual responsible for a specific process within an organization. In Agile, a process owner supports defining the measurable success criteria of a project and can be part of the development team.

service manager: a manager responsible for a collection of functions within an organization. The service manager supports the creation of the project vision and mission, facilitates the measurable success criteria of an Agile project, and can supply resources.

service owner: an executive responsible for a collection of functions within an organization. In Agile the service owner is responsible for the vision and mission of the project, and signs off on the project success criteria. The closest parallel to a service owner is an executive sponsor for a waterfall project.

silo: a closed management system that does not interact or operate with other silos, or divisions, within an organization

stakeholder log: a log used to capture and categorize internal stakeholders based on their department, process owners, and organizational processes they support but do not own

DISCUSSION QUESTIONS

1. What knowledge areas of the PMI methodology does organizational decomposition support? How is organizational decomposition similar to these PMI knowledge areas and how is it different?
2. Why is the concept of *genchi genbutsu* important in enterprise Agile projects? What principles does it support?
3. How is an Agile project charter different from a PMI waterfall project charter? Describe and explain the similarities and differences.
4. Should Agile be adapted for large, complex organizations, or should organizations that are interested in adopting Agile modify their organizational structure before they attempt to conduct Agile projects? Explain your answer.
5. Why does it become necessary to utilize software tools to manage enterprise Agile projects? Is the use of tools contrary to Agile principles? Explain your answer.

NOTES

1. K. Rubin, *Essential Scrum: A Practical Guide to the Most Popular Agile Process* (Boston, MA: Addison-Wesley Professional, 2012).
2. C. Protzman, F. Whiton, and D. Protzman, *Implementing Lean* (Productivity Press, 2018).

4 Capturing and Prioritizing User Stories through the Value Stream

CHAPTER OVERVIEW

In chapter 4 we introduce the Lean tool: value stream mapping. Value stream mapping, or current state mapping, builds on organizational decomposition concepts discussed in chapter 3. Mapping activities are used to identify requirements that can be used by Agile frameworks to organize and prioritize into user stories.

User stories will be covered in greater detail, including best practices for user story creation. This includes how user stories can be created by utilizing Lean techniques and approaches to creating effective user stories.

By the end of the chapter, readers will understand how value stream mapping can be used to support Agile, how effective user stories are created, and how outputs of value stream mapping can be imported into software tools designed to support Agile frameworks.

WHAT IS VALUE STREAM MAPPING?

Value stream mapping is a Lean management technique that analyzes the current state of a process to identify and remove waste. The goal of value stream mapping is to design a more efficient **future state process**.[1] To understand a value stream map, it is easiest to imagine a literal stream and its flow of water. A stream flows most efficiently when there are no obstructions to affect its current. Therefore, a **current state process** map maps the flow of a process, its steps, and its organizational interactions, which can help identify any obstructions that negatively affect a process's efficiency. These obstructions can be any one of the three forms of waste: *mura, muda, muri*, or non-value activities. A future state process is a re-envisioned process with obstructions removed to achieve better efficiency, or flow, resulting in greater customer value.

Value stream maps provide a visual representation of a process. By having a visual map, obstructions can be more readily identified along with improvement opportunities. As a result, like any map, value stream maps use image conventions to represent different types of activities.

A common feature amongst value stream maps is that they comprise nodes and connections. Node icons can vary; figure 4.1 is not an exhaustive list. The key to any value stream map is to use a node to capture when that action occurs. Once the action is complete, a directional connection is made to the next activity, or node, to occur in the process. Connections include a single node to a single node connection, a single node to multiple node connections, and multiple nodes to a single node connection. Value stream maps vary in complexity.

Another common feature amongst value stream maps are icons that identify where waste has been identified. This can be represented by a *kaizen* burst as depicted in figure 4.1. However, there are many ways to represent waste. When waste, or opportunity for process improvement, is identified in a value stream map, it usually represents a commitment to further investigate the improvement opportunity.

Process box: a discrete activity performed either manually or through automation

Data box: exchange of information

Initiator or terminator: represents the beginning or end of a process

Manual document: represents a physical form of media that could be created manually or through automation and passed through the process

Pre-defined process: a group of activities that have been previously captured

Decision box: represents a manual or automated intervention where process flows diverge or loop

Data repository: represents a system, storage, and/or retrieval action

Kaizen burst: represents an area in the process where improvements may be possible. Usually highlights where more investigation will occur.

Electronic flow connecting two nodes in a process

Directional flow of the process and interactions among nodes

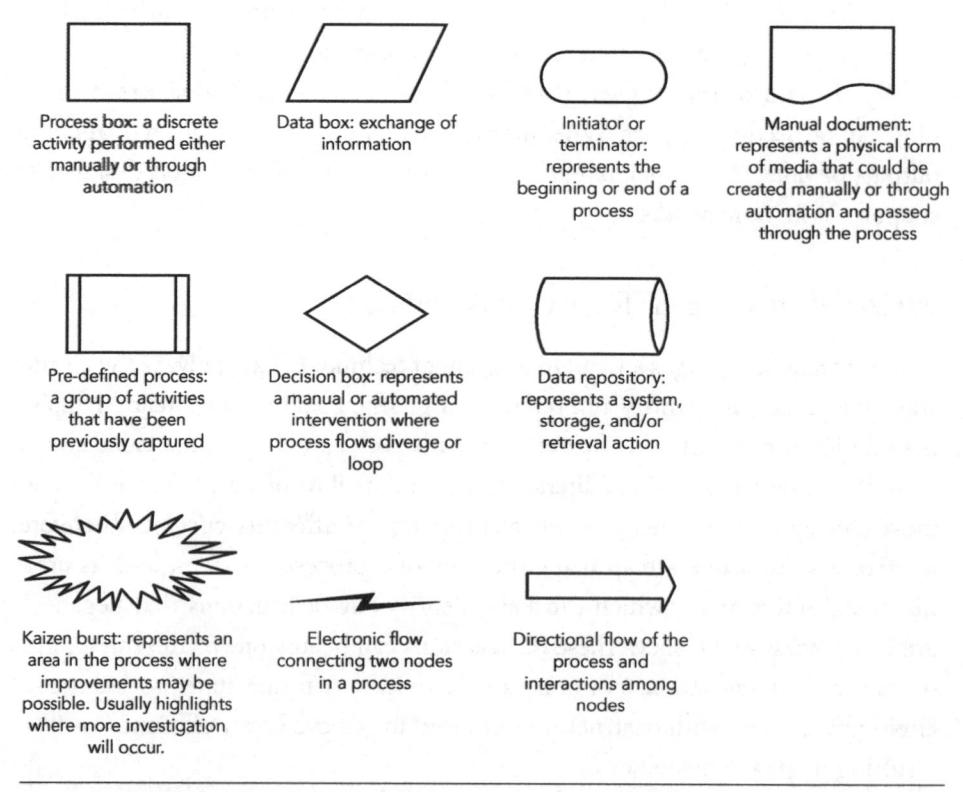

Figure 4.1 • Common Value Stream Icons

CREATING VALUE STREAMS

Value stream, or current state, maps can be created through **observation, collaboration,** or a hybrid of both. Observation supports the concept of *genchi genbutsu*, or "go and see." Project team members can perform a **gemba walk,** which involves going to where the process occurs and observing the process in action. By doing so, project team members can ask questions in real time, take notes, and return to document the map based on their observations. This process can be effective in organizations where processes are physical and can be easily observed without disrupting an organization's operations.[2]

Observational approaches are not always the most effective or realistic method of capturing a process map. Organizations that operate largely through information technology may have processes that are not readily observable by performing a gemba walk. In addition, for some organizations, such as healthcare, observing a process could be disruptive or even dangerous in the case of administering

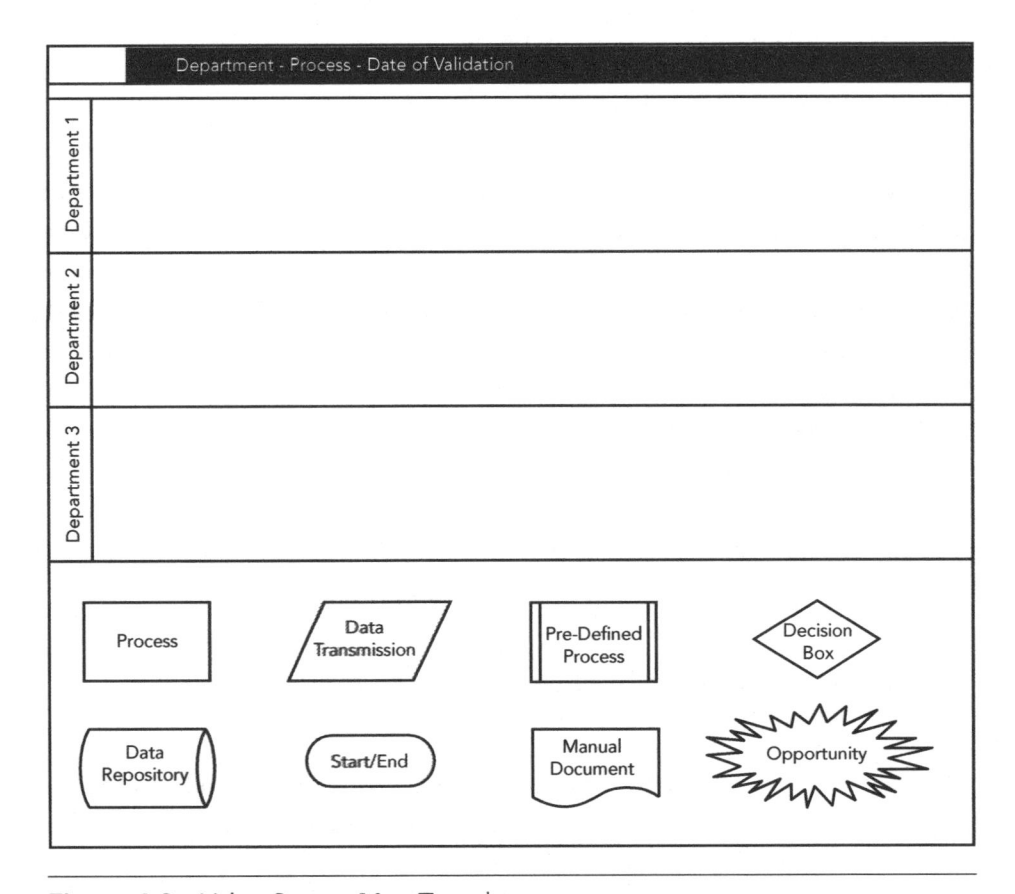

Figure 4.2 • Value Stream Map Template

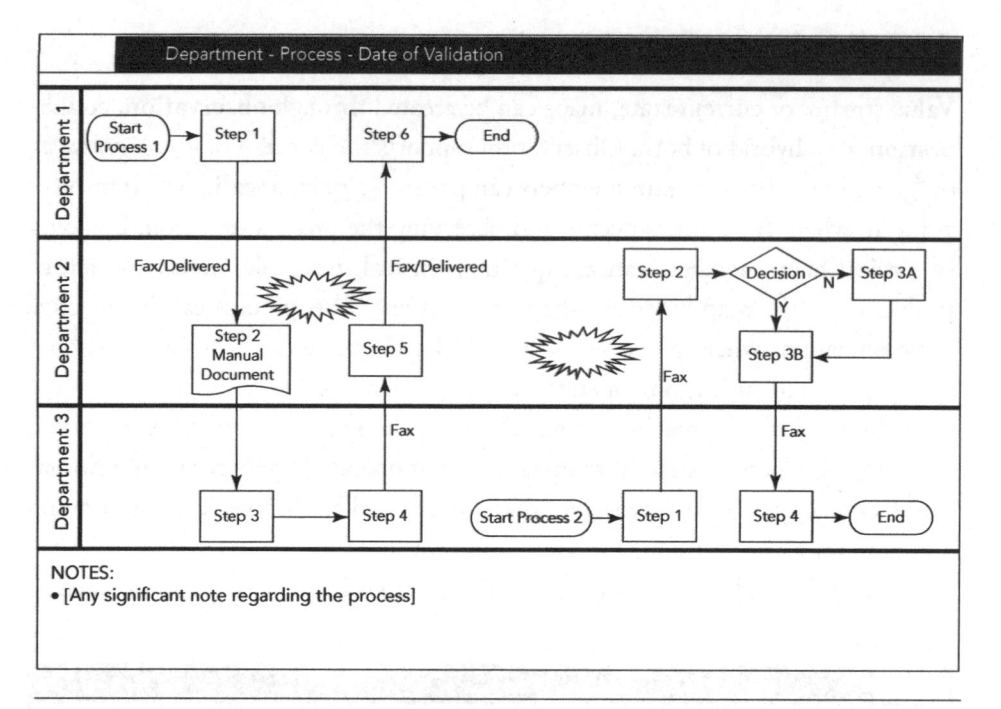

Figure 4.3 • Value Stream Example

life-saving health treatments. Under these scenarios, collaboration may be a more effective approach. Collaboration refers to the technique of gathering subject-matter experts into a process mapping session in which a process is mapped out end to end. This occurs *away* from the "action" but involves experts familiar enough with the process that physical observation by the project team is not required. At the completion of the value stream process mapping exercise, the facilitator will "walk" the process with participants to ensure correctness as well as to solicit opportunities for improvement.

Value streams are typically captured in a template. The template is usually divided into **swim lanes**. Swim lanes represent departments and help illustrate cross-functional interaction. Templates usually capture node and connection conventions.

COMBINING VALUE STREAM MAPPING WITH AGILE PRINCIPLES

Through value stream mapping, teams can collect requirements and user stories. During the value stream mapping process, owners and subject-matter experts can identify key functions that must remain. This does not mean that the key functions that are identified cannot be replaced with an alternative approach; however, the function is mandatory. Consider the example of financial reporting. In the current state a file must be prepared and sent to an external accounting firm. As part of the current state there could be multiple manual inputs that create inefficiencies. This process may be automated through the project; however, the output file must remain.

Once requirements and user stories have been collected, project teams must come to understand the relative importance of each. The **MoSCoW** prioritization model, developed under the **Dynamic Systems Development Method (DSDM)** Agile framework, helps to organize and structure requirement and user story priority. *MoSCoW* is an acronym that breaks requirements into categories:

Must-have requirements—These requirements are mandatory. The project cannot launch unless they are fulfilled.

Should-have requirements—These requirements are high priority. Their absence may not prevent a project from launching but may prevent an organization realizing the full benefit of the project or affect the measures of success outlined in the Agile project charter.

Could-have requirements—These requirements aren't as high in priority but could represent additional value. Could-have requirements are also known as "exciters" in the Kano customer satisfaction model, which will be discussed later in this chapter.

Won't-have requirements—These requirements will not be included in a release or project. They can be included in later phases, but for the purpose of the project are removed from planning and further discussion.[3]

For the purposes of planning, requirements should be distributed across categories.

Must-have requirements should not exceed 60 percent of the overall distribution. A greater percentage can add additional risk to the project. Could-have requirements should not exceed 20 percent of the overall distribution; more than this would indicate that the project may not be achieving business value and numerous superficial features or requirements are being implemented. Should-have requirements should represent the difference between the must-have and could-have requirements.[4]

[Bar chart showing MoSCoW requirements distribution: Must Have ≈ 60, Should Have ≈ 20, Could Have ≈ 20]

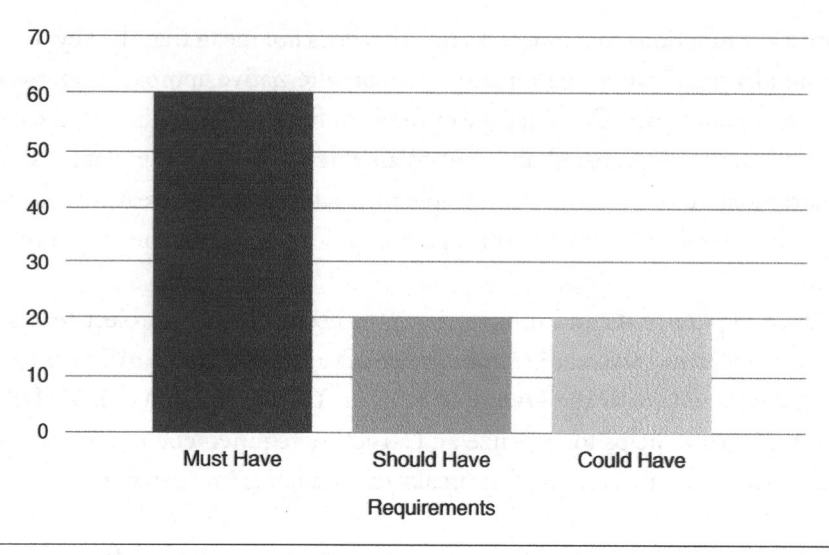

Figure 4.4 • MoSCoW Requirements Distribution

> **Case Study 4.1** • Converting Collaboration to Requirements
>
> Imran utilized the sticky-notes session to build a schedule of current state mapping activities. He used the process view of the organization to schedule mapping sessions that included the process owner and functional managers and were supported by project analysts.
>
> Imran facilitated mapping the process flow across departments using value stream mapping techniques and icon conventions. During the sessions, Imran found he was hearing requirements and needs from both the process owners and functional managers. He decided to have the project analysts capture the requirements using the MoSCoW technique. In addition, Imran realized he could use the opportunity to capture the requirements as user stories for later planning.
>
> Imran used a template that would help capture user stories, their relative priority, and their contribution to waste reduction. He knew he would be able to use the template to later import this information into Agile software to create a backlog.

USER STORIES

As explained earlier in the text, user stories are short, simple descriptions of a feature or requirement, told from the perspective of the person who will benefit from the new capability. This can be a user of or stakeholder in the solution. User

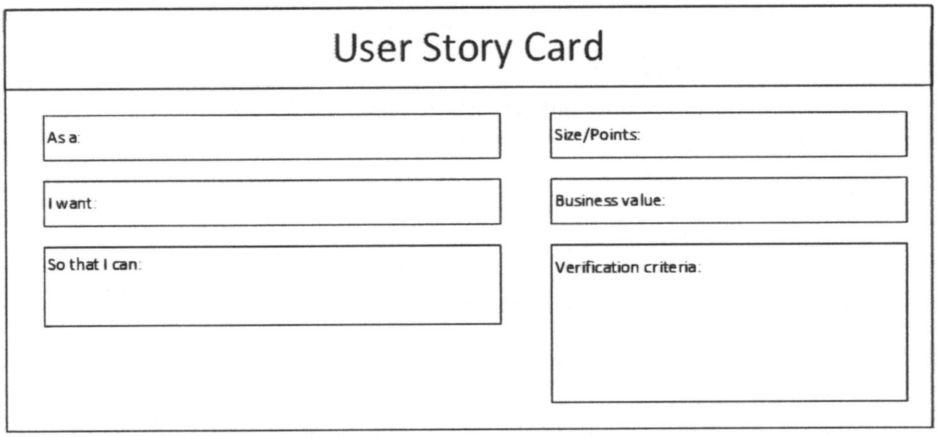

User Story Card
As a: / I want: / So that I can: Size/Points: / Business value: / Verification criteria:

Figure 4.5 • User Story Card

stories typically follow a simple template: As a < type of stakeholder >, I want < some goal > so that < some reason >.[5] User stories aren't the only form in which work can be represented in Agile frameworks, although they are one of the more common approaches and, as a concept, can be utilized in most Agile frameworks to capture the work to be performed.

Although user stories are often created by product owners, corporations that are not familiar with Agile or software development may need to leverage process owners or functional managers—those who are closest to being able to describe the need and reason for a story—to create them.

User stories are often captured in cards.

Additional elements of a user story include the following:

- *Size/points*—These are used to help estimate the user story for planning purposes and will be covered in chapter 6.
- *Business value*—This captures the value the user story contributes to the organization, project mission, or customer and can help prioritize the story.
- *Verification criteria*—These capture how the user story can be verified as complete and will be covered later in this chapter.

User stories should follow the **INVEST** guideline. INVEST is an acronym that outlines the attributes that define high-quality user stories.

Independent—The story is discrete and can be fulfilled independently of other user stories.

Negotiable—The story is open to negotiation of how it can be best fulfilled by the development team.
Valuable—The story contributes to customer value, the project mission, and/or achieving organizational goals.
can be Estimated—The story can be estimated by the development team. Estimation refers to the effort required to complete it.
Small—The story is discrete and incremental in achieving value. When stories are too large, they often have to be broken into smaller units for planning and estimating purposes. This will be covered at greater length in chapter 6.
Testable—The story can be verified and validated. Often the steps are included in the story so the development team can understand what is needed to verify that the story has met product owner expectations.[6]

INVEST supports the three Cs of good user-story creation:

Concise/card—The user story is short enough to fit on a 4 × 6 card.
Conversation—The user story is supported by a conversation or is a starting point for a conversation between business and project teams.
Confirmation—The user story should include acceptance criteria to help the development team better understand the requirement and expectations of the story.[7]

In addition to the three Cs, Agile user stories need to be specific enough to estimate. Therefore, stating that a user would like to manage customers using a single interface may not be broken into sufficient detail for the development team to estimate. When considering how to further decompose a user story, the CRUD approach can be used. CRUD is an acronym that represents standard functions for most software:

Create—The action of adding a new entry into a system
Read—The action of being able to retrieve and review a system record
Update—The action of modifying an existing system record
Delete—The action of removing, hiding, or disabling a system record[8]

Including testable criteria within the user story supports a concept borrowed from the **Extreme Programming (XP)** Agile software development framework referred to as **test-driven development**, or **TDD**. Test-driven development requires the verification criteria to be created before the code; this approach can help developers ensure they build a feature that will pass verification.[9]

In contrast to TDD, waterfall generates requirements that are often passed along to developers to begin coding. The passage of requirements often occurs simultaneously with testers beginning to write test plans and scripts. The two groups often work on their respective functions independently, which can pose challenges if the groups interpret the requirements differently and could result in code that does not pass verification.

TDD supports the Lean concept of *jidoka*. *Jidoka* is a Japanese term. The goal of *jidoka* is to support activities that "build in" quality. Rather than identifying defects after a product has been completed, the goal of *jidoka* is to minimize defects from occurring in the first place by fixing the defect-causing behaviour at its source.[10]

When defects are discovered after a product has been built, the discovery could come "too late" and the defect could cause costly and inefficient re-work, which could delay other important activities. Therefore, by building in quality at the source, a level of automation is introduced that supports a continual throughput of activity and efficiency. If we consider the stream or flow-of-water analogy, defects represent obstacles that disrupt the current and optimal efficiency of a stream. This is true for cross-functional processes as well. By including TDD within the story itself, quality criteria have been built into the development task, which should minimize the occurrence of defects downstream.

Business value is another key concept to both a good user story and Lean. Lean defines a value-added activity as one that meets these criteria:

- It transforms the product or service
- Customers are willing to "pay" for it
- It must be done correctly the first time

Some of the above criteria may be difficult to quantify. To help visualize value, user stories can be placed in a **Kano model**. The Kano model is a product development and customer satisfaction approach. The Kano model breaks products into categories that help identify activities that drive customer satisfaction and business value.[11] There are three qualities associated with the Kano model:

1. *Must-be or needs qualities*—This category captures the elements that customers often take for granted and that, if not fulfilled, create customer dissatisfaction. These types of qualities can include non-functional needs

such as product performance, scalability, sustainability, reliability, maintainability, safety, and security, as well as functionality, or core functions that enable business operations.

2. *One-dimensional or wants qualities*—This category is linear. Customers are satisfied if their wants are fulfilled and are dissatisfied if their wants are left unfulfilled. These types of qualities are often functional in nature and specific to a project. For example, an organizational unit being able to generate automated reports that were once manual illustrates customer expectations. If the project does not fulfill the expectation, the customer will be dissatisfied with the project.

3. *Attractive or delighter qualities*—This category provides satisfaction when fulfilled but does not generate dissatisfaction if left unfulfilled. This is because customers aren't expecting these qualities in their product and, as a result, are pleasantly surprised by them. These types of qualities can be cosmetic, an unexpected feature or function that improves efficiency, and so on. It is important to note that once a delighter quality has been experienced, it often becomes a one-dimensional or must-be quality in future releases.[12]

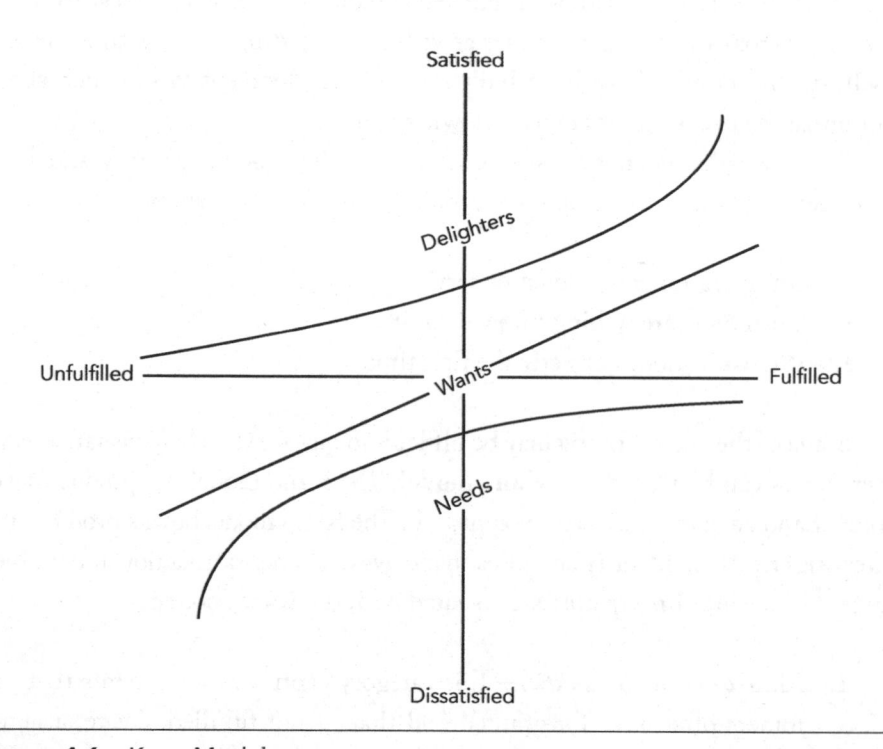

Figure 4.6 • Kano Model

Another method of identifying value is the elimination of waste. Value stream mapping identifies obstacles that are impeding a process from achieving optimal flow. Business value can be assigned to a story by identifying the type of obstacle(s) a story removes. Lean identifies **seven forms of waste**:

1. *Transportation waste*—Materials, information, or resources are unnecessarily moved to fulfill a process.
2. *Waiting waste*—Resources are idle while they wait for a dependent process or activity to be completed.
3. *Overproduction waste*—Resources are producing more than necessary to achieve customer needs.
4. *Defect waste*—The process results in an unacceptable outcome.
5. *Inventory waste*—Additional resources or work-in-progress items do not directly contribute to or impede a process's ability to achieve customer value.
6. *Movement waste*—Materials, information, or resources are excessively moved to complete a specific process activity.
7. *Extra processing waste*—Work is performed that is not required to satisfy the customer need.

Stories can remove single or multiple obstacles from the flow of a process. However, if a story does not contribute to the removal of waste or fulfill one of the Kano model's needs or wants, then it does not have a clear business value. When stories do not contribute to generating value, they should be reviewed by the product owner and stakeholders to determine whether they should be considered as part of the project deliverables.[13]

For large corporate projects, it may be difficult to capture all the variables associated with user stories through the use of cards. Often, templates are used that can be loaded into Agile software tools. The following illustrates a user story template.

USER STORIES SUPPORTING PROCUREMENT PROCESSES

Capturing user stories not only adds business value, but can support additional processes such as procurement. For a large and complex enterprise project, it may be necessary to tender qualified vendors. This can be performed through a **request for proposal** (**RFP**) process. An RFP is a formal purchase request to qualified vendors. It typically represents a commitment that an organization will be purchasing a solution or services to achieve a business need. Vendors respond to RFPs by stating their

User Story Template

Department	Process	Process Owner	User Story Name	Current System (System Name/ Manual/NA)	Type (Function, Validation, Reporting)	Description	Verification	Kano Scale	Priority (Must Have, Should Have, Could Have, Won't Have)	Transportation	Waiting	Overproduction	Defects	Inventory	Movement	Extra processing
Organizational department	Process the story supports	Process owner or customer to have follow-up discussions if needed	Name of story	How the requirement is being fulfilled in the current state	The goal of the story to fulfill a function, action, validation, or report	User story template: As a: <User> I want to: <some goal> So that I can: <some reason>	How the development team will know whether they fulfilled the story	Need Want Delighter	MH, SH, CH, WH							

Figure 4.7 • Enterprise User Story Template

organization's or product's capabilities. A vendor's response is organized against the purchaser's set of requirements, usually contained within the RFP. By capturing value associated with story, organizations can better evaluate vendor responses and select a solution or service that will achieve the greatest value.

AGILE TOOLS: USER STORIES

User stories can be created individually or via import.

Creating an Individual Story

Select the Create button at the top-right navigation.

The Create issue window will appear. Ensure the correct project is selected. Story should be selected as the issue type.

Enter in the user story summary and description. Select Create.

Confirming User Story Creation

There are a variety of ways to verify that the story has been created. The `Your work` button will show work the user has completed. However, to ensure the story has been linked to the correct project, using the Filters function is most consistent with the previous versions of Jira.

Select `Filters` from the navigation bar. Select `View all filters`.

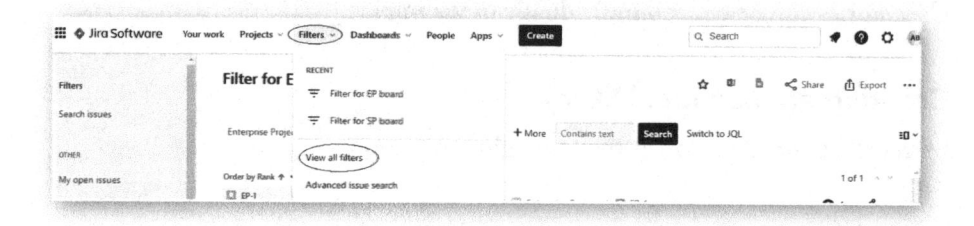

The Filters pane will appear. Select the project the user story was created for. The recently created user story can be seen.

Note: The term *issues* is equivalent to user story in Jira.

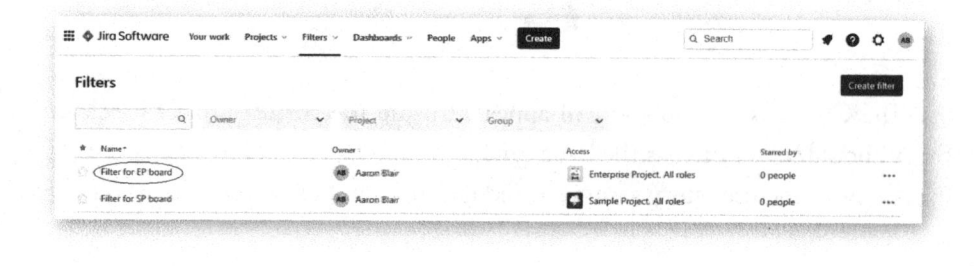

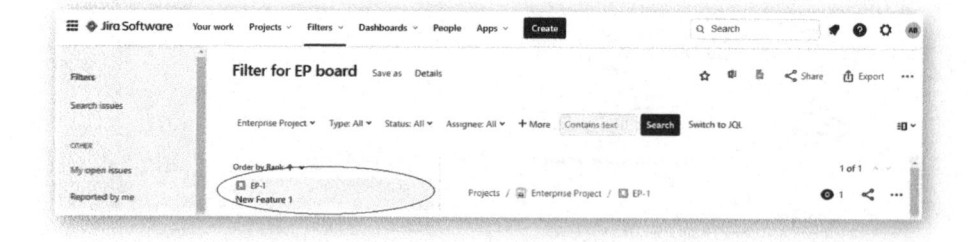

Creating Multiple User Stories

To create multiple user stories in Jira, prior to selecting the `Create` button, select the `Create another` radio button.

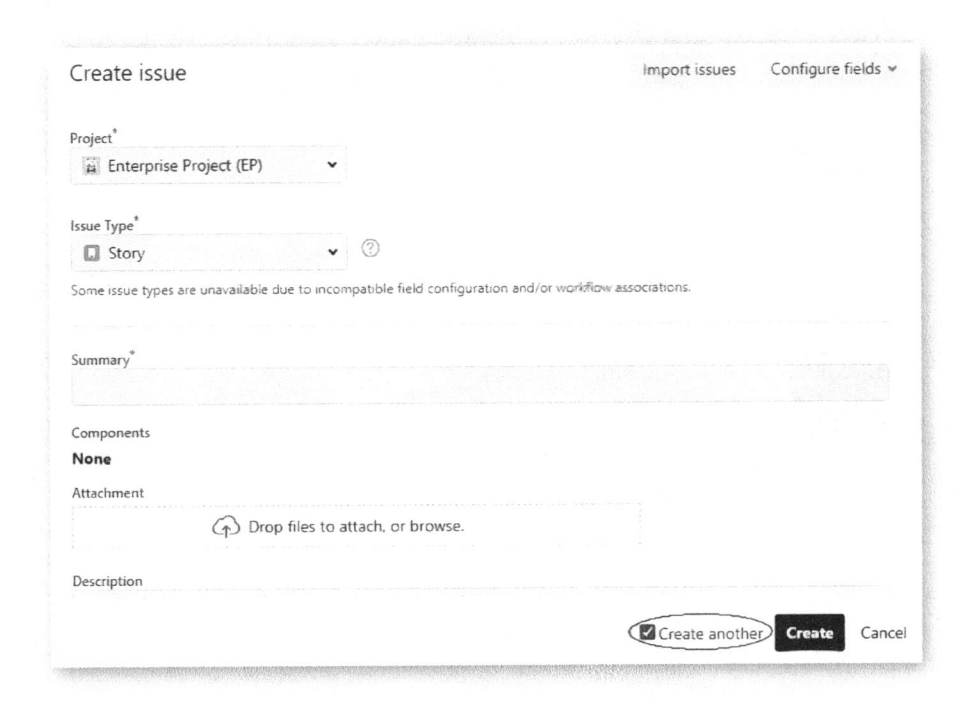

Chapter 4 • Capturing and Prioritizing User Stories through the Value Stream   79

Importing User Stories—File Preparation

When importing user stories into Jira, it is first necessary to prepare the file for import. This instruction will highlight how to prepare a Microsoft Excel file for import.

From your open user stories Excel form, select the `File` tab.

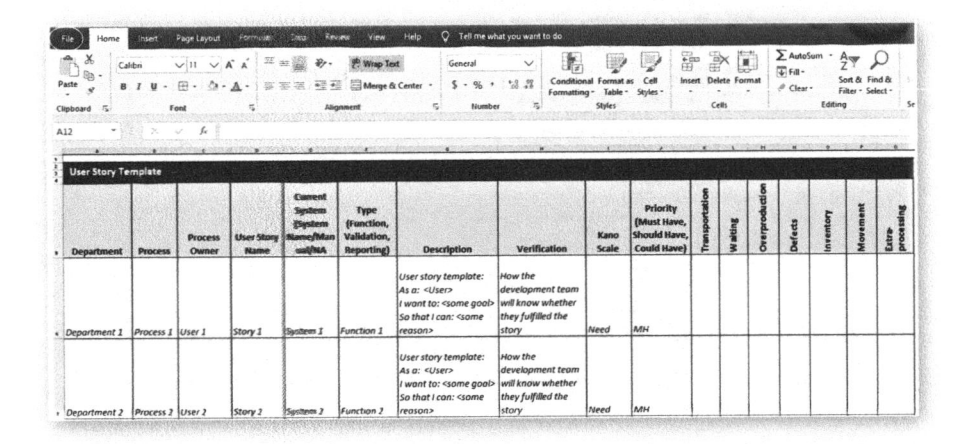

AGILE PROJECT DELIVERY

Select Save As, and choose the file destination. Remember where it is saved. Jira will require you to navigate to the file location as part of the import process.

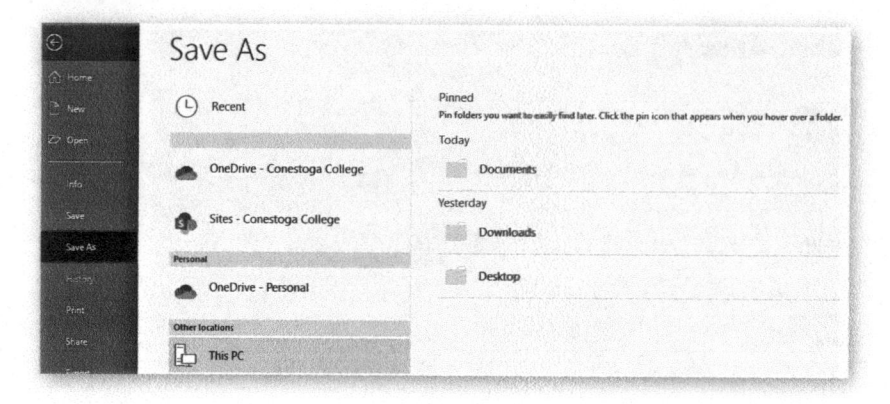

From the Save As dialogue box, select the Save as type pull-down menu.

From the options, select the CSV (Comma delimited) file and select Save.

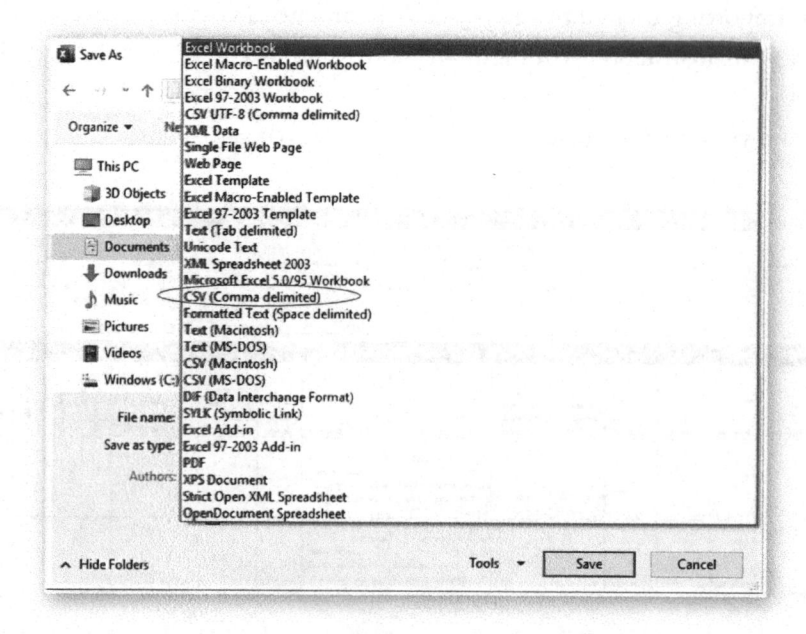

Note: Prior to importing the CSV file, all non-data rows, columns, and fields should be removed. There should only be a single header row. The header cannot include any punctuation.

Jira Preparation for Import

Jira must have target values for all the elements that will be imported. This means if users are being assigned via the import, they must be added in Jira first. In addition, components or custom fields need to be created for non-standard Jira fields.

Components are useful to group stories. However, they are unique per project and need to be updated for each new project. In addition, components have limited functionality, as they are simply labels or tags assigned to the user story.

Custom fields can be created. However, these are set at a global level. Therefore, when searching issues, it is important to ensure that stories are not confused across projects. Custom fields have a wide variety of functionality, including multi-line and pick lists.

Creating Components

Select the cog icon from the navigation bar. Select Projects from the pull-down menu.

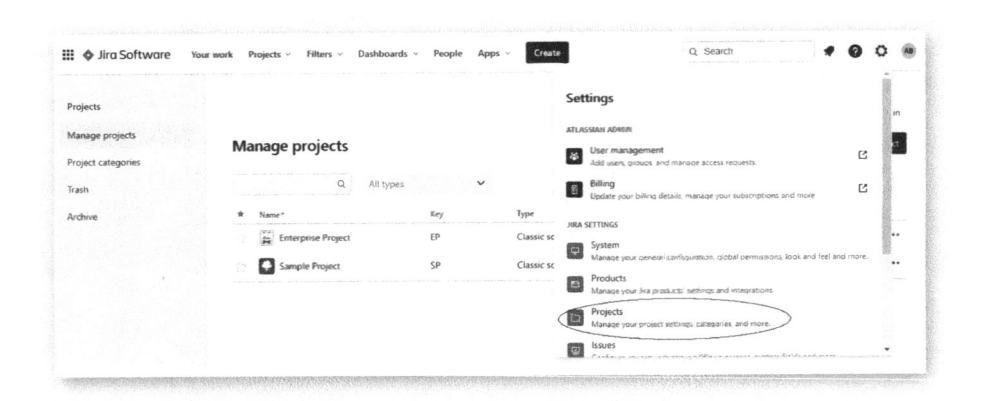

The Manage projects pane will appear. Select the project where components are to be created.

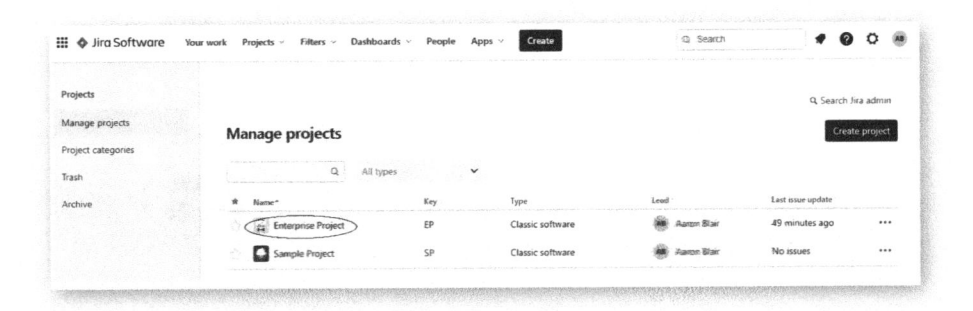

The project screen will open. Select the Components menu option, and then select the Create component button.

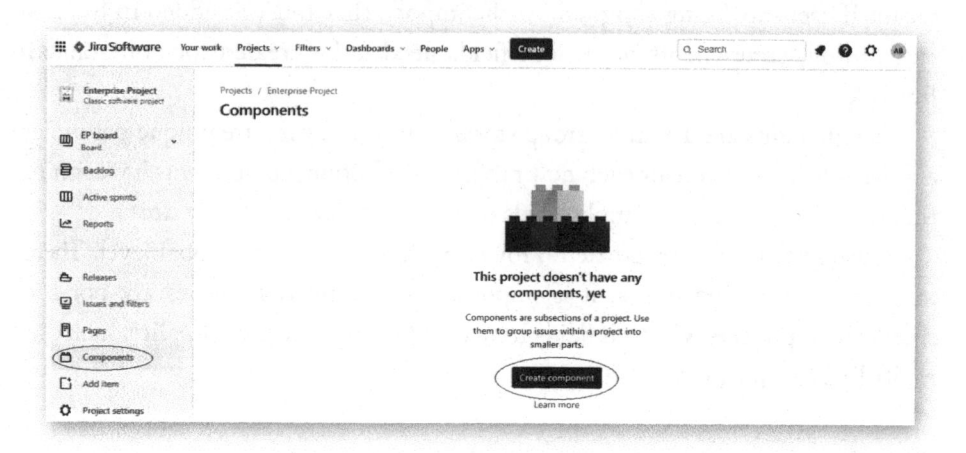

Enter the component name and description, and select Save.

Note: Components are single labels. Therefore, import values must have a one-to-one relationship if they are mapped to components. For example, if using MoSCoW (must have, should have, could have) values from an import file, a component will need to be created for each option.

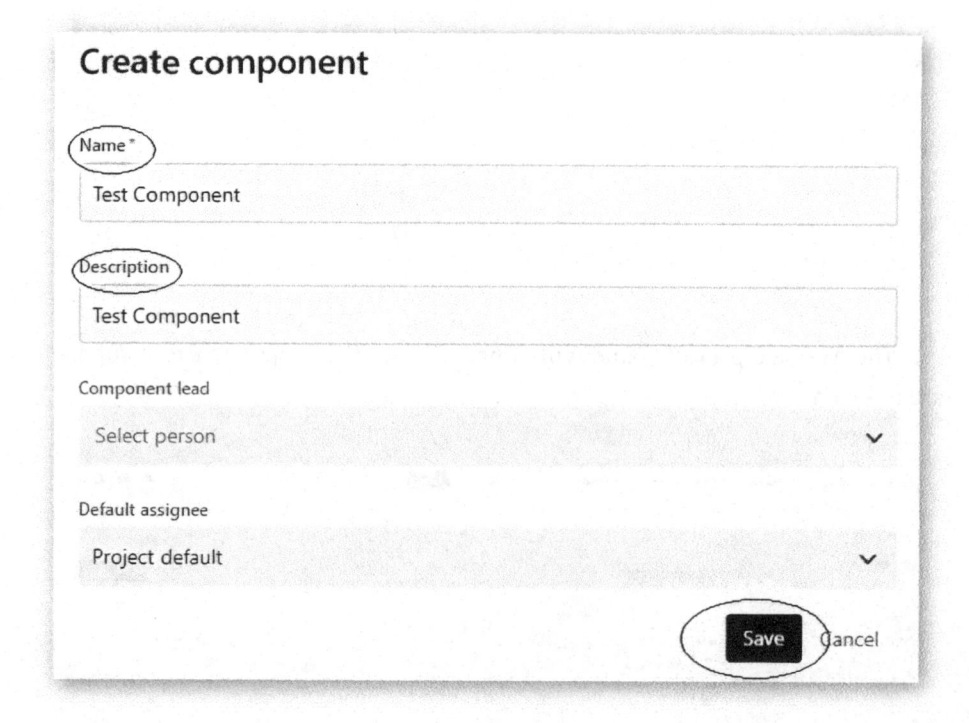

Chapter 4 • Capturing and Prioritizing User Stories through the Value Stream 83

The component will be added to the project. To create additional components, use the `Create component` button located at the top right of the screen.

Creating Custom Fields

To create custom fields, select the `cog` icon in the navigation bar. Select the `Issues` menu option.

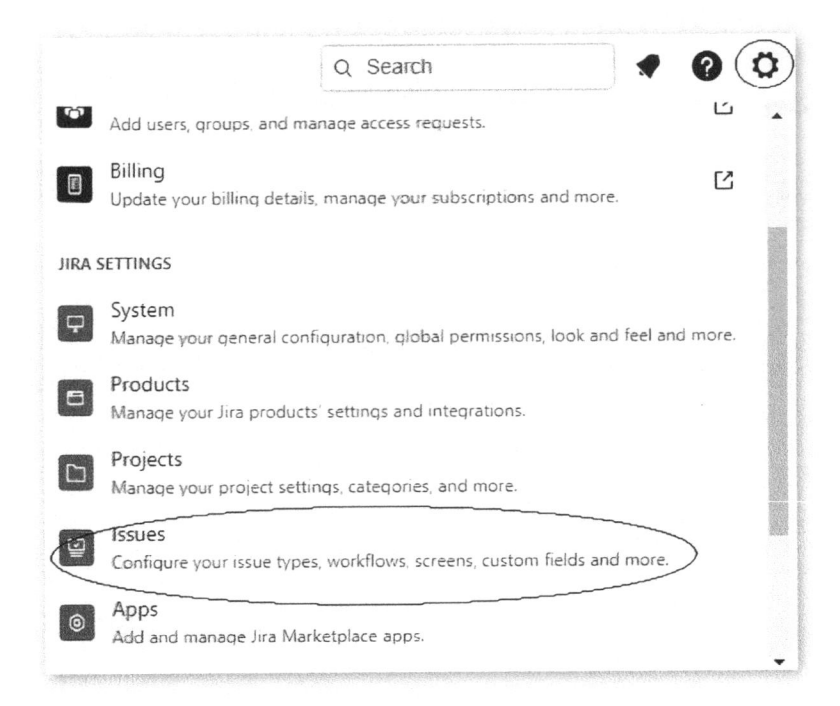

The Issues Settings menu will appear. Scroll down and select the `Custom fields` menu option. From the Custom field screen, select the `Create custom field` button.

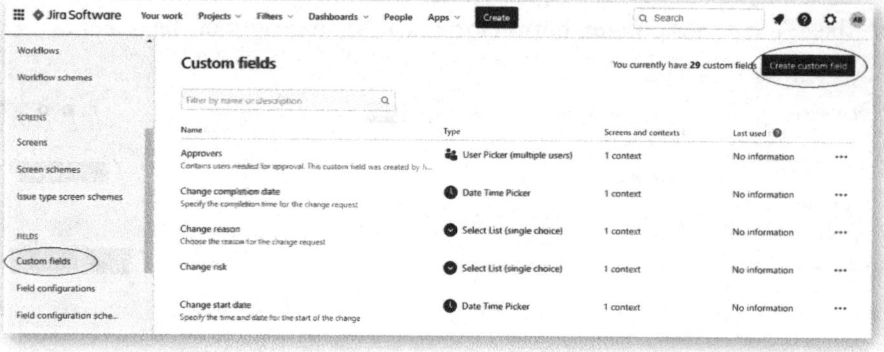

The custom-field creation wizard will appear.

Note: There are a number of options. This text will not explain the function of each option. Refer to Atlassian documentation available from Atlassian.com.

Select the appropriate field type to be created, and select `Next`.

The creation window will appear. Enter the field name and description and select `Create`.

For multi-select options, enter the expected values and select the Add button until all options are added.

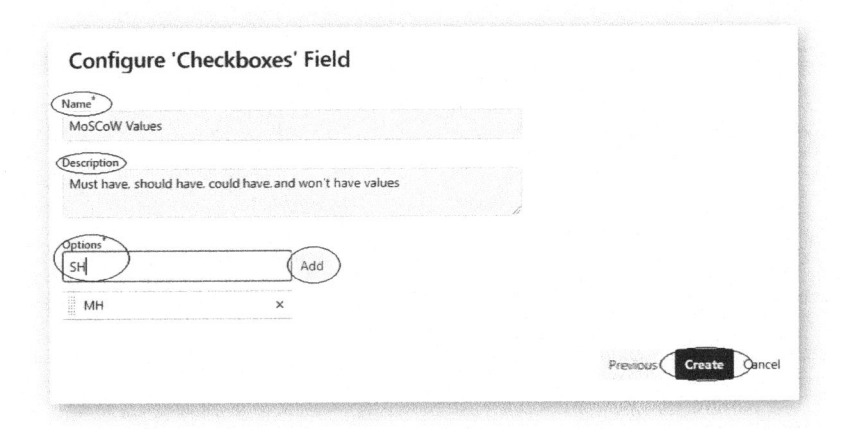

Note: Values must match the data import exactly; otherwise, the import will have failures.

The verification screen will appear. Select the screens that the field will be available to and select Update.

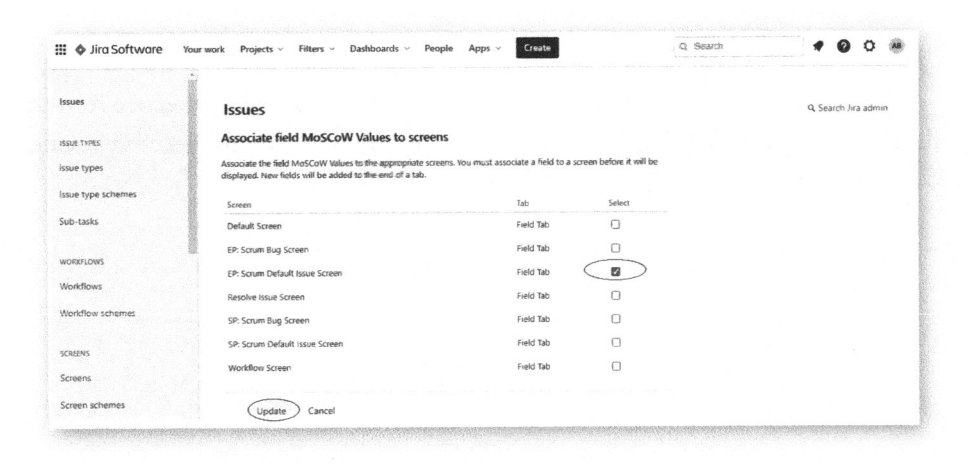

Note: For global fields from the user story template, the field should be available in all screens.

Importing User Stories in Jira

From the Create issue function, select `Import issues`.

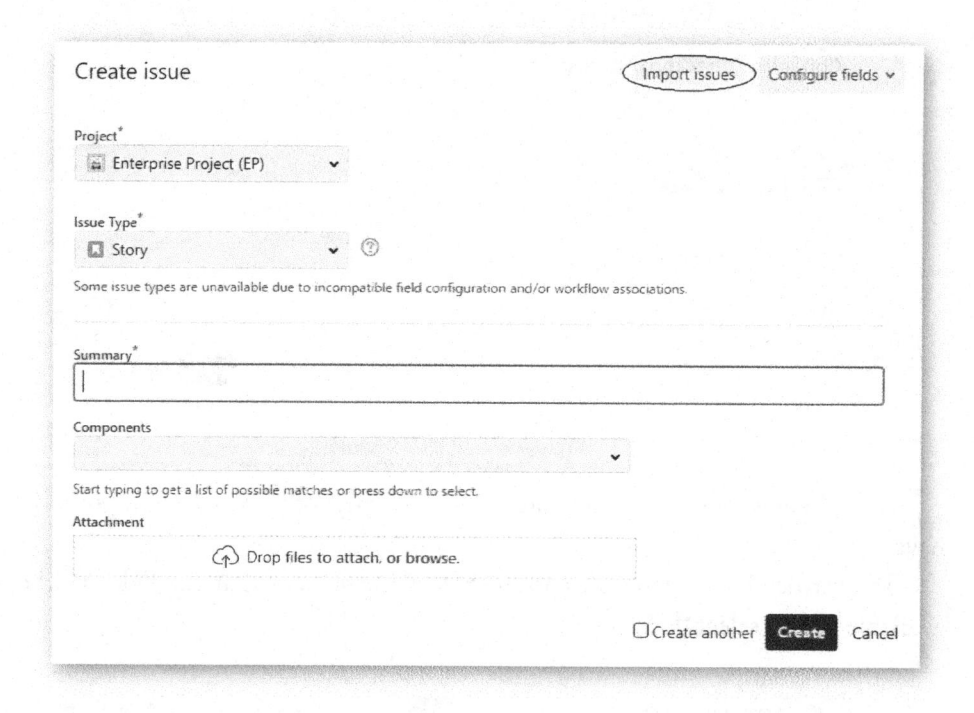

The Import issues function will take you to the Bulk create screen. From the Bulk create screen, select the `Choose file` button to locate the recently created CSV file.

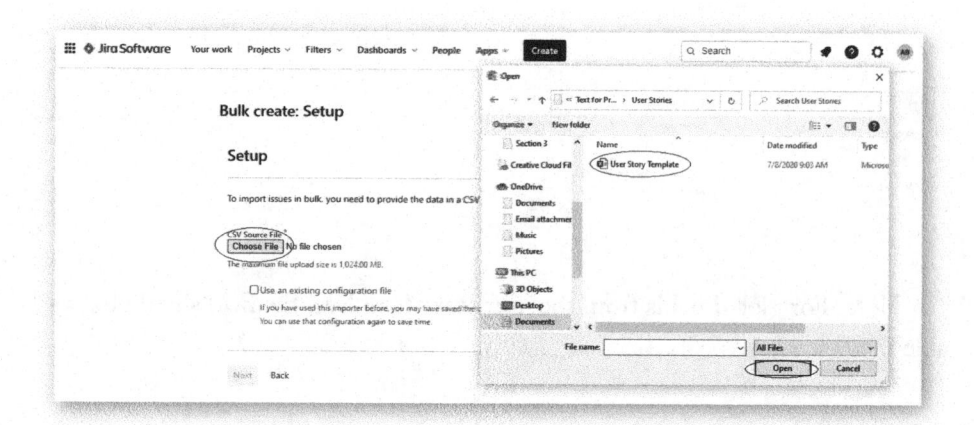

Once the file has been selected, the `Next` button will activate. Select the `Next` button.

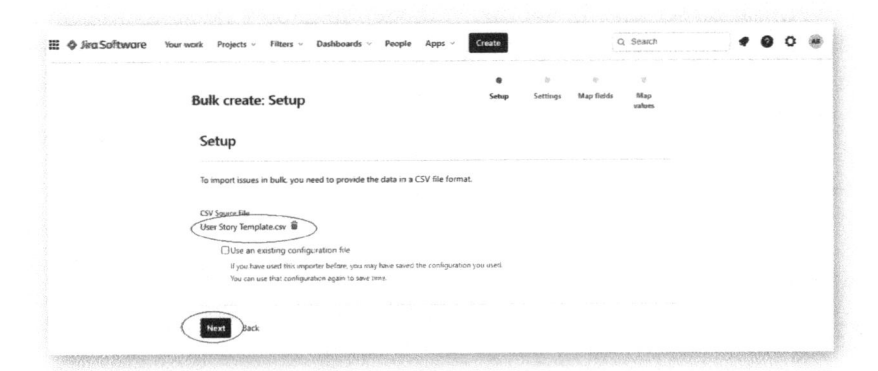

Chapter 4 • Capturing and Prioritizing User Stories through the Value Stream   87

Select the project to which the stories are to be imported. Note: The default options for delimiter and encoding should remain. The date format should be updated to the organizational standard. Then select Next.

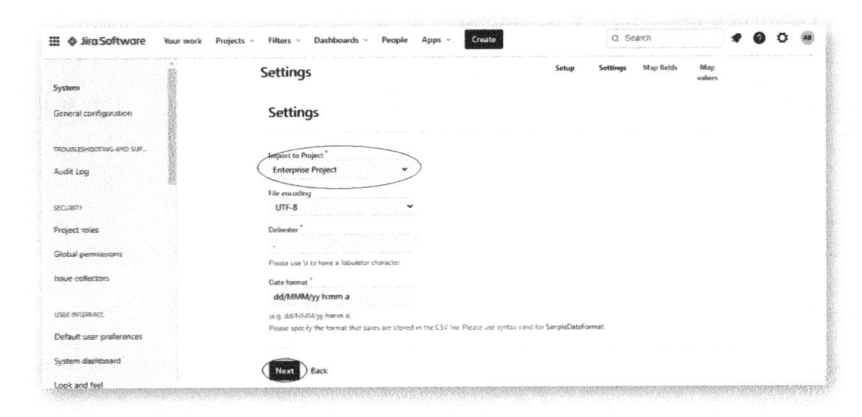

In the Map fields screen, map the CSV fields to Jira fields and select Next.

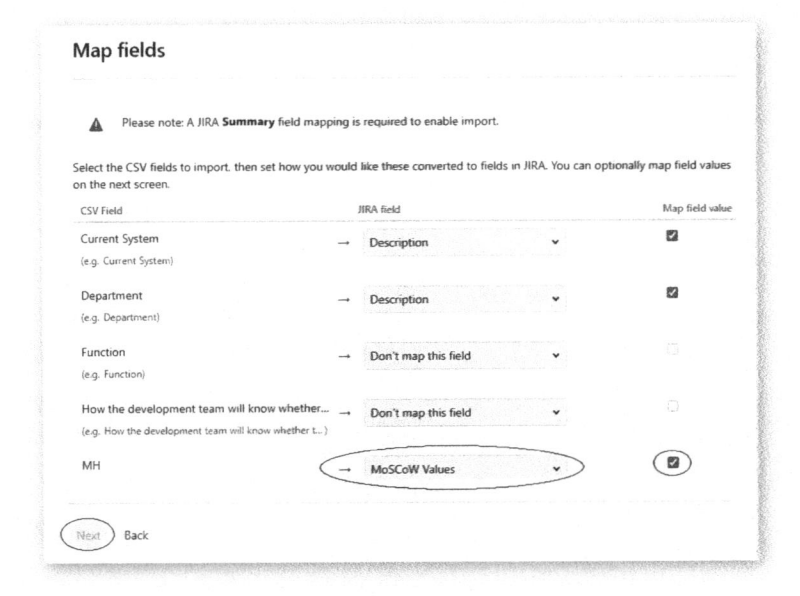

A verification screen will appear. Validate the import values and select `Begin Import`. Otherwise, return to the previous step.

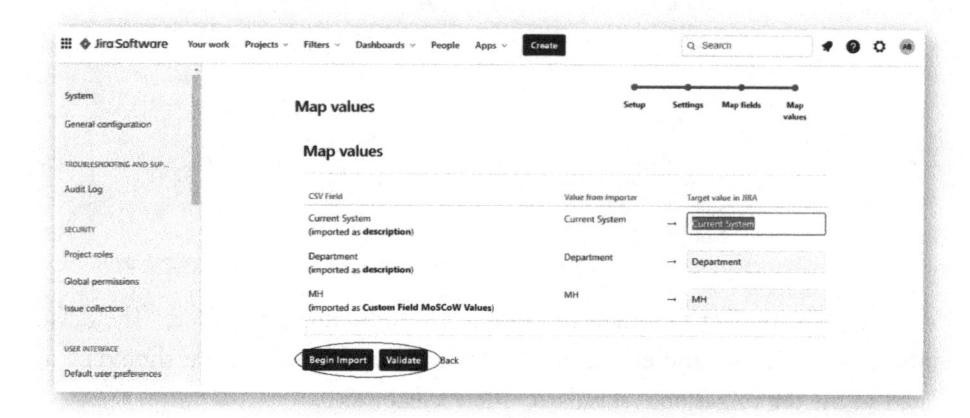

A confirmation screen will appear.

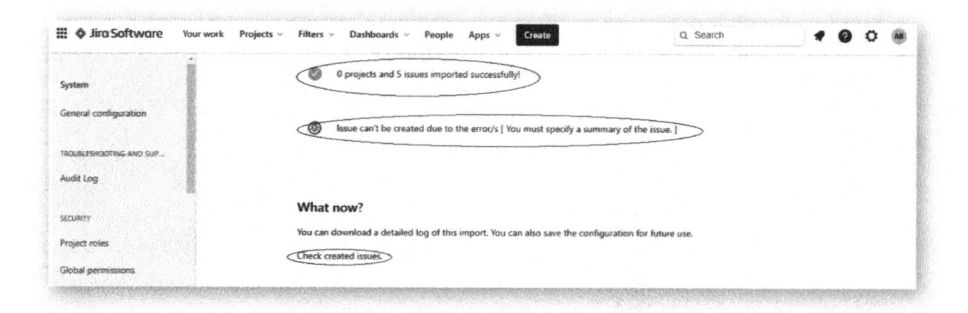

Confirming User Story Import

The CSV user story import can be validated by the same method as a single story creation.

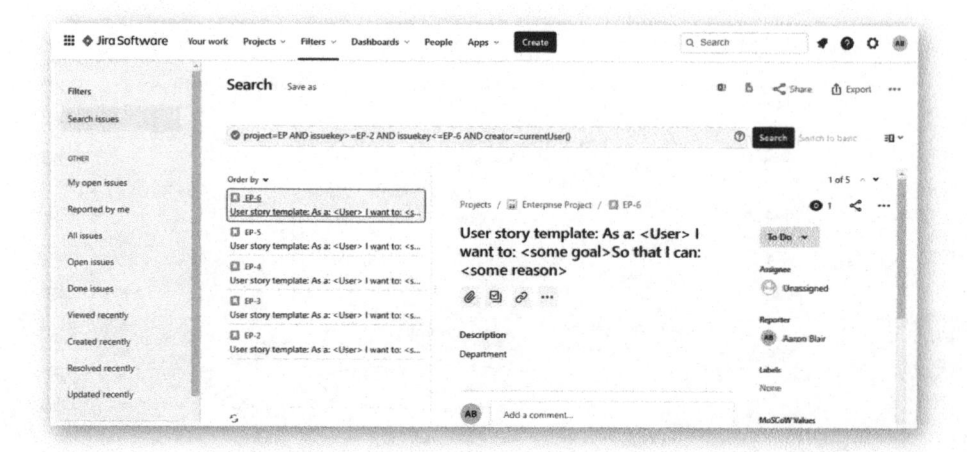

Although there are a variety of methods for mapping fields, to achieve the above results the following table outlines the recommended field mapping for the user story Excel template described in this text.

Table 4.1 • Recommended Field Mappings for User Story Template

Field Name	Mapping	Type
Department	Component	Create a component per department
Process	Custom field	Text value (single line)
Process owner	Custom field	Text value (single line)
User story name	Summary	Standard
Current system	Custom field	Text value (single line)
Type	Custom field	Select list (single choice): function, report, validation
Description	Description	Standard
Verification	Custom field	Text value (multi-line)
Kano scale	Custom field	Select list (single choice): need, want, delighter
MoSCoW	Custom field	Select list (single choice): MH, SH, CH, WH
Affinity mapping	Custom field	Select list (single choice): XS, S, M, L, XL

SUMMARY

- Value stream mapping is a Lean process to identify obstacles that impede optimal process flow. By working with subject-matter experts, process owners, and functional managers, project teams can create a visual current state process map that can be used to identify process waste.
- Value stream mapping outputs can be used to identify user stories, their relative priority, and their value. To identify priority, project teams can use the MoSCoW approach. MoSCoW prioritizes user stories by placing them in must-have, should-have, could-have, and won't-have categories. User story value can leverage the Kano model, which prioritizes user stories into customer needs, wants, and delighters.
- Lean identifies seven forms of waste: transportation, waiting, overproduction, defect, inventory, movement, and extra processing. Project teams can

assign the form of waste eliminated by a user story through value stream mapping. This can also aid in assigning value and priority to user stories.
- User stories are brief and should follow the INVEST acronym. User stories are meant to be short and concise and to fit on a single card. In large and complex organizations performing enterprise projects, user story cards may not be the most efficient method of organizing user stories. Therefore, using templates to collect user story data is a preferred approach. User story templates should be structured to enable import into Agile tools.
- Agile borrows from the XP Agile software development method by including test-driven development concepts in user stories. TDD captures the verification criteria within user stories to minimize defects. This approach supports the Lean concept of *jidoka*.

KEY TERMS

collaboration: a process mapping technique where project team members work with subject-matter experts to create a process map. The collaboration approach is used when observation is not viable.

current state process: captures how an organization performs an existing process

DSDM: an acronym for Dynamic Systems Development Method

Dynamic Systems Development Method: an Agile framework that focuses on completing the minimum work required to move to subsequent steps and phases

Extreme Programming: an Agile software methodology

future state process: once a value stream is analyzed, the project team proposes an optimized process model referred to as the future state.

gemba walk: a process discovery technique where project team members go to where the process occurs and observe the process in action

INVEST: an acronym describing the attributes that define high-quality user stories: independent, negotiable, valuable, can be estimated, small, and testable

jidoka: a Japanese term that strives to minimize defects from occurring by fixing the defect-causing behaviour at its source

Kano model: a product-development and customer-satisfaction approach that categorizes satisfaction into the following categories: must-be or needs qualities, one-dimensional or wants qualities, and attractive or delighter qualities

MoSCoW: an acronym that breaks requirements into categories: must have, could have, should have, and won't have

observation: a process mapping technique where project teams observe a process in action. This can be done through job shadowing or by physically attending when the process occurs.

request for proposal: a formal purchase request to qualified vendors. It typically represents a commitment that an organization will be looking to purchase a solution or services to achieve a business need.

RFP: an acronym for request for proposal

seven forms of waste: Lean's waste categories: transportation waste, waiting waste, overproduction waste, defect waste, inventory waste, movement waste, extra processing waste

swim lanes: a visual representation of cross-functional process interaction

TDD: an acronym for test-driven development

test-driven development: a process that requires the verification criteria to be created before the code

value stream mapping: a Lean management technique that is used to identify process waste

XP: an acronym for Extreme Programming

DISCUSSION QUESTIONS

1. Are Lean's seven forms of waste applicable to all industries? How could they be modified? Identify the industry and rationale.
2. The concept of *jidoka* looks to build quality into activities. TDD is one example. Can you think of another? Explain your answer.
3. Consider your approach to your studies. Create a value stream. Identify where there may be waste.
4. Performing a gemba walk, or in-person observation, is not always an option when creating a value stream. Identify process scenarios when observation versus collaboration is preferred. Identify three processes for observation and three for collaboration. Explain your rationale.
5. Procurement is an organizational process that can benefit from value stream mapping. Can you think of another non-project organizational function that could benefit from value stream mapping outputs? Explain your answer.

NOTES

1. K. Martin and M. Osterling, *Value Stream Mapping: How to Visualize Work and Align Leadership for Organizational Transformation* (New York, NY: McGraw-Hill, 2013).
2. Ibid.
3. P. Measey, *Agile Foundations: Principles, Practices and Frameworks* (London, UK: BCS, The Chartered Institute for IT, 2015).
4. Ibid.

5. Ibid.
6. Ibid.
7. R. Black and G. Coleman, *Agile Testing Foundations: An ISTQB Foundation Level Agile Tester Guide* (London, UK: BCS, The Chartered Institute for IT, 2017).
8. M. Cohn, *Agile Estimating and Planning* (Upper Saddle River, NJ: Prentice Hall, 2007).
9. Measey, *Agile Foundations*.
10. C. Protzman, F. Whiton, and D. Protzman, *Implementing Lean* (Productivity Press, 2018).
11. C. Wright, *Fundamentals of Assurance for Lean Projects* (Cambridgeshire, UK: IT Governance, 2017).
12. Ibid.
13. Protzman et al., *Implementing Lean*.

PART III

AGILE PROJECT PLANNING

In part III of the text, the focus shifts to the planning stages of a project utilizing Agile frameworks. User stories are the key input to project estimation. One goal of Agile is to use empirical data when planning sprints, predicting team velocity, and setting realistic customer expectations.

Some of the challenges associated with large and complex environments are addressed in this section. Many Agile frameworks recommend small teams that are both dedicated to the project and co-located in the same physical space. This can pose a challenge in large and complex environments that may be distributed and utilize matrix management. A number of Agile at scale frameworks will be referenced; however, Agile at scale at an organizational level requires significant change management and is outside the scope of this text.

Part III will build on concepts from part II while demonstrating how Agile can adapt to meet some of the challenges in non-software development corporate settings. In addition, Agile tools will continue to be expanded for estimation and sprint planning.

By the end of part III, readers will be familiar with different approaches to managing teams, user story estimation techniques, and the sprint planning event.

5 Building the Agile Team

CHAPTER OVERVIEW

In chapter 4, user stories were created by the project team. In chapter 5, user stories will be assigned. This requires the creation of the development team; once the team has been assembled, user stories can be estimated and then added to sprint planning.

Chapter 5 covers how team composition can be adapted for corporations, the role of the scrum master, and the vendor product owner relationship. We review Agile at scale frameworks and some of the characteristics these frameworks recommend to succeed when managing large initiatives and numbers of people at an enterprise level.

By the end of the chapter, readers will be familiar with matrix-managed environments, how to manage virtual and distributed Agile teams, the role of a scrum master as a servant leader, and why large enterprise projects will at times use a vendor product owner. In addition, readers will learn how to add users and assign user stories in Agile tools.

AGILE AT SCALE

Agile is designed to maximize productivity amongst a small group of dedicated resources. Large organizations that design complex software solutions for enterprise needed ways to adapt Agile to meet their needs. As a result, a number of frameworks emerged. These include the Scaled Agile Framework (SAFe), large-scale Scrum (LeSS), and disciplined Agile delivery (DAD). Agile at scale frameworks are typically applied at the organizational level, which is outside the scope of this text. However, these frameworks do employ a number of themes that are consistent with approaches necessary to apply Agile techniques to non-software development corporate projects.

Michael Cohn developed a common acronym used for implementing Agile frameworks: ADAPT.

- A—Creating *awareness* that there is room for improvement. This can be achieved through the use of metrics, as well as by communicating that the status quo is not working and providing exposure to Agile to new people throughout the organization.
- D—Creating a *desire* for change. This can be achieved through creating a sense of urgency, creating pilot projects where Agile is used, and addressing the natural fears that come with change.
- A—building the *ability* to work in an Agile manner. This can be achieved through coaching and training, sharing information, and setting reasonable targets.
- P—*Promoting* early successes to build momentum and gain followers.
- T—*Transferring* the impact of Agile throughout the organization. If this is not done effectively, organizational gravity will pull an enterprise back to the status quo.[1]

To help scale Agile at an enterprise level, organizations can create an enterprise transition community (ETC) to provide energy, resources, guidance, and occasional direction to ensure all elements of ADAPT are applied.[2] The ETC should be supported at the highest level of the organization and help remove impediments that are preventing the transition to Agile. Once the transition is complete, the ETC should be disbanded. If issues arise with newly transitioned Agile practices, organizations can form improvement communities (ICs), which form around the passion of a small number of practitioners charged with the real work of improving how the organization uses Agile. ICs usually work in improvement iterations that are consistent with sprint length of two to four weeks and are disbanded once the improvement goal has been achieved.[3]

When scaling, Agile organizations will often encounter resistance. Resistance can be either active or passive and rooted in the desire to maintain the status quo. Cohn identifies four types of resistance:

- *Diehards*—Active resisters who are committed to the status quo. To manage resistance from diehards, organizations need to align organizational objectives, confront fear, and create dissatisfaction with the status quo.
- *Followers*—Passive resisters who support the status quo. To manage resistance from followers, organizations should change team composition, model and praise the desired behaviour, involve followers in the process,

and determine the root cause of resistance, whether it is awareness, desire, or ability.
- *Skeptics*—Passive resisters who dislike Agile. To manage resistance from skeptics, it is recommended to appoint a champion skeptic. This will help solicit peer anecdotes as well as build awareness. Organizations should provide training to skeptics as well as continue to push the desire for change. Finally, once an organization has effectively transitioned to Agile and is experiencing success, time will remove the barriers generated by skeptics.
- *Saboteurs*—Active resisters who dislike Agile. To manage resistance from saboteurs, it is recommended to reinforce the organizational commitment to Agile, move them, and, in extreme cases, fire them.[4]

Many Agile at scale frameworks use Scrum as the foundation of their team structure. However, rather than having a single Scrum team, many teams may contribute to the project.[5] Having multiple Scrum teams working autonomously creates a coordination challenge. Teams need to work towards a unified goal, and if all are working autonomously, there is risk that teams are working at cross-purposes. To mitigate this risk, Agile at scale frameworks often utilize cross-team coordination techniques as well as organizing teams into feature teams or autonomous team structures that minimize issues that could arise from teams being interdependent.[6] Agile at scale frameworks often synthesize elements from software development and continuous improvement methodologies such as Lean, XP, and Crystal.[7] Because Agile at scale frameworks can be applied at the organizational level, they can often involve expanding access to additional stakeholder groups to participate directly in the development team or providing some level of governance to help direct the development team.[8]

As we progress throughout chapter 5 and beyond, this text will be utilizing some of the lessons learned from Agile at scale frameworks to identify different techniques to help navigate non-software development corporate projects.

MATRIX-MANAGED VERSUS DEDICATED TEAMS

Many corporations employ **matrix management**, or organizational structures where resources report to multiple managers. This can also be referred to as dotted line reporting.

In a matrix-management structure, resources can split time between operational and project activities. This means that a resource who is a help-desk expert

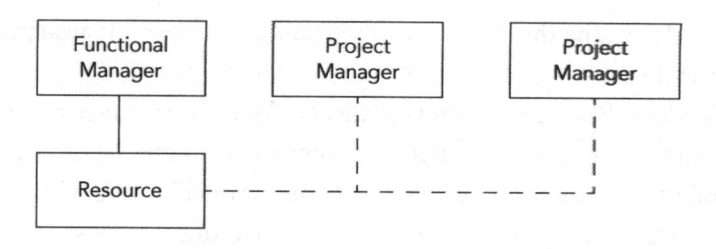

Figure 5.1 • Matrix Management

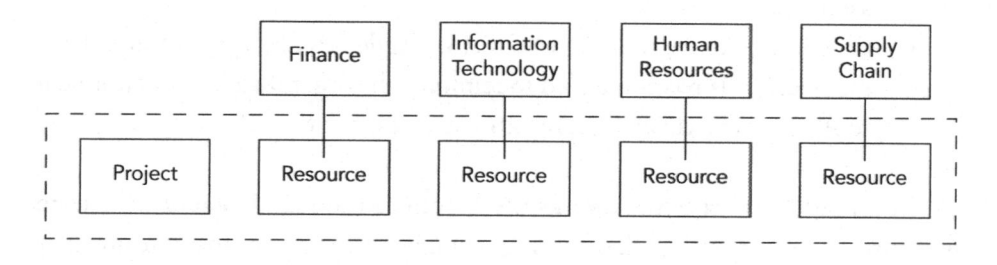

Figure 5.2 • Matrix-Managed Resources Assigned to a Project

and is assigned to an Agile project may spend time answering help-desk calls as well as acting as a help-desk expert on a project team including project activities such as process design. In addition, the help-desk expert may also be providing help-desk expertise to other projects. There can be a number of challenges with this approach. Because the distribution of time is estimated across numerous responsibilities, if any one of the assigned projects or operational duties is in urgent need of support, this may decrease the resource's availability to meet all of their time commitments. As the number of resources assigned to the project grows in a matrix-managed environment, the permutations and complexities also grow.

A matrix-managed team can lead to an unevenness of throughput. As team members are pulled toward different priorities, their ability to provide a constant amount of output can suffer.

Matrix management may not seem to align with some of the core Agile principles:

4. Business people and developers must work together daily throughout the project.
5. Build projects around motivated individuals. Give them the environment and support they need, and trust them to get the job done.

6. The most efficient and effective method of conveying information to and within a development team is face-to-face conversation.
8. Agile processes promote sustainable development. The sponsors, developers, and users should be able to maintain a constant pace indefinitely.

Consider the complexity of an enterprise project that may utilize dozens of resources. Managing availability cycles can become quite challenging. Business representatives may also be allocated to multiple initiatives, which further challenges the predictability of time and work commitments to a project. In addition, large and complex organizations that would like to manage projects using an Agile methodology may find it difficult to modify their staffing models and dedicate resources to projects. This creates a project constraint, or a limitation that a project must manage.

To manage a matrix-managed staffing constraint, it is recommended that Agile teams use **skilled generalist** resources.[9] Skilled generalists are resources that are interchangeable and can perform multiple functions on a project if a development team member becomes unavailable or additional effort is required. Although skilled generalists may not be readily available in an organization, one goal of Agile teams is to "skill up" team members. Skilling up refers to development team members acquiring technical and functional knowledge that supports building skilled generalist resources.[10] In addition, Agile concepts such as velocity and

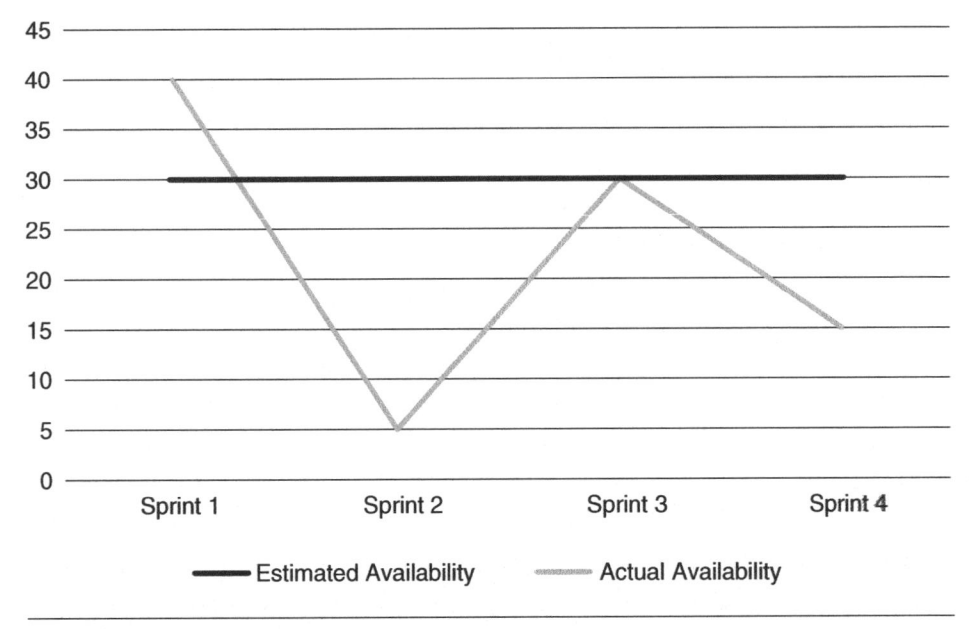

Figure 5.3 • Actual versus Estimated Resource Availability

information radiators can assist in securing resources when they are most needed. These topics will be covered later in the text.

Dedicated or **projectized teams** are resources that are fully allocated to a project. Resources can be hired by an organization for the purpose of the project, **seconded** to the project from another function, or supplied through a contract instrument from an external vendor. Dedicated project teams are consistent with Agile values and principles. However, recommending the use of dedicated teams as a best practice for projects is not unique to Agile methodologies; PMI also recommends a dedicated project team when a project is high priority and cannot afford timeline variation.[11]

Hybrid teams are common in non-software development corporations undertaking enterprise projects. A portion of the team is dedicated, while some resources are supplied through matrix management.

DISTRIBUTED VERSUS CO-LOCATED TEAMS

Agile teams are ideally **co-located,** sharing a single space. Co-location supports Agile values:

- *Individuals and interactions* over processes and tools
- *Customer collaboration* over contract negotiation

Co-location also supports Agile principles:

4. Business people and developers must work together daily throughout the project.
6. The most efficient and effective method of conveying information to and within a development team is face-to-face conversation.

The **Crystal** software development methodology is part of the Agile software development family. The Crystal methodology developed the concept of **osmotic communication** and the importance of ease of access to experts. Osmotic communication refers to knowledge being acquired simply by hearing team member conversations. By sharing space, team members can become skilled generalists through osmosis. Co-location also supports the Crystal value of access to experts. When all team members are in a single room, or war room, they can interact freely. Issues can be resolved informally and incidental interaction can result in increased productivity.[12]

Case Study 5.1 • Securing Commitment in a Matrix-Managed Environment

As part of the current state mapping activities, Imran created a schedule and presented it to the functional management team. The schedule included the time commitments needed by both the SMEs and functional managers. Imran estimated that current state mapping would take three cycles: draft, review, finalize.

Although Imran's SMEs and functional managers were matrixed, providing the weeks their time was needed and breaking sessions across three meetings made the commitment easier for the business to provide. In addition, Imran knew he had dedicated project analysts for the project and looked at the current state mapping sessions as an opportunity to skill up his team.

Imran's approach enabled him to create current state mapping sprints for his project team and provided transparency to business stakeholders in manageable time increments, which resulted in business commitment. Once commitment was secured, Imran had the sessions scheduled to secure space and SME/functional manager time with enough contingency to move sessions if needed.

Table 5.1 • Pre-Defined Business Resource Schedule

Process	Business Resources Required	Session 1	Session 2	Session 3
Process 1	SME 1, functional manager 2	DD/MM/YYYY	DD/MM/YYYY	DD/MM/YYYY
Process 2	SME 1, functional manager 2	DD/MM/YYYY	DD/MM/YYYY	DD/MM/YYYY
Process 3	SME 2, functional manager 1	DD/MM/YYYY	DD/MM/YYYY	DD/MM/YYYY
Process 4	SME 2, functional manager 1	DD/MM/YYYY	DD/MM/YYYY	DD/MM/YYYY
Process 5	SME 3, functional manager 3	DD/MM/YYYY	DD/MM/YYYY	DD/MM/YYYY
Process 6	SME 1, SME 2, functional manager 1	DD/MM/YYYY	DD/MM/YYYY	DD/MM/YYYY
Process 7	SME 1, SME 2, functional manager 1	DD/MM/YYYY	DD/MM/YYYY	DD/MM/YYYY
Process 8	SME 2, functional manager 1	DD/MM/YYYY	DD/MM/YYYY	DD/MM/YYYY
Process 9	SME 1, functional manager 2	DD/MM/YYYY	DD/MM/YYYY	DD/MM/YYYY
Process 10	SME 1, functional manager 2	DD/MM/YYYY	DD/MM/YYYY	DD/MM/YYYY

However, co-location does not guarantee that teams will benefit from osmotic communication. Team spaces should encourage interaction independent of roles and be rich with project information about the project, its progress, and any open questions or issues. Negative team space can usually be recognized by the following attributes:

- Minimal interaction
- People organized by job functions, resulting in cliques or a lack of skilled generalist resources
- Lack of project information, or lack of up-to-date information
- Team member isolation, either through room layout or through technology barriers such as wearing headphones
- Poor and unattractive room layout

Large, complex organizations that may not be able to co-locate teams face additional challenges. Multinational organizations may have numerous physical locations across many time zones. When team members are located in separate geographies they are referred to as a **distributed team**. Distributed teams can still be successful using an Agile approach. Therefore, just as it is important to create a physical space conducive to interaction, similar approaches should be used to create a virtual space, including the following:

- Creating a shared online presence, such as a web page on an organization's intranet
- Using Agile software that replicates physical space, such as online information radiators and Kanban or scrum boards
- Ensuring online information is current
- Using document collaboration tools, such as wikis, to share knowledge and allow multiple members to contribute
- Using unified communication technologies that promote team conversation and result in osmotic knowledge acquisition
- Conducting scrums at times of the day when all teams can participate

Distributed team communications occur either **synchronously**, where all team members meet at the same time, or **asynchronously**, where team members see and contribute information at different times. It is important to understand

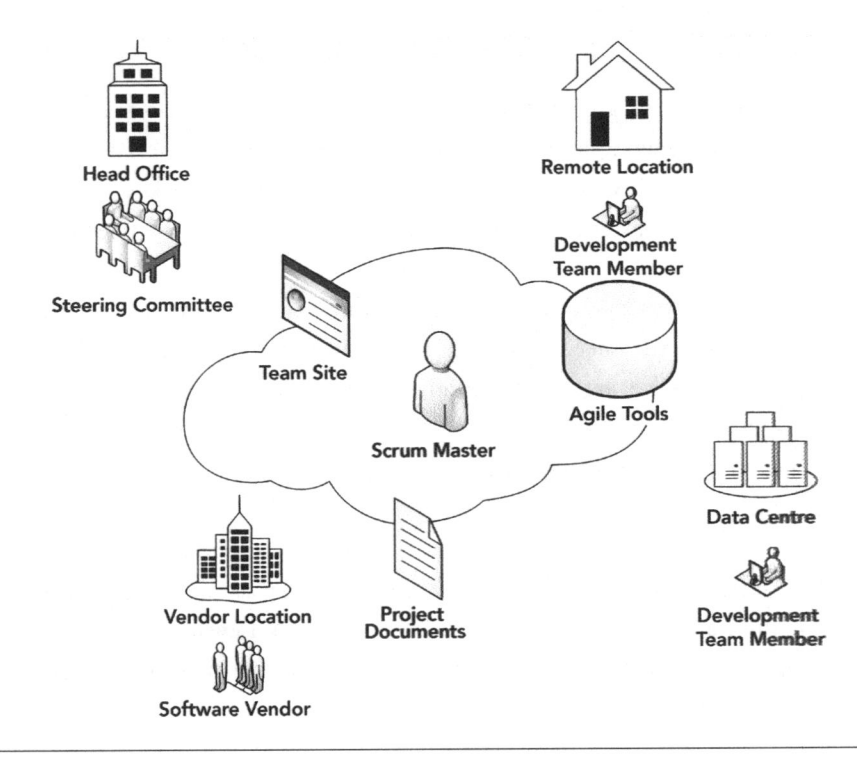

Figure 5.4 • Distributed Agile Team

which types of communication amongst the team should occur synchronously versus asynchronously to establish team communication norms.

Some additional factors are important when using distributed teams:

- Having an agreed upon approach to estimating
- Ensuring there is a shared understanding of the "definition of done"
- Not grouping teams by specialty, such as testing or development, and keeping teams cross-functional regardless of geographic location. This will ensure silos do not emerge and will promote "skilling up" the team.
- Not creating artificial barriers such as single points of communication
- Agreeing on update times for code check-ins or document updates

By establishing positive virtual spaces and having a shared understanding of expectations, distributed teams can be just as successful as co-located teams using Agile methodologies.

SCRUM MASTER AS A SERVANT LEADER

The scrum master plays a central role in coordinating an Agile team. Although the scrum master is seen as a project leader, it is important to understand the type of leadership that is expected from the scrum master role. Some key principles in satisfying the scrum master role can be found in the 12 Agile principles:

5. Build projects around motivated individuals. Give them the environment and support they need, and trust them to get the job done.
10. Simplicity—the art of maximizing the amount of work not done—is essential.
11. The best architectures, requirements, and designs emerge from self-organizing teams.

A foundational concept of the Agile methodology is that teams should be self-organizing, and the scrum master must monitor and ensure that the team is functioning in an Agile way.[13] Therefore, the scrum master functions as a mentor and coach to the team.

- The scrum master is not a functional, or line, manager who assigns work.
- The scrum master is not authoritarian: they do not tell the team what is to be done and when.
- The scrum master does not decide how a solution will be designed or act as a technical authority.
- The scrum master does not approve the product or direct the development team to make product changes at the end of a sprint. Team members, product owners, and stakeholders make project decisions.

A scrum master is a **servant leader** who tends to the needs of the team. The goal of a servant leader is to put employees at the centre of decision-making by sharing power and ensuring employees achieve their maximum potential.[14] In Agile, servant leaders do the following:

- Remove obstacles
- Coach the team, product owners, and sponsors/stakeholders about the Agile process
- Facilitate scrums and other Scrum events

Agile uses a **participatory decision-making** (**PDM**) model. In PDM, organizations identify the degree to which employees will inform organizational decisions. PDM in Agile includes several key elements:

- *Input*—All members of the team are encouraged to provide input on decisions.
- *Collaboration*—All members participate in deriving the project solution.
- *Command*—Final approval is achieved by review with a smaller group of customers or the product owner.

PDM is consistent with the Crystal approach, which values **personal safety** or the ability to speak about work without fear of ridicule. A safe and open environment helps to ensure positive interaction from the team, which supports the input component of PDM.

The preferred model of decision-making is through negotiation, where teams are free to negotiate a user story to achieve a win-win outcome. This approach is called **collaborating**, which differs from some waterfall approaches that use an **accommodating** approach. Accommodating approaches yield to the customer, which can result in cost, scope, and schedule overruns.[15]

DEVELOPMENT TEAM COMPOSITION

The term *development team* suggests a focus on software development. However, although Agile was developed for software development projects, it is not limited to them. When building a development team, it is important to consider the concept of *jidoka* from the previous chapter. A development team must comprise all the people necessary to ensure a user story is fully completed. This could include the following:

- Architect
- Developers
- IT staff
- Support staff
- Trainers
- Testers
- Technical writers
- Business analysts
- Business leads

Including the right mix of team members as part of the development team supports another important Lean concept associated with customer value: completing an activity right the first time. In addition, a cross-functional mix of resources will help develop team members into skilled generalists who may be able to support other team member work if the need arises.

Size is an important consideration when building Agile teams. If an Agile team becomes too large, it ceases to be agile. Scrum recommends that team sizes are limited to six, plus or minus three, members. A larger and more complex project will not grow the development team but rather will require the Agile project to have multiple development teams running multiple sprints concurrently, usually no more than eight teams running concurrently.[16] Enterprise projects can often involve multiple teams broken out by feature or module consistent with the Agile at scale framework LeSS, an approach that will be used in the case study throughout the text.

THE VENDOR PRODUCT OWNER

In a large and complex product or software development organization, the product owner role can often be fulfilled by internal staff. However, if an organization is procuring an outside service or product from a vendor, it may be appropriate for the vendor to designate a product owner or owners to the project.

The product owner is the resource that should be the most knowledgeable about the product and service and can provide clarification and prioritization for user stories. In a purchased solution, the vendor may be best equipped to fulfill the product owner role as they are most familiar with the product or service; they have likely implemented a similar project in the past and, as a result, understand what is necessary for a user story to be carried out successfully.

When the product owner role is fulfilled by a vendor, it is important that they are partnered with a business resource that can provide organizational context. Although the **vendor product owner** may be knowledgeable about their product, they will not be aware of organizational context that could influence how to best complete a user story. In this scenario, it is important to add a business role to the development team.

AGILE TOOLS: ADDING USERS

Adding People

To add people to the project, on Jira select the People menu item from the navigation bar.

If the user identity can't be found, use the people search function. Select the user.

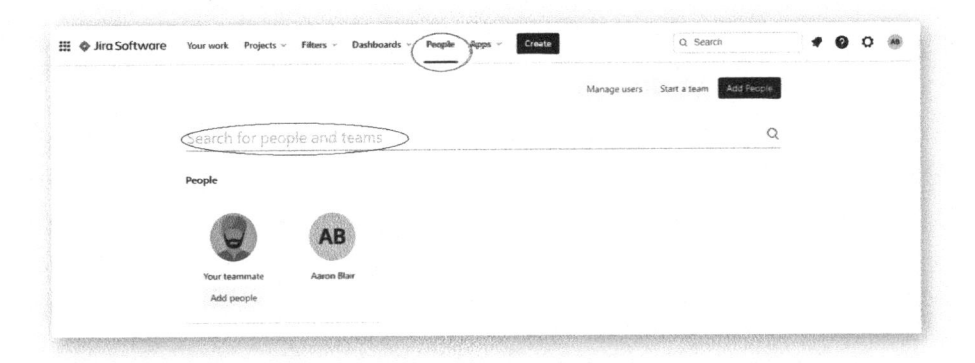

This will take you to the user details screen, which will provide more information about the user.

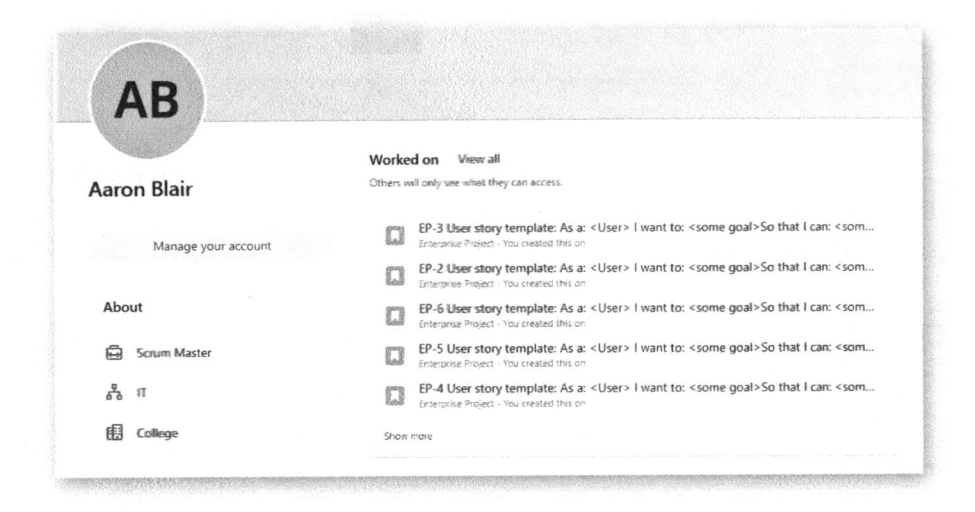

To add a user, return to the People home screen. Select either `Add people` button. This will generate the Add People dialogue box.

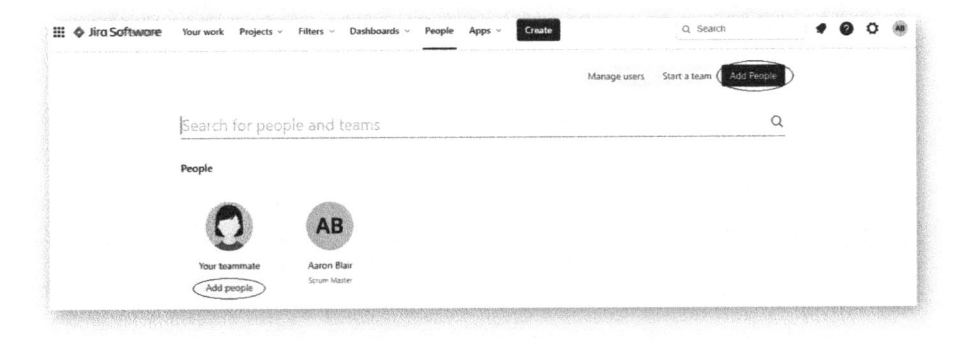

Enter the email address(es) of the user(s) to be added and select Send.

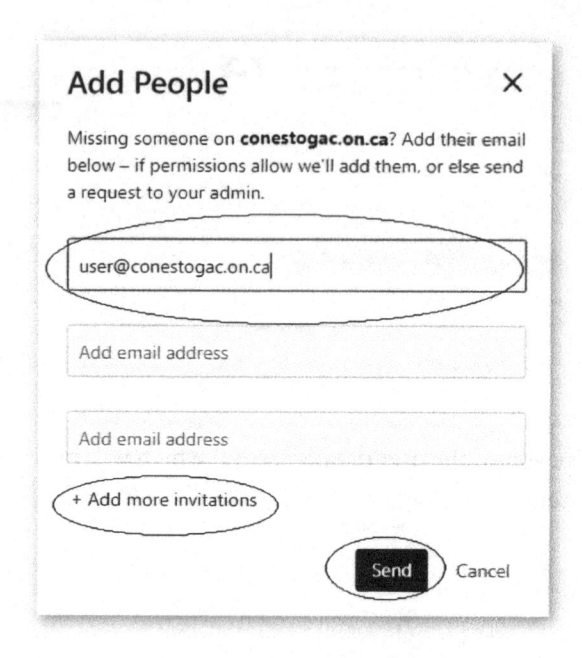

Note: Users will only be added to the project if Jira has them on file. If not, the request will go to the administrator, who will receive a notification that a user request has been made.

Creating Teams

You can also create a team from the People home screen.

Select either Start a team button. The Start a new team dialogue box will appear.

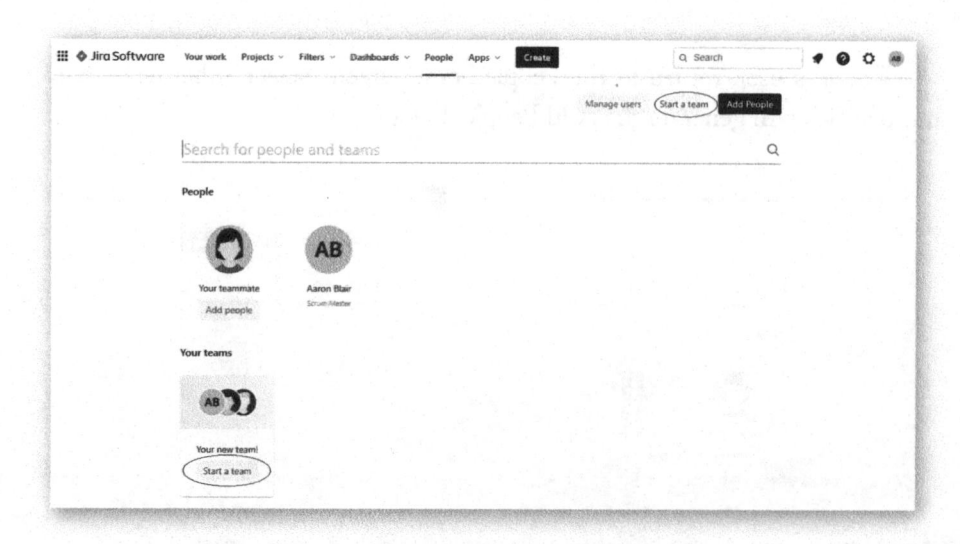

Enter the team name. Invite team members. Select the `Start` button.

Note: Only 10 team members can be added at a time. This is consistent with Agile team-size best practices.

Once created, the team window will be displayed showing the team name, its members, and any user stories assigned.

Note: The team window layout can be configured with different widgets; the default is consistent with virtual team best practices.

Team members can be added directly from the team page. Select `Add people`. The Add team members window will appear. Add the team members' names and select `Confirm`.

Note: To add team members from the team page, users **must** already exist in the Jira instance.

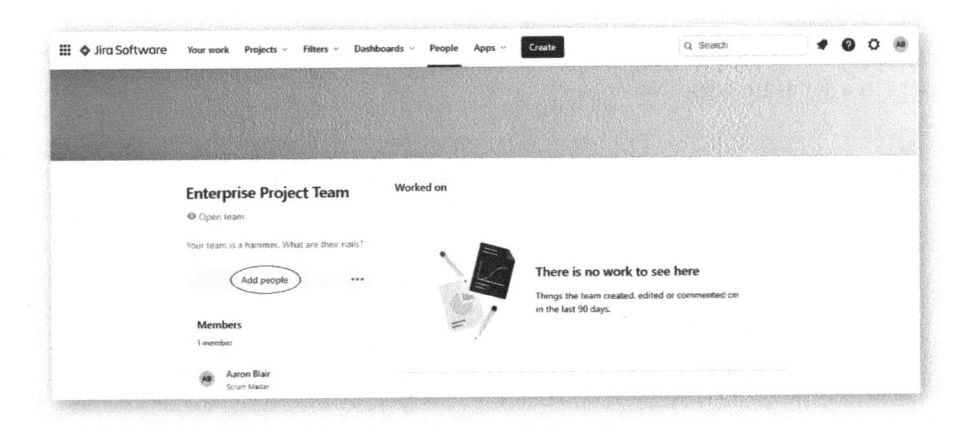

110   AGILE PROJECT DELIVERY

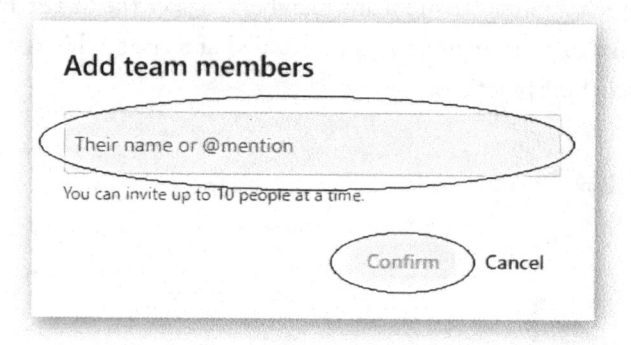

If no longer needed, the team can be deleted. Select the `ellipsis`, or three dots, then select `Delete team`.

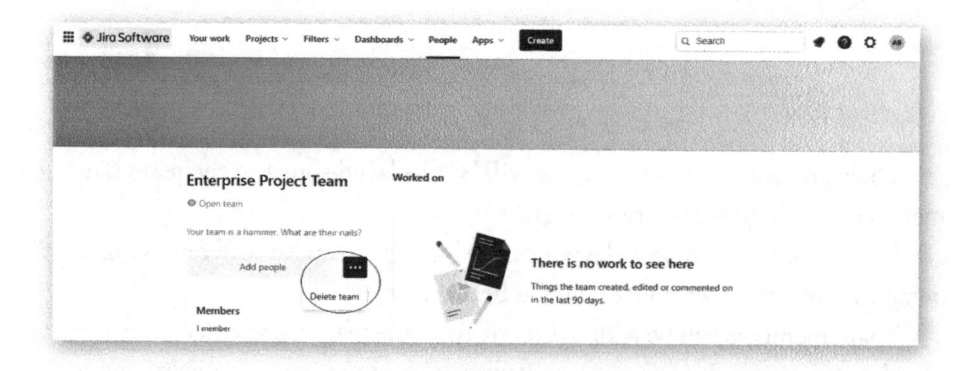

Managing Users

The Manage users function may only be available to administrators of the Jira instance.

From the People home screen, select the `Manage users` button. This will take users to a separate window.

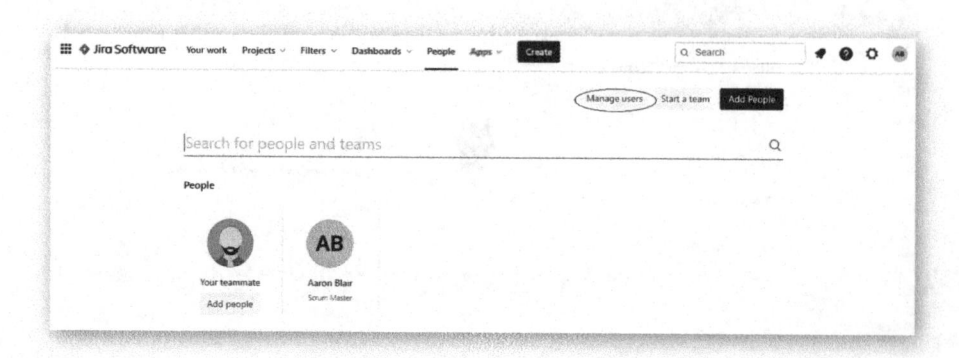

From the manage user administration screen, users can be added by entering their email address. User status appears at the lower section of the screen. Managing individual users can be initiated by selecting the `ellipsis`.

To invite new users to the Jira instance, such as external vendors, select the `Invite users` button at the top right of the screen. This will open the Invite users window.

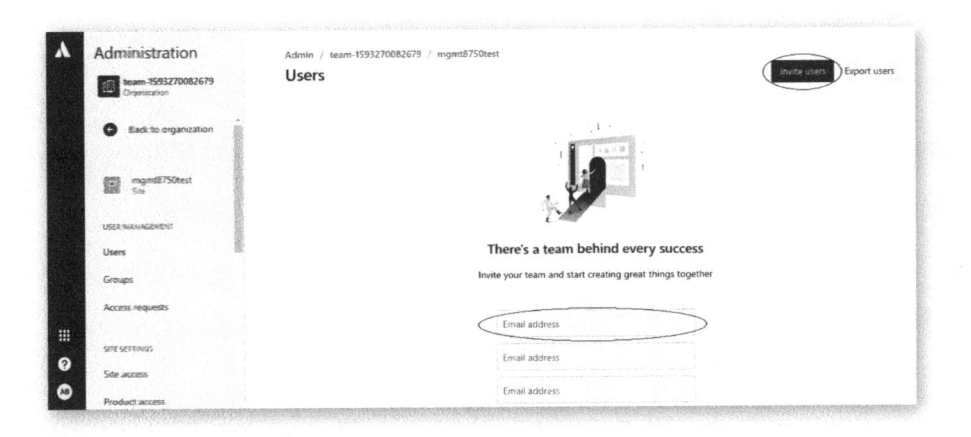

Enter the user email address, and select `Invite user`.

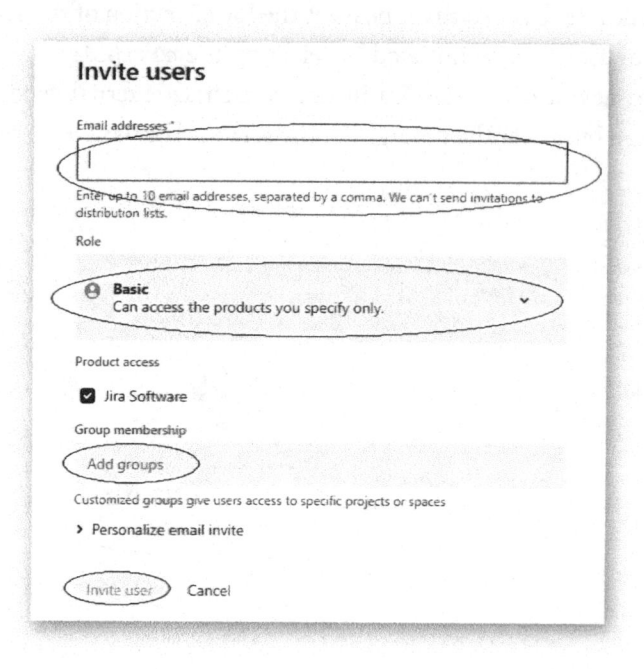

Note: There are additional advanced user-management functions that will not be covered in this text. To review advanced user-management functions, refer to Atlassian documentation.

SUMMARY

- Large and complex organizations often employ matrix-management resource management techniques. Matrix management can affect Agile team project dedication.
- Matrix management often means project team resources are allocated at a percentage of their available time.
- Additional operational and project responsibilities can impact resource availability.
- Co-located teams share space and benefit from osmotic communication. Shared physical space is important to encourage team interaction.
- Interactive teams create skilled generalist resources who can work interchangeably on user stories.
- Large and complex organizations often have distributed teams. This requires virtual spaces to be created that promote interaction amongst team members.

- Scrum masters are servant leaders. They are process coaches that remove obstacles to maximize team efficiency and throughput.
- Development teams should consist of all the resources needed to fully complete a user story.

KEY TERMS

accommodating negotiation approach: a negotiation approach that yields to the customer

asynchronous communication: team members see and contribute information at different times.

collaborating negotiation approach: team members are free to negotiate a user story. The goal of this approach is to achieve a win-win outcome.

co-located team: a team sharing a single space

Crystal: a software development methodology that is part of the Agile methodology family

dedicated/projectized teams: resources that are fully allocated to a project

distributed team: team members are located in different geographies or different locations within a building.

hybrid team: a team that has some dedicated resources and some resources supplied through matrix management

matrix management: organizational structures where resources report to multiple managers. This can also be referred to as dotted line reporting. This approach is common amongst large and complex organizations.

osmotic communication: knowledge being acquired by hearing team member conversations and informal team interaction

participatory decision-making: organizations identifying the degree to which employees will inform organizational decisions

PDM: an acronym for participatory decision-making.

personal safety: the ability to speak about work without fear of ridicule. Part of the Crystal methodology values.

seconded: resources that are supplied to the project from another function within the organization. A seconded resource is typically a dedicated project resource.

servant leader: a leader who puts employees at the centre of decision-making by sharing power and ensuring that employees achieve their maximum potential

skilled generalists: resources that are interchangeable and can "stand in" to perform multiple functions on a project

synchronous communication: all team members meet and communicate in real time.

vendor product owner: a vendor designate in a purchased product or solution scenario. The vendor product owner is the most knowledgeable project resource about the product and/or services purchased. However, they may lack organizational context and will need to be partnered with a business representative.

DISCUSSION QUESTIONS

1. Why can't organizations that engage in Agile simply use dedicated teams?
2. If geographical barriers can negatively impact project outcomes, why do organizations have distributed teams?
3. What are some disadvantages to being a servant leader? Explain your response.
4. Why does Agile value the collaborating negotiation approach? What Agile values or principles are consistent or inconsistent with a collaborating negotiation approach? Explain your response.
5. Do you think it is important for organizations to use a participatory decision-making model? What are some of the advantages versus disadvantages of PDM?

NOTES

1. M. Cohn, *Succeeding with Agile* (Addison-Wesley Professional, 2009).
2. Ibid.
3. Ibid.
4. Ibid.
5. C. Ebert and M. Paasivaara, "Scaling Agile," *IEEE Software* 34, no. 6 (2017): 98–103.
6. F. Dumitriu, G. Meșniță, and L. D. Radu, "Challenges and Solutions of Applying Large-Scale Agile at Organizational Level," *Informatica Economica* 23, no. 3 (2019): 61–71.
7. Ibid.
8. Ibid.
9. K. Rubin, *Essential Scrum: A Practical Guide to the Most Popular Agile Process* (Boston, MA: Addison-Wesley Professional, 2012).
10. Ibid.
11. D. C. Barrett, *Understanding Project Management: A Practical Guide* (Toronto, ON: Canadian Scholars, 2018).
12. A. Cockburn, *Agile Software Development: The Cooperative Game*, 2nd ed. (Boston, MA: Addison-Wesley Professional, 2006).

13. Rubin, *Essential Scrum*.
14. Ibid.
15. J. A. O. G. Cunha, H. P. Moura, and F. J. S. Vasconcellos, "Decision-Making in Software Project Management: A Systematic Literature Review," *Procedia Computer Science* 100 (2016): 947–954.
16. C. Larman and B. Vodde, *Large-Scale Scrum: More with LeSS* (Boston, MA: Addison-Wesley Professional, 2016).

6 User Story Estimation

CHAPTER OVERVIEW

In chapter 6 we introduce user story estimation techniques. User story estimation is a necessary input to sprint planning. Understanding the different approaches common to user story estimation enables teams to determine which estimation approach is most applicable to their environment. The goal of sprint planning is to determine sprint duration and the number of user stories to be completed within a sprint, based on empirical data.

In the early stages of a project using Agile frameworks, estimation techniques create a baseline calculation for user story effort. The baseline is used to determine a team's velocity, or the amount of user stories the team can complete in a given sprint. Understanding team velocity will help projects leveraging Agile frameworks determine how many sprints are necessary to meet the project launch criteria.

By the end of the chapter, readers will understand different approaches to user story estimation, how they contribute to sprint planning, and how Agile tools can be used to capture user story estimation data.

ESTIMATING CHALLENGES

Estimation is a challenge regardless of the project methodology being utilized. Part of this challenge can be attributed to **Parkinson's law**. Parkinson's law suggests that work expands to fill available time. This tendency is often partnered with people's tendency to overestimate, or create a buffer, to ensure that they have enough time to complete a task. If tasks are overestimated yet the maximum time is used to finish a task, then—due to Parkinson's law—teams are not completing tasks as efficiently as possible. In addition, estimation tends to be individual. What may take one resource an hour to complete may take another resource a day, and so estimation is inherently inconsistent.[1]

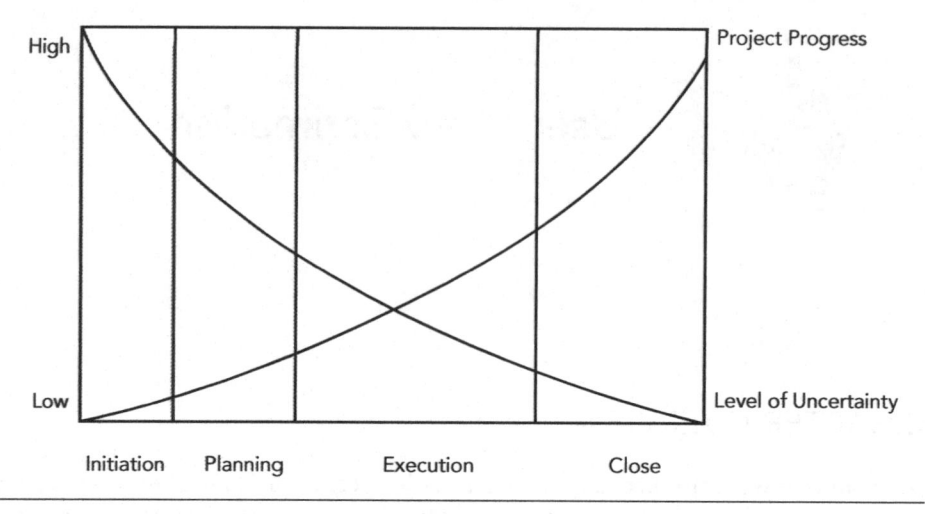

Figure 6.1 • Decreasing Uncertainty as a Project Progresses

Estimation challenges are further compounded by the **cone of uncertainty**. In the early stages of a project there is greater uncertainty.[2]

Figure 6.1 illustrates the inverse relationship between uncertainty and project progress. As more time elapses, more information is known about the project, creating greater estimate accuracy. This is also referred to as **progressive elaboration**. The cone of uncertainty captures the variability of estimation as the project progresses.

The cone of uncertainty illustrates the degree of variability when attempting to estimate user stories during the early stages of a project. Therefore, it is recommended that project teams not commit to features to be included in an overall Agile project until there has been sufficient elaboration. Once a feature has been fully elaborated, the project team is in a better position to provide commitments.[3]

It's important to note that Agile project variability is not associated with the timeline or budget of a project but rather with the number of user stories that will be completed in a sprint, release, or launch. This is due to the timeboxing approach to planning.

THE TIMEBOXING APPROACH TO PLANNING

Waterfall projects are often driven by scope completion. If the scope is not completed, additional time and budget may be required. It is challenging for project teams to accurately estimate a budget and schedule early in the project. The cone of uncertainty illustrates that as more time elapses, understanding increases, which results in greater accuracy.

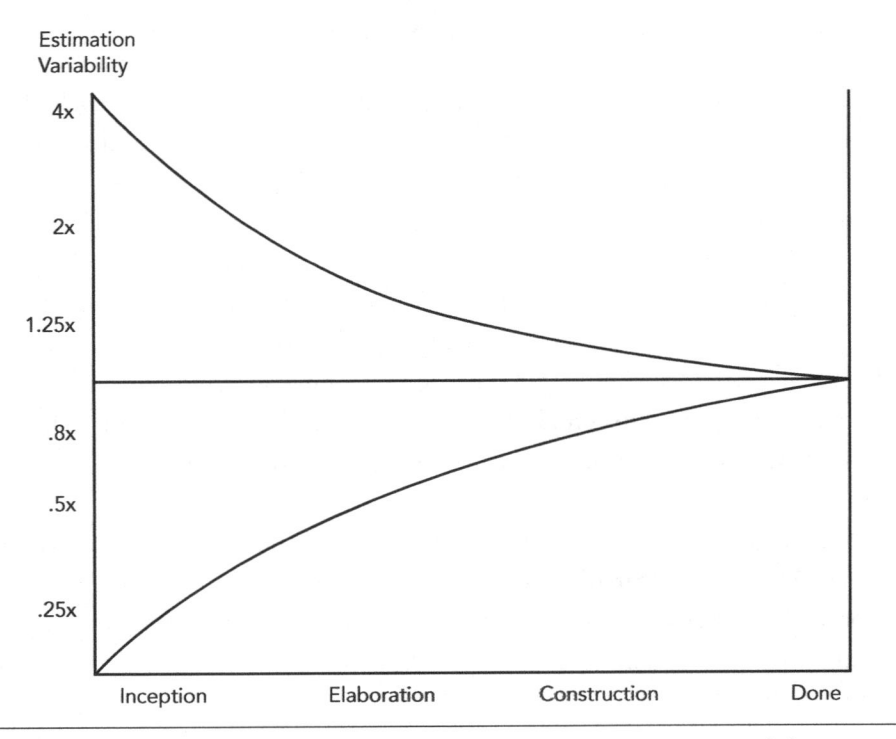

Figure 6.2 • Cone of Uncertainty and Its Impact on Estimation Variability

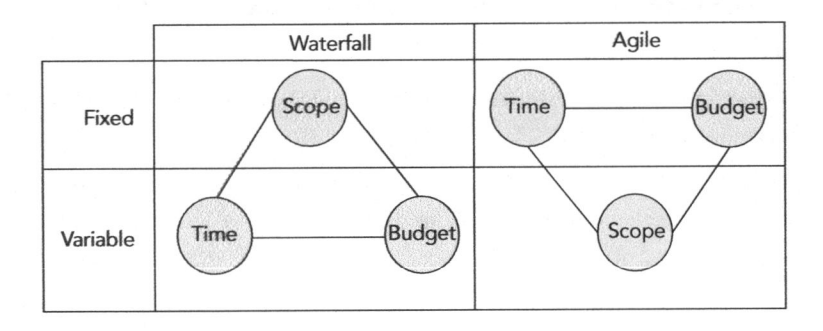

Figure 6.3 • Timeboxing Planning Approach

To mitigate this challenge, the Agile methodologies look to fix the budget and schedule rather than being driven by scope.[4]

By fixing the schedule and budget, a project team gives the project a definite end date and cost. What will be delivered is variable. This places the importance on ensuring that must-have and should-have user stories are prioritized correctly, which will enable the team to focus on delivering the core scope necessary for project launch. Scope that has not been completed by the project can be added to future projects or phases.

IDEAL TIME VERSUS STORY POINTS

When estimating user story effort, Agile frameworks use two key approaches: **ideal time** and **story points**. The ideal time approach estimates effort based on the ideal time it would take to complete the work. Ideal in this context refers to time that is uninterrupted and completely focused on completing work. In addition, ideal time assumes that everything needed to complete work is available to the resource.

As with other forms of estimating, ideal time can differ between team members. However, in addition to individual variability, it is important to understand that ideal time is *not* the real time needed to complete a user story. To calculate the real time required to complete a user story, distractions need to be factored in. Distractions include breaks, team interactions, meetings, and so on. Therefore, ideal time + distraction time = real time.

For large and complex corporate settings that use matrix-management techniques, ideal time estimation is further challenged. Because resources are only allocated for a percentage of their time, their other commitments can contribute to additional distraction time as well as impact the total elapsed time to complete a user story.

Ideal Time Estimation for Matrix-Managed Projects

Ideal time = 20 hours
Distraction time = 4 hours (assume 20 percent distraction above ideal time)
Real time = 24 hours
Matrix-management allocation = 30 percent = 2.4 hours per day allocated to the project, assuming an 8-hour day.
Elapsed time = 10 days

The Ideal Time Estimation for Matrix-Managed Projects illustrates the impact matrix management can have on task completion. What would potentially take three days for a dedicated resource could take 10 days for a matrix-managed resource. This can be a challenge for project leaders to communicate to the business. However, when quantified, presenting the impacts of a non-dedicated team can influence leadership to make more resources dedicated or look at eliminating wasteful activities that contribute to resource distraction.

The other approach to user story estimations is assigning story points to user stories. Points are assigned to a user story based on its complexity. The more time it will take to complete a user story, the more points it will receive. Therefore, a user story with 10 points will take longer to complete than a user story with five. However, story points do not represent hours, so a 10-point user story may not necessarily take twice as long as a user story with five points.

The goal of story points is to assign a relative value to each story. When moving to sprint planning, the team agrees on the stories it feels it can complete. Story points are aggregated. At the completion of the sprint, the team confirms the number of user stories that were completed. The story points associated with the completed user stories are tallied. The total number of story points completed during a sprint creates a baseline velocity of the team's capacity. For future sprint-planning sessions, the baseline velocity is used to confirm which, and how many, stories can be completed within the sprint.[5]

Story points can pose a challenge to project leaders because they are a more abstract concept, which makes them more difficult to explain to business partners. However, story points contribute to empirical measurement. Story points are a pure estimate that does not have to factor in distraction or elapsed time. Team performance becomes easier to estimate once a baseline is established. In addition, story point estimation can be more accurate than individual estimation and performed more quickly.

PLANNING POKER

A common approach utilized for story point estimation in Agile methodologies is **planning poker**. Planning poker is an approach based on the wideband Delphi model. The following are the steps to **wideband Delphi**, which is an interactive approach to estimation:

- Participants are presented with a specification and form.
- A meeting is called to discuss estimation issues and seek clarification.
- Participants complete the form anonymously.
- Estimates are summarized and distributed.
- A follow-up meeting is called to review items with significant variation.
- Experts complete the forms anonymously.

The last three bullets continue in a loop until a consensus estimate emerges per item.[6]

Planning poker is structured similarly; however, instead of forms a card system is used. Each participant is provided a card with a number. The numbers are

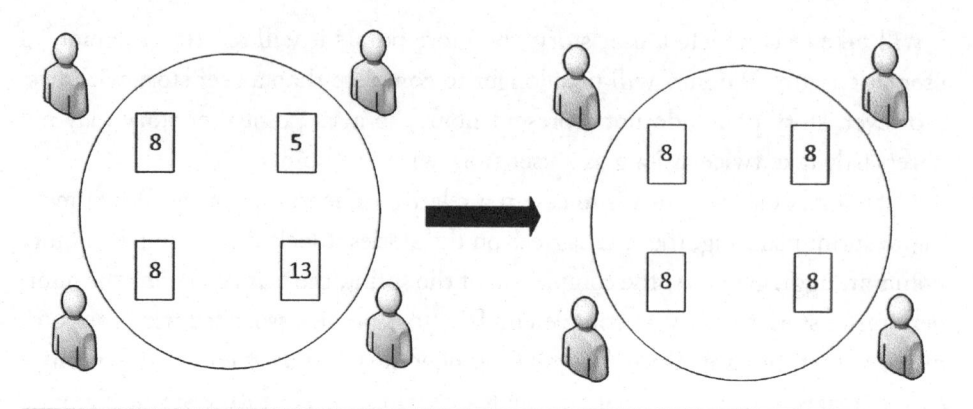

Figure 6.4 • Planning Poker Example

based on a modified **Fibonacci series**. A Fibonacci series is a series in which each number represents the sum of the previous two numbers. For example, 1, 2, 3, 5, 8, 13, 21, and so on. Participants are given seven cards from 1 to 21. Then a meeting is called that resembles the wideband Delphi approach.[7]

- Each user story is read out by the product owner.
- The participants ask clarifying questions.
- Participants select a card that best represents the number of points, or degree of difficulty, associated with completing the user story.
- The selected card is placed face down.
- Participants present their scores.
- Variations are discussed openly.
- Participants re-select a card based on a revised understanding from the joint discussion.

The last four bullets repeat until a consensus emerges.

Unlike the wideband Delphi approach, estimates are generated in real time, and story points can be added to the user story once a consensus is reached.

AFFINITY ESTIMATION

Affinity estimation, also known as T-shirt sizing, is an estimation technique that groups user stories into sizes. Like T-shirts, sizes begin at extra small and grow to extra large.

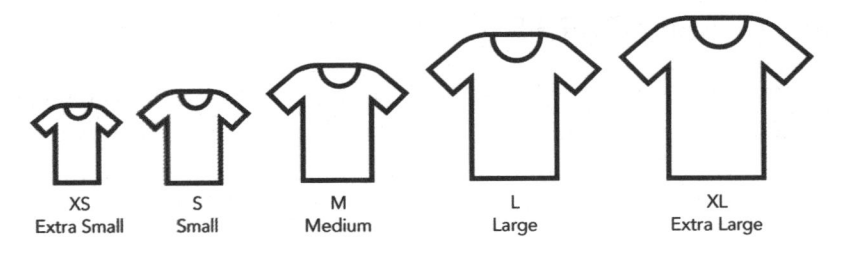

Figure 6.5 • T-Shirt Sizing Example

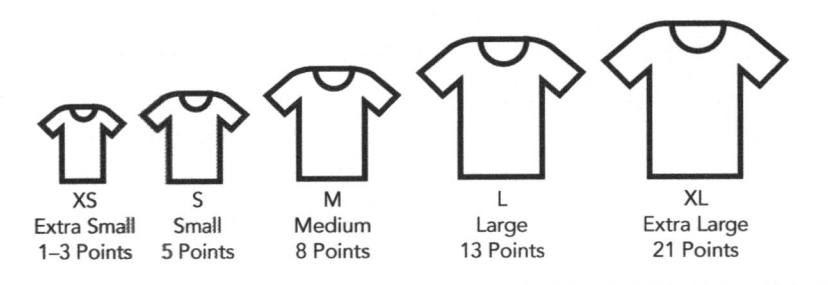

Figure 6.6 • T-Shirt Sizing with Points

Table 6.1 • User Story Log

User Story	Size	Points
User story 1	S	5
User story 2	M	8
User story 3	XL	21
User story 4	M	8

Once a baseline of story points associated with each category, or size, has been established, points can be rapidly assigned to all user stories.[8]

The affinity estimation technique is helpful when there are a large number of user stories for a project. Planning poker could take a significant amount of time if it's done for every user story. By quickly applying sizes to user stories using T-shirt sizes, a significant number of user stories can be estimated in a short period of time. It is important to note that when performing affinity estimation there is a higher risk that the size may not fit the story, because the process of **elaborating** each user story was not performed. This can result in a higher degree of variability.

LARGE USER STORIES

User stories must be able to be completed within a single sprint. If the team feels that the user story is too large to assign a value to, further decomposition of the story is required. The product owner will help the team break the story into smaller components.

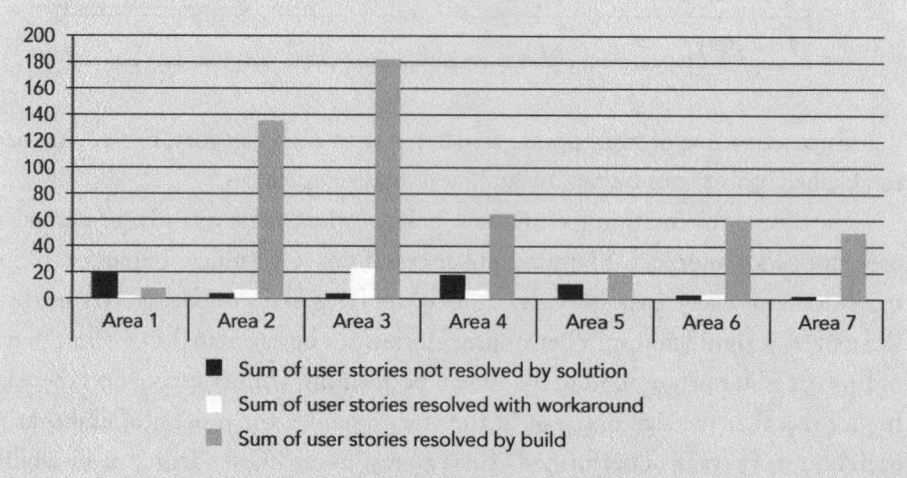

> **Case Study 6.1 • Using Affinity Mapping for Large Vendor Projects**
>
> The winning software vendor was announced. The requirements that were gathered through the value stream mapping activities helped identify the vendor that would best meet the organization's needs. Imran and his team had mapped hundreds of current state processes and recorded thousands of requirements. The winning vendor initiated a kick-off meeting with the entire project team. As part of the kick-off meeting, the vendor shared their proprietary project-task tracking tool along with their project approach. There were to be four waves of configuration. Each wave represented more than one hundred items per module.
>
> Imran exported the list of tasks from the vendor tool. There was a significant volume of tasks to complete within a wave. Imran scheduled a meeting with his team. Imran included in the meeting the vendor representatives for each of his team's modules and his team members who were responsible for configuring the modules. Together they quickly assigned values to each of the tasks based on T-shirt sizes from extra small to extra large. The team also leveraged the opportunity to associate each vendor task with the requirements captured during the value stream mapping exercise.
>
> [Bar chart showing Areas 1–7 with three series: Sum of user stories not resolved by solution; Sum of user stories resolved with workaround; Sum of user stories resolved by build. Y-axis ranges from 0 to 200.]

> By associating tasks with stories, the team was able to forecast the requirements that would be fulfilled by the vendor solution and highlight where the solution would not resolve a requirement. This would be important when considering vendor customizations and implementing workarounds, as well as setting expectations with stakeholders.

AGILE CONTRACTING

Agile contracting is a procurement approach for acquiring and managing Agile resources. In waterfall approaches, procurement can be a substantial activity; significant time and effort can be spent on creating proposals and contracts. This is often called a fixed-price contract, where the entire scope of a project is described in procurement documents. Vendors then respond to the written scope, and a contract is negotiated based on the documented scope, resulting in a dollar-figure agreement. Changes to the contract or scope often result in formal change requests, which can increase project cost and time. The fixed-price approach is in conflict with the following Agile principle:

> 2. Welcome changing requirements, even late in development. Agile processes harness change for the customer's competitive advantage.

Therefore, Agile contracting uses **time and materials contracts**. Time and materials contracts refer to an agreement between customer and vendor. Vendor resources charge a fixed hourly rate along with any material cost associated with work completion. There can be stipulations about a minimum number of hours or a time cap, so that a certain amount of time will not be exceeded by a vendor resource. This enables Agile teams to quickly procure resources. As per the timeboxing approach covered earlier in the chapter, once the project has fixed the budget number and/or timeline, resources can be procured. When the budget or schedule has been reached, the vendor resources can be released and the project is completed. Because of the unpredictable nature of Agile projects and the willingness to accept change, time and materials contracts offer the necessary flexibility for teams to add and release resources as needed.[9]

CREATING AN AGILE BUDGET

Agile budgets are often focused on the expenditure of team effort. Enterprise projects can often have infrastructure expenditures such as creating space, expanding a technology footprint, or upgrading telecommunications. Large enterprise projects often have dedicated infrastructure workstreams that may or may not be using Agile techniques (infrastructure tends to be a reliable and repeatable activity with well-defined scope that supports the waterfall approach). When cloud technologies are used, infrastructure activities are often managed by a vendor and requests are performed operationally. The IT service desk can take an infrastructure service request, and the cloud vendor fulfills the request within days. For these reasons, Agile budgets are often focused on capturing resource time and the costs associated with utilizing those resources during a sprint.

Costs to use a resource include both **direct** and **indirect costs**. Direct costs can be tied directly to the production of a product or service. In an Agile project, a direct cost is the resource labour but could include equipment such as the computers resources use to perform their work. Indirect costs are not tied directly to project activity but are incurred by the project. This could include items such as insurance, utilities, or rent. For large and complex organizations, there is often a **loaded cost** to use a resource. A loaded cost includes the resource's hourly rate including an amount that represents the resource's impact on indirect costs. For example, resource 1 has a direct labour cost of $50 per hour. However, their loaded cost includes rent, utilities, insurance, computer lease, and service provider costs. The organization calculates that the actual cost to use the resource is $85 per hour. This is their loaded cost.[10]

To build an Agile budget, the scrum master must use resource loaded costs as well as resources' hour allocation for participating in the project. For example, if a resource is allocated at 50 percent using matrix management, then for a 40-hour workweek they would be allocated to the project for 20 hours per week. The following table illustrates a sample Agile budget.

Table 6.2 • Sample Agile Project Budget

Resource	Loaded Rate	Hour Allocation	Weekly Cost	Sprint Cost
Resource 1	$80	20	$1,600	$6,400
Resource 2	$100	30	$3,000	$12,000
Resource 3	$120	40	$4,800	$19,200
Resource 4	$80	40	$3,200	$12,800
Resource 5	$80	20	$1,600	$6,400
Resource 6	$60	15	$900	$3,600
Total	$520	165	$15,100	$60,400

The Agile budget focuses on the cost per sprint. Using the timeboxing planning approach, if there is a fixed budget, it will determine the number of sprints the team can afford. Alternatively, if there is a fixed timeline, then the cost per sprint can be extended across that period to determine the project cost. Finally, if team velocity is known, then the costs and number of sprints can be calculated based on the time it will take to complete the prioritized user stories.

AGILE TOOLS: ASSIGNING STORY POINTS TO USER STORIES

Updating a Single User Story

From the navigation bar, select `Projects`. Then select the desired project from the Projects workspace.

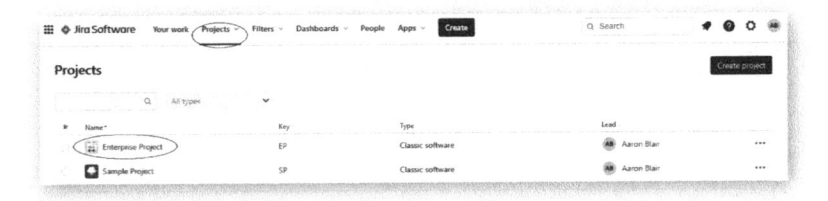

The project will open. Select `Backlog` from the Project menu. Then select the user story to add story points to.

Once the story has been selected, scroll using the story details pane on the left of the screen until the Story Points field has been reached. Enter the appropriate value in the Story Points field.

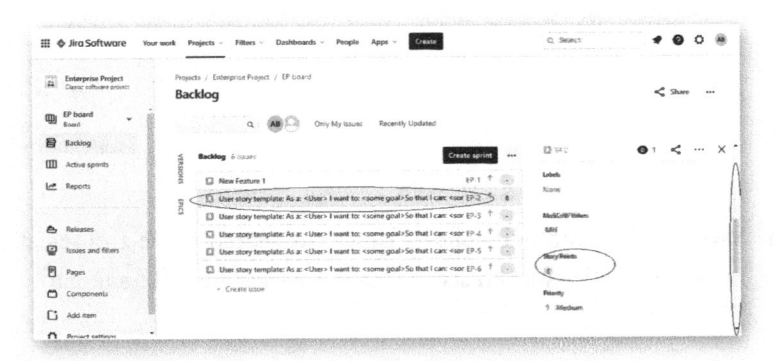

Creating Saved Searches/Filters: Basic

To create saved searches, select `Filters` from the navigation bar. Select `Advanced issue search`.

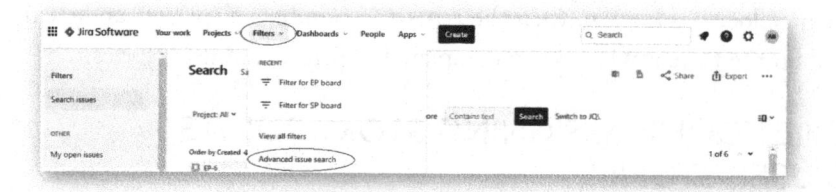

Issue filters can be applied to the project, issue type, progress, and/or ownership as well as any fields in the issue table. This includes any fields that were customized for the project, such as MoSCoW.

The Contains text attribute allows the filter to be further refined. As an example, if the MoSCoW custom field was created with MH, SH, and CH values for must have, should have, and could have, then using the text filter for MH will only show the must-have stories. Once satisfied with the search criteria, select `Save as`.

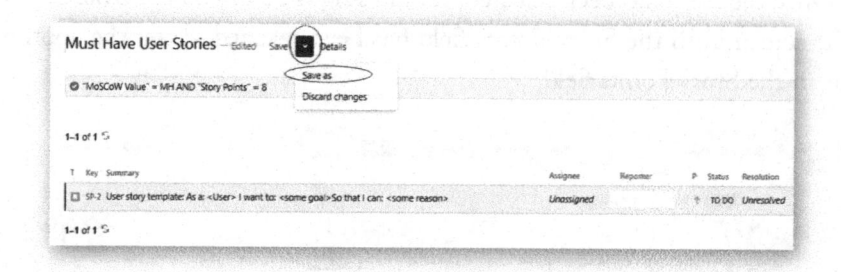

The Save Filter screen will appear. Enter the search name and select `Submit`. It will now appear in the starred section of the Issues and filters menu.

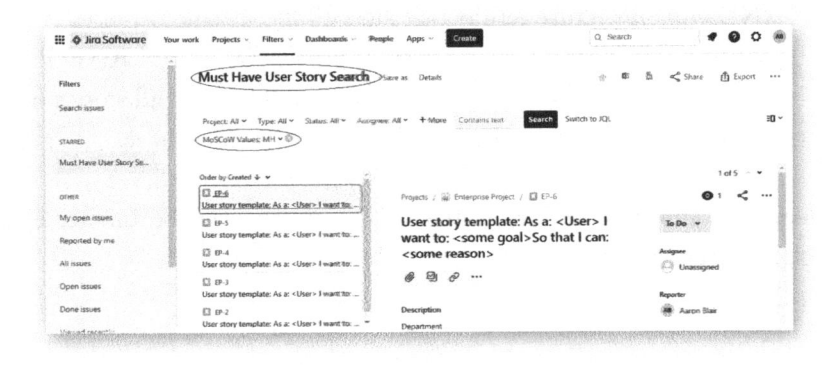

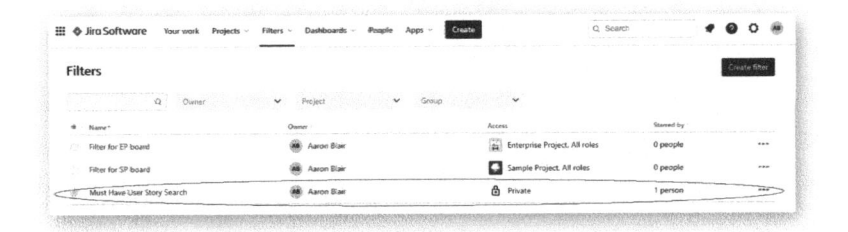

Creating Saved Searches/Filters: Advanced

To create advanced searches with multiple criteria, select `Switch to JQL`.

JQL is a search language. JQL comprises fields, operators, values, and keywords:

Fields are search components available within Jira such as Priority, Story Points, and Assigned To.

130 AGILE PROJECT DELIVERY

Operators provide direction to the query. Common operators include equals (=), does not equal (!=), and is less than or greater than (< >). An operator for a query may include searching all stories that are field: Assigned To = Specific User.

Values are the actual data in the query. In the previous example, the Assigned To value was the Specific User.

Keywords are specific words in JQL that help further refine searches by combining fields and values. Common examples are AND, OR, and IS. Building on the previous example, a keyword may be used to search all stories for Project = X AND Assigned To = Specific User AND Status = Done. Using AND will only return results that meet all the specified criteria. An example using OR could be to search all stories for Project = X AND Priority = High OR MoSCoW = MH. This query would return all stories from the specified project with a high priority or listed as must have.

Note: The above is just an example. JQL queries can be further explored through Atlassian user guides.[11]

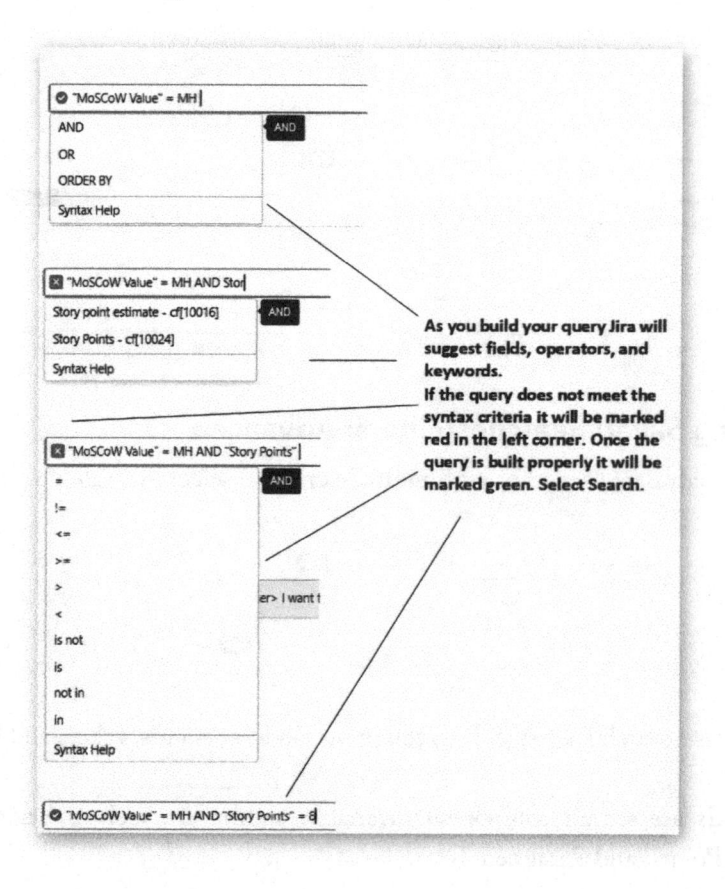

Once the JQL search has been completed, the results will appear in the search window. Previously created searches can be modified and saved as new searches by selecting the pull-down menu and selecting `Save as`.

If saved, the JQL search will appear in the Issues and filters menu in the same manner as the basic search under starred.

Editing Multiple User Stories

When there are hundreds of user stories that need to be updated, doing them one by one is not feasible. Consider the affinity mapping technique. This is a quick way to assign a relative sizing value to many user stories. To have these reflected in Jira, you will want to use the bulk change function.

From the Filters pane, select the appropriate search criteria to identify the list of user stories that require editing. Once satisfied with the results, select the `ellipsis` at the top right corner and select the `Bulk change` function.

Select the user stories to be edited. Select the `Next` button.

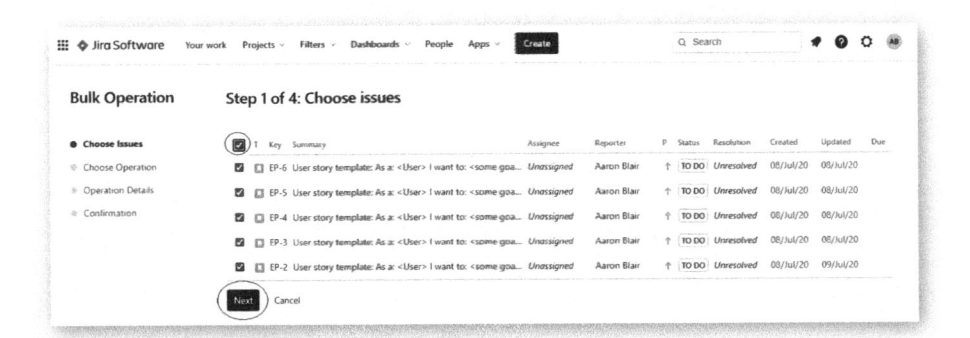

Not all user stories will be the same size. Once user story points have been defined, you can use the bulk edit function to apply story point values to a number of user stories in a single function. Select all the stories that apply to the desired value being edited. If affinity mapping was applied, there may be a number of stories that meet the "large" criterion. These stories would be assigned a value of 12. The bulk change function would apply the value of 12 to all the user stories selected in the bulk change function. This step would need to be repeated for each affinity mapping category. Users can only bulk edit a specific field value one at a time. For example, user story points cannot be updated with 8, 3, and 5 in a single operation. The operation would need to be performed each time a new value is being updated.

Users can update multiple fields in a bulk edit as long as the values are consistent. Therefore, if all story points that are 3 are also considered a low priority because they should be relatively easy to complete and they pose minimal risk, the priority for all user stories that have been labelled as 3 can also be updated to low during the same bulk change operation.

Once the user stories have been selected along with Next, you will be taken to step 2 of the bulk edit routine. To bulk edit stories select Choose issues. Then select Next.

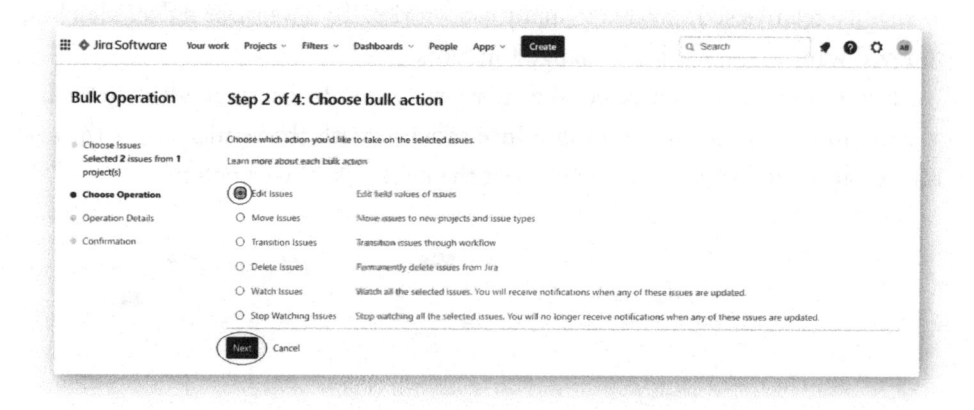

In step 3 of the routine, scroll to the desired field(s) to be edited and select the radio button. Enter the desired value and select Next.

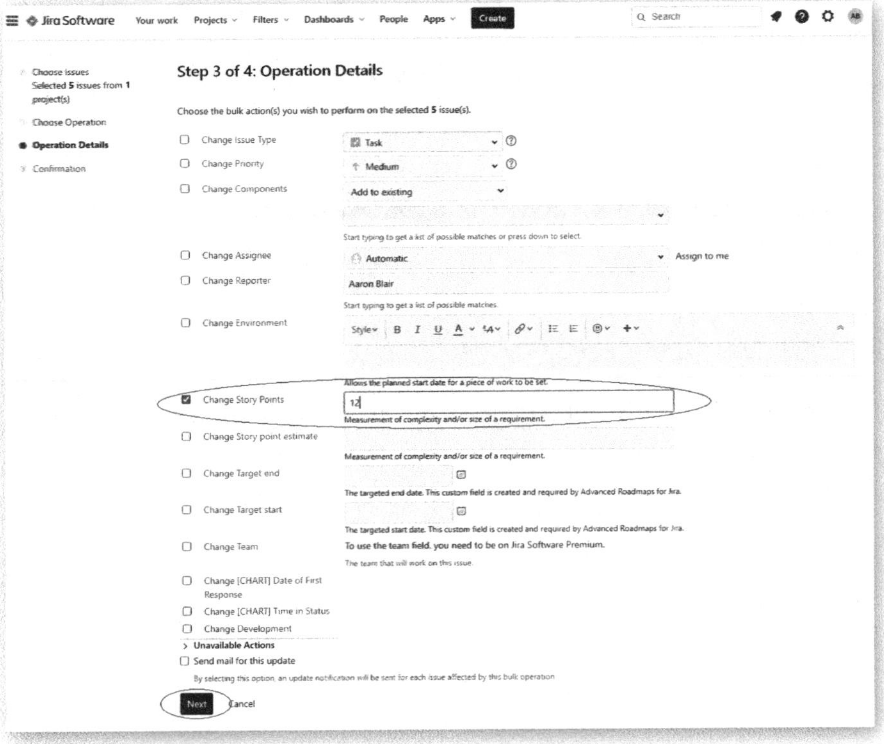

Step 4 will present you with a confirmation. If satisfied with the results select `Confirm`.

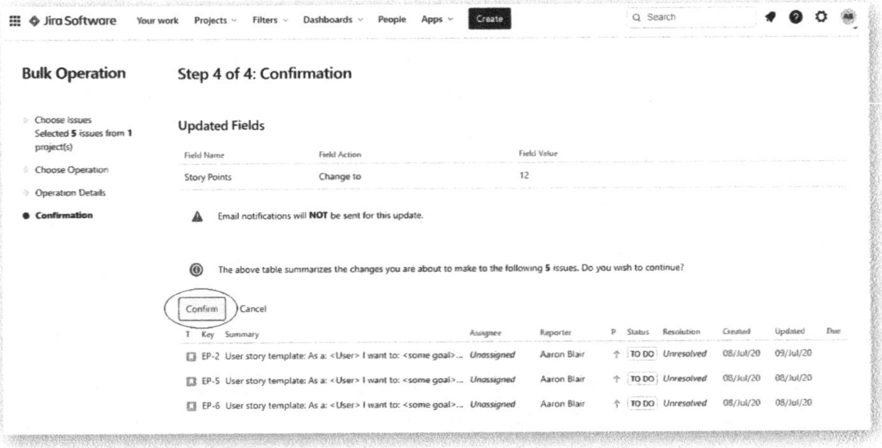

You will be taken to a progress screen. Once complete, select Acknowledge.

Once selected, you will be returned to the Issues and filters screen with the updates applied.

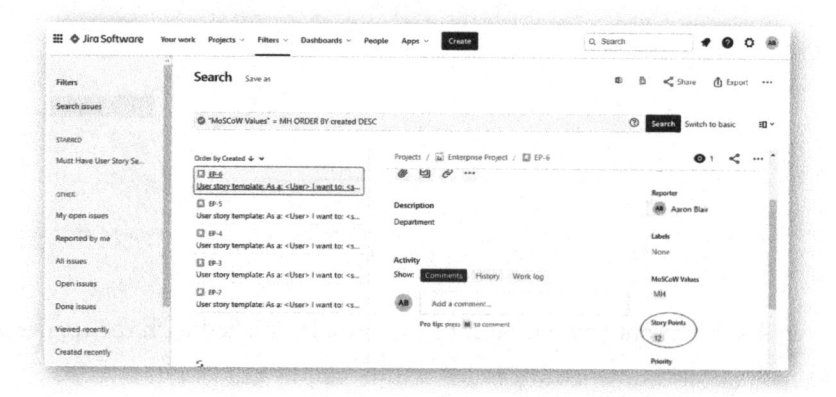

SUMMARY

- All projects contain uncertainty. As a project progresses, things that were once uncertain become clarified.
- Uncertainty contributes to estimation accuracy. The more uncertain the requirement, the less accurate the estimate. This is referred to as the cone of uncertainty.
- Agile estimation can be done in ideal time or story points. Ideal time does not necessarily indicate how long a task will take to complete; distraction time needs to be factored on top of the ideal time estimate to appreciate the elapsed time a task will take. Story points is a purer estimate and supports empirical performance measurement that can be used during sprint planning sessions.
- Planning poker is an Agile approach to assigning story points to a user story. Planning poker is a consensus-driven estimation technique that uses a series of card values to assign size and complexity to a story.

- Affinity estimating can be used to quickly categorize a large number of stories. However, because affinity mapping is performed quickly, it does not benefit from the conversations and clarifications that come with planning poker.
- User stories need to be completed in a single sprint. User stories that are too large to be completed in a short interval should be further decomposed into smaller stories.
- Agile fixes schedule and budget to reduce the risk of exceeding these thresholds. Scope becomes the variable, placing the importance on ensuring that user stories are prioritized correctly.
- Agile contracting uses time and materials contracts to quickly add resources and release resources if budgetary limits for the project have been reached.

KEY TERMS

affinity estimation: an estimation technique that quickly groups user stories into size categories; also known as T-shirt sizing or estimation

Agile contracting: the use of a time and materials procurement approach to acquiring Agile resources

cone of uncertainty: the tendency for estimates to have less variability as a project progresses towards its goal

direct costs: costs that can be tied directly to the production of a product or service. In an Agile project, a direct cost is the resource labour but could include equipment such as the computers resources use to perform their work.

elaborating: development team members learning more about user stories so they can validate their estimates and complete their work to meet customer expectations

Fibonacci series: a series of numbers where each number in the series represents the sum of the previous two numbers

fields: a JQL search component. Fields available within Jira include Priority, Story Points, and Assigned To.

ideal time: an estimating technique that assigns an hour value based on the ideal time it would take to complete a user story. Ideal time is time that is uninterrupted and completely focused on work. It assumes that everything a resource needs to complete a user story is readily available.

indirect costs: costs that are not tied directly to project activity but are incurred by the project. This could include items such as insurance, utilities, or rent.

JQL: a search language used in Jira to build custom filters. JQL comprises fields, operators, values, and keywords.

keywords: specific words in JQL that help further refine searches by combining fields and values. Common examples are AND, OR, and IS.

loaded cost: the resource's hourly rate including an amount that represents the resource's impact on indirect costs

operators: a JQL search component that provides direction to a query. Common operators include equals (=), does not equal (!=), and is less than or greater than (< >).

Parkinson's law: stipulates that work expands to fill the time available for its completion

planning poker: an Agile estimation technique that uses cards arranged in a Fibonacci series. Participants use the cards to assign a value to a user story. The process is iterative until a consensus is reached.

progressive elaboration: refers to uncertainty being reduced as a project progresses throughout its lifecycle

story points: a point system used for user stories. Points are assigned to a user story based on its complexity. The more time it will take to complete a user story, the more points it will receive.

time and materials contract: an agreement between customer and vendor where vendor resources charge a fixed hourly rate along with any material cost associated with work completion

values: a JQL search component. Values are the actual data in the query, such as the search field must equal a certain value.

wideband Delphi: an interactive approach to estimation whose goal is to achieve consensus amongst its participants. Planning poker is based on the wideband Delphi approach.

DISCUSSION QUESTIONS

1. Consider types of projects that may not benefit from a wideband Delphi or planning poker approach. Identify the types of projects and provide your rationale.
2. Identify a variety of daily, weekly, and monthly activities. Assign a value to each based on a Fibonacci series. Explain your rationale for the number assigned.
3. Why would ideal time be more challenging to estimate in a matrix-managed environment? Explain your answer.
4. How do you think story points contribute to empirical data? How do you imagine this information is used by project teams? Explain your answer.

5. User stories too large to be completed in a single sprint need to be broken down into smaller pieces. Relate this concept to a personal experience on a project, at work, planning an event, etc. Explain your answer.

NOTES

1. H. Kerzner, *Project Management: A Systems Approach to Planning, Scheduling, and Controlling*, 11th ed. (Hoboken, NJ: John Wiley & Sons, 2013).
2. P. Measey, *Agile Foundations: Principles, Practices and Frameworks* (London, UK: BCS, The Chartered Institute for IT, 2015).
3. Ibid.
4. K. Rubin, *Essential Scrum: A Practical Guide to the Most Popular Agile Process* (Boston, MA: Addison-Wesley Professional, 2012).
5. Ibid.
6. Ibid.
7. Ibid.
8. Ibid.
9. Kerzner, *Project Management*.
10. Ibid.
11. www.atlassian.com

7 Sprint Planning

CHAPTER OVERVIEW

In chapter 7, we review the sprint planning process. Sprint planning builds on the cumulative understanding of user stories from previous stages. Sprints are populated with user stories based on their size, complexity, and the team's capacity, or velocity. During early stages of the project it can be a challenge to accurately forecast a team's capacity. Approaches such as benchmarks or expert input can be used until empirical performance data has been collected.

Sprints should be populated with the number of user stories that can be completed within the allocated timebox. If there are too many user stories, sprints will consistently not meet their sprint goal. This chapter will review the approaches Agile frameworks use to maximize the potential of a sprint while remaining realistic.

By the end of the chapter, readers will understand how sprint planning meetings are facilitated and the roles and responsibilities associated with sprint planning. Readers will be able to describe the concept of the planning onion, the definition of done, and the difference between a product backlog and a sprint backlog. In addition, readers will understand how to use Agile tools to populate a sprint with user stories.

THE PLANNING ONION

When determining how many sprints should be part of a project, it is important to understand how each user story and release contributes to achieving an overall strategic goal of an organization. This can be referred to as the planning onion. The **planning onion** refers to the layers associated to strategic project planning.

The planning onion contains the following layers:

Strategy—the organizational strategy and mission to deliver products and services to its customers

Portfolio—a collection of projects that contribute to achieving the organizational strategy

Figure 7.1 • The Planning Onion

Product/project—the specific products or projects that will deliver customer value

Release—the incremental rollout of project or product features that will deliver customer value

Sprint—an iteration cycle required to complete the necessary features/scope to be included in a release

Day—the daily activities necessary to successful sprint completion[1]

Large corporations can have a significant number of products, projects, and releases that may be managed concurrently. Team members are often supplied through matrix management and can be geographically dispersed, or distributed. Large and complex organizations often use a number of tools that can help them track progress along with business value realization. Scrum masters often have to become familiar with an organization's standard suite of tools to ensure the organization has the necessary visibility into project progress. These approaches will be covered at greater length later in this text.

Because large corporations can have multiple products or projects running concurrently, large, complex organizations can have diverse and complicated portfolios.

To accommodate this complexity, Agile frameworks use **themes, initiatives, releases,** and **epics** to help manage enterprise projects. There can be some variation in definition of these categories. This text uses the Atlassian definitions, as the company's tool, Jira, is used to manage complex initiatives in this text.

> *Themes*—large focus areas that span the organization. These could be process improvement or innovation. Projects that fit within these categories would be listed under the appropriate theme.
> *Initiatives*—a collection of epics and/or stories that help a team drive toward a common goal. Initiatives can be synonymous with a project or new product introduction.
> *Releases*—points in time where functionality is made available for broader use. This could refer to customer use, but it could also refer to making functionality readily available to other projects or members of a project team.
> *Epics*—large bodies of work that can be broken down into a smaller collection of activities or stories. Epics could be used for enterprise initiatives where there are a number of components being delivered as part of the overall project or program.[2]

Case Study 7.1 • Using Epics to Manage Modules across an Enterprise Project

Once the affinity mapping exercise was complete, Imran looked at the totality of work. His team was responsible for multiple application modules: health information, finance, housekeeping, and human resources. Tracking all the user stories under a single project did not seem feasible, nor would it enable Imran to assess the performance of his team.

Imran decided to use epics to represent each module for which his team was responsible. When he completed organizing the user stories into epics, Imran noticed some discrepancies with work distribution. He only had one resource assigned to the health information module, but the volume of work expected to be completed during the same period was more than that for Imran's other modules. Additionally, health information had a high number of medium to large stories.

Imran questioned his vendor product owner. The product owner assured him that the work had been performed in previous projects at other organizations with the same work complement. Without his own empirical data, Imran decided to trust his product owner's input, but flagged it as a risk to his project sponsor. Once his team had completed a sprint, Imran would have more data to determine whether the resource risk was in fact an issue and would require corrective action.

142 AGILE PROJECT DELIVERY

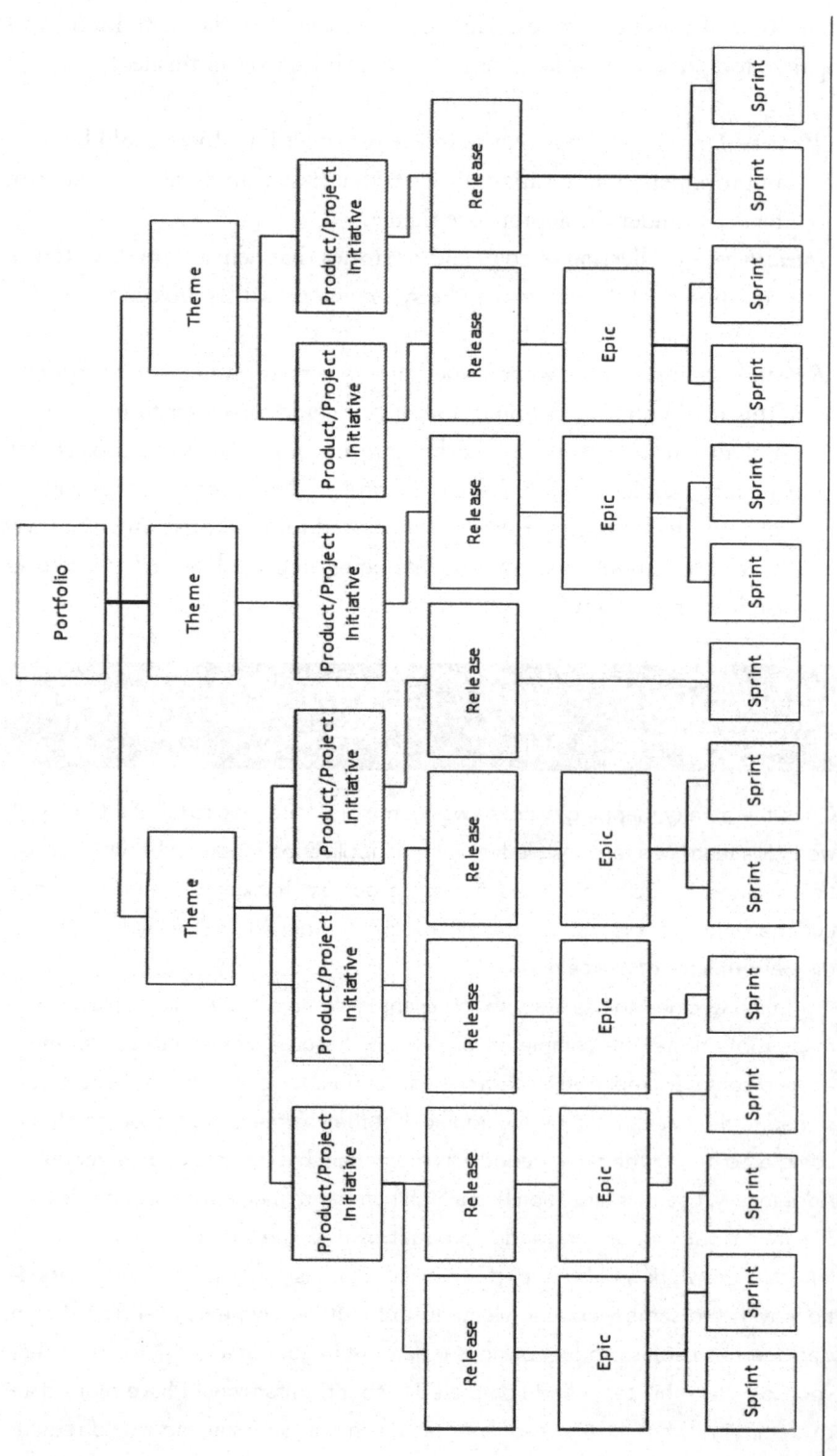

Figure 7.2 • Sample of a Large Corporation's Project Portfolio

PLANNING THE SPRINT

Sprint planning is one of the four Scrum events, where user stories are placed into a **timebox**. A timebox is a fixed unit of time. It cannot be exceeded. If user stories are not completed within the timebox, they are carried over to a future sprint. Timeboxes are based on the size and complexity of a project. The length of timeboxes can vary; however, best practice is to have timeboxes limited to two to four weeks. Sprint planning sessions are driven by timebox length.

- Sprint = Two to four weeks
- Sprint planning = Two hours for each week of the sprint

Therefore, a four-week sprint would have its own eight-hour timebox for the sprint planning session.[3]

If we recall from the planning onion, sprints contribute to releases. Releases typically refer to promoting working software to production for customer use. For corporations conducting enterprise projects, the term *release* may not refer to promoting working software to production. Instead, releases may involve promoting key functionality that is a **dependency** for other initiatives or epics. A dependency is a condition that must be satisfied before the next step can begin. In the case of an enterprise software implementation, a dependency may refer to a core set of features—such as the necessary components for an interface or integration team to begin their work—being available. Project dependencies are not limited to software development and configuration; they can apply to all projects. For example, in construction, a hole must be dug before concrete can be poured. The concrete foundation must have time to set before structural framing begins. All projects are made up of dependent activities.

Therefore, prior to the sprint planning session, it is important to understand the overall release plan and whether there are key user stories that are needed to fulfill dependencies for other epics or initiatives.

As part of sprint planning, teams should clarify the **release goal**. The release goal is the conditions a release must fulfill to achieve its business objective. Product owners define the release goal based on the business priorities and development team capacity. For enterprise software projects, vendor product owners are often in the best position to identify key dependencies and release goals based on their experience implementing their product in the past.[4]

In addition to a goal, a **release date** should be identified. A release date is a defined point in time when functionality is made available. Establishing a predefined release date helps teams understand sprint duration. A release date also helps prioritize user stories to meet the release goal.

Because there can be many sprints that contribute to a release, establishing a **sprint goal** is also important. A sprint goal captures the desired outcome of an iteration, which helps teams create a sprint backlog.[5]

THE DEFINITION OF DONE

Part of the sprint planning phase is creating the **definition of done**. The definition of done is the set of criteria that must be met for a user story to be considered complete. Often, the definition of done appears in the form of a checklist.

The definition of done is an important artifact. It helps build a common understanding of what constitutes the work necessary for a user story to be considered completed. This tool can help manage customer expectations as well as drive consistency across the team or, in large and complex organizations, teams. Definitions of done span time zones and geographies, so it is an important tool for distributed and virtual teams.[6]

In addition to building consistency amongst team members, the definition of done also supports sprint planning by enabling the team to break user stories into **tasks** that will be managed throughout the sprint. Tasks are the items that need to be completed for the user story to meet the definition of done criteria. Therefore, if a user story simply states "allow users to search by address," user story tasks may include creating test scripts, updating test automation tools, creating user documentation, creating training documentation, and so on. The

Table 7.1 • Definition of Done Checklist

Definition of Done	
User story configured and loaded with no errors	
User story peer-reviewed	
User story tested	
User story support document created	
User story training material created	
User story reviewed and approved	

definition of done helps provide a checklist of the tasks necessary to complete a user story.

PRODUCT BACKLOG VERSUS SPRINT BACKLOG

As discussed in chapter 2, there is both a product or project backlog and a sprint backlog. The product or project backlog is a collection of *all* the user stories to be completed. The sprint backlog is the specific set of user stories that will be completed within a single sprint. The product or project backlog is dynamic. It changes with every sprint and can be reprioritized at any time. The sprint backlog, however, is a commitment. Once the sprint has begun, there should be no changes to the sprint backlog. New user stories are added to the product or project backlog to be considered in future sprints.[7]

When creating the sprint backlog, understanding a team's **velocity**—the amount of work a team can complete within a sprint—is crucial. This can be calculated in ideal time, in real time, or by story points. For example, if the team's historical performance indicates that it can only complete 50 story points within a sprint, then the user stories in the sprint backlog should not exceed 50 points. As mentioned throughout the text, in Agile frameworks, planning is based on empirical data.[8]

In the absence of historical data, the first sprint will help establish a baseline velocity that can be used for future sprint planning sessions. A vendor product owner may be able to supply velocity data based on previous implementation experience, as highlighted in the text's case study.

CONDUCTING THE SPRINT PLANNING MEETING

The sprint planning meeting is often divided into two parts. The first part of the sprint planning meeting is dedicated to these items:

- Confirming the release goal
- Prioritizing user stories based on the release goal
- Creating a definition of done (Once the definition of done has been established, it should be reusable for future sprint planning sessions.)
- Defining the sprint goal
- Prioritizing the release-goal user stories into sprints
- Validating previous user story estimates

- Determining what the team can commit to delivering within the sprint
- Creating the sprint backlog

Several additional items are focused on in the second part of the sprint planning meeting:

- Decomposing user stories into tasks
- Re-validating that the team can commit to delivering user stories within a sprint
- Team members identifying which tasks they will focus on first[9]

The sprint planning session allows the team to co-create the sprint. Building consensus helps drive ownership across all team members and ensures there is a common goal and common success criteria for the sprint and all of its tasks.

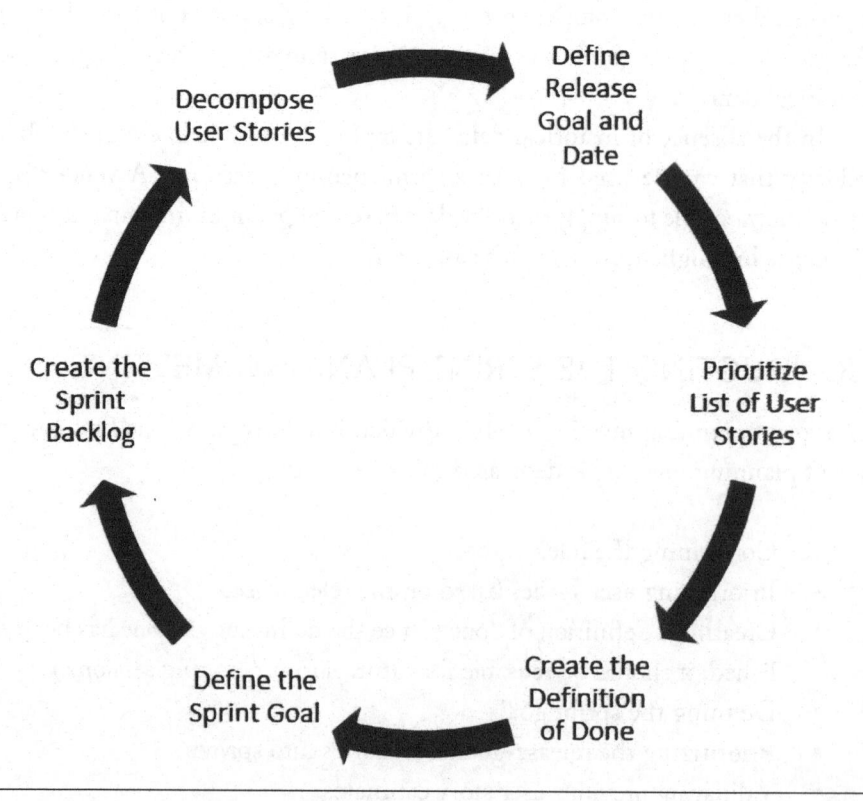

Figure 7.3 • Sprint Planning Meeting

AGILE TOOLS: CREATING THE SPRINT BACKLOG

Creating Releases in Jira

To create a release, select `Projects` from the navigation bar. Select the appropriate project.

From the project sub-menu, select `Releases`. Then select the `Create version` button.

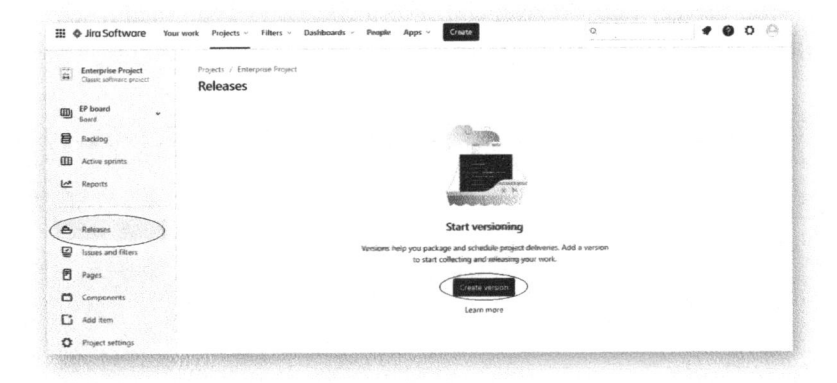

The Create version window will appear. Enter the release name, the release date, and a release description. When complete, select `Save`.

Once saved, the release will appear as an entry on the Releases screen. To create additional releases, select `Create version` and repeat the previous steps.

Creating an Epic

Epics can be created in numerous locations within Jira. Wherever an issue can be created, an epic can be created as well.

Select the `Create` button from the navigation bar. Select the appropriate project from the Project pull-down menu. From the Issue Type menu, select `Epic`. Enter the epic details and select `Create`.

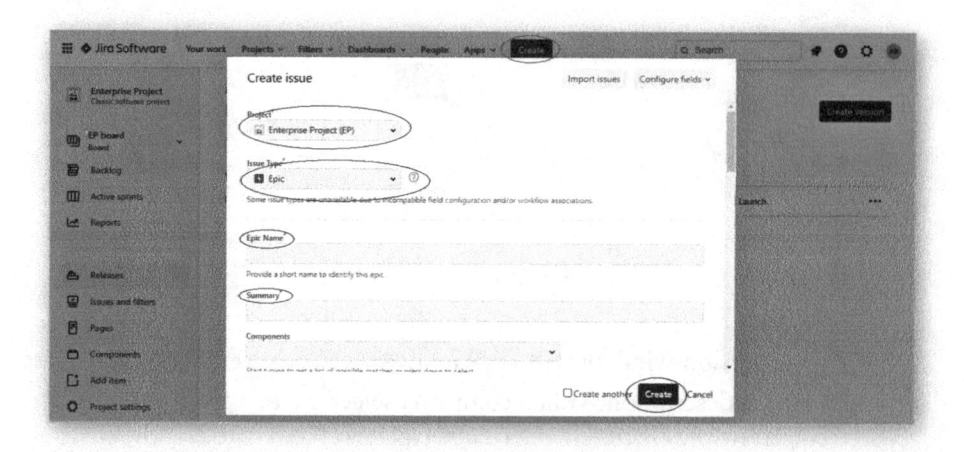

Adding User Stories to an Epic

To add user stories to an epic, select `Projects` from the navigation bar and select the appropriate project.

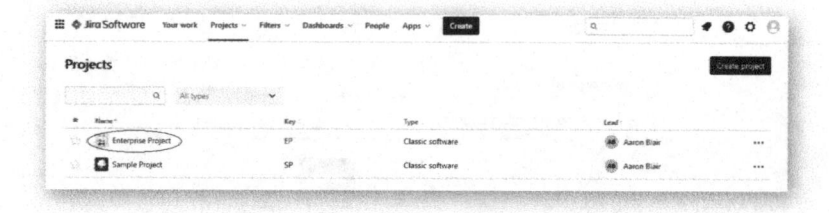

Select `Backlog` in the Project sub-menu. Incomplete user stories will appear on the Backlog screen. Select `EPICS` on the user stories side bar. Select user stories and drag them to the appropriate epic. Once a user story is added to an epic, it will have the epic label assigned.

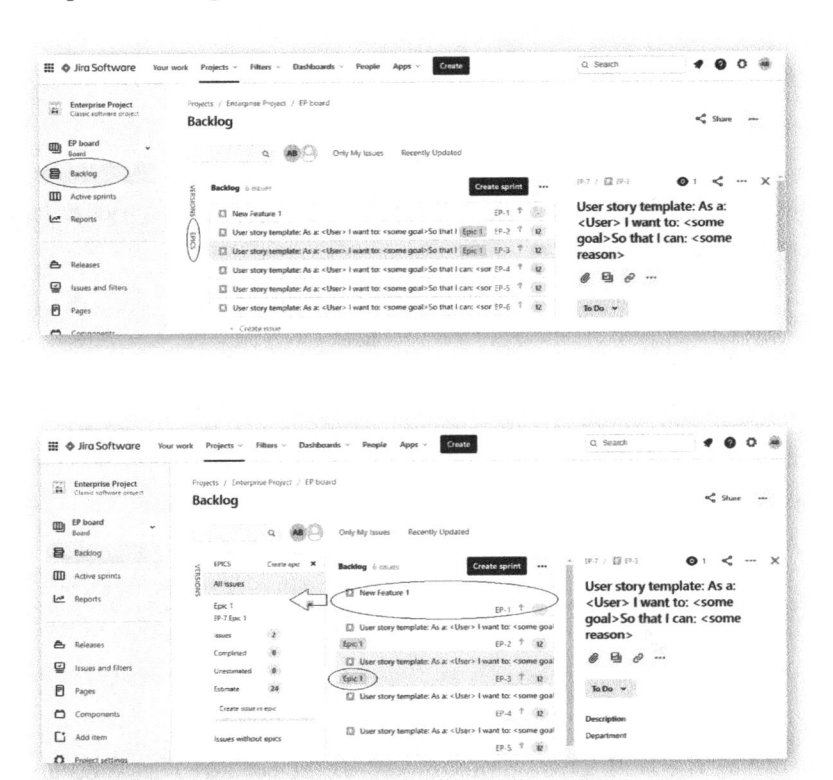

Assign User Stories to Epic Using Bulk Change

For large projects, dragging user stories into the appropriate epic one at a time can be time-consuming. Using the bulk change operation can help assign a number of user stories to an epic in a single function.

From the navigation bar, select `Filters`. The Filters pane will appear. Select the search criteria to identify the user stories to be moved. Then select the Bulk change function on the Filter screen by selecting the `ellipsis` in the top right.

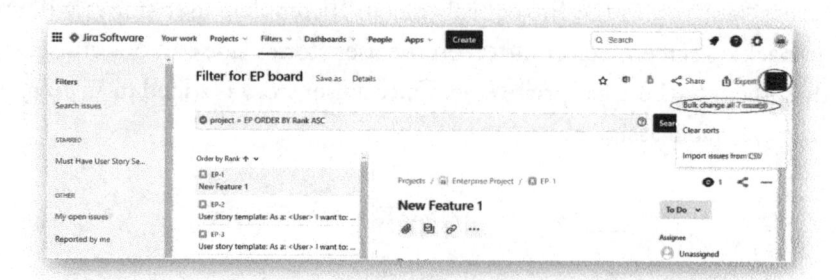

Step 1 of the Bulk Operation will appear. Select the user stories to be moved and select Next.

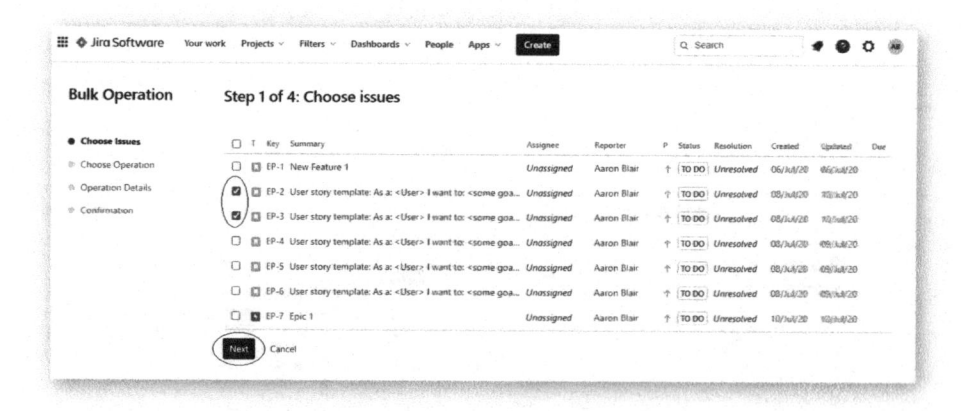

Step 2 of the Bulk Operation will appear. Select Edit Issues and select Next.

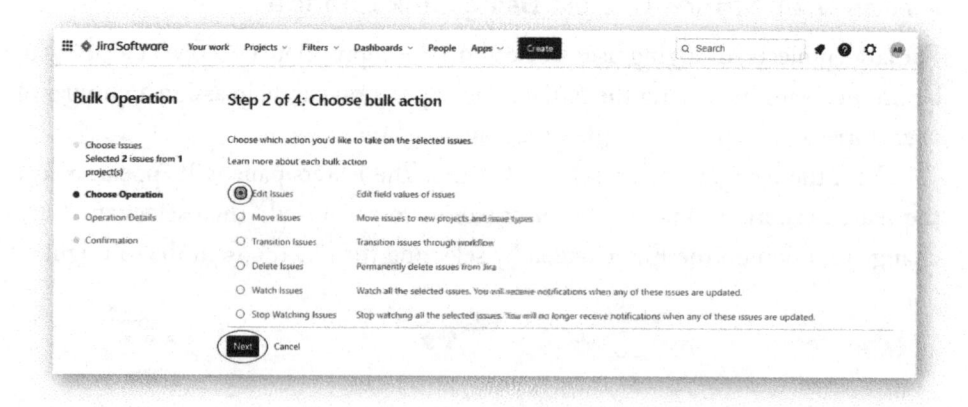

Step 3 of the Bulk Operation will appear. Select `Change Epic Link`. Select the appropriate epic to link to the user stories.

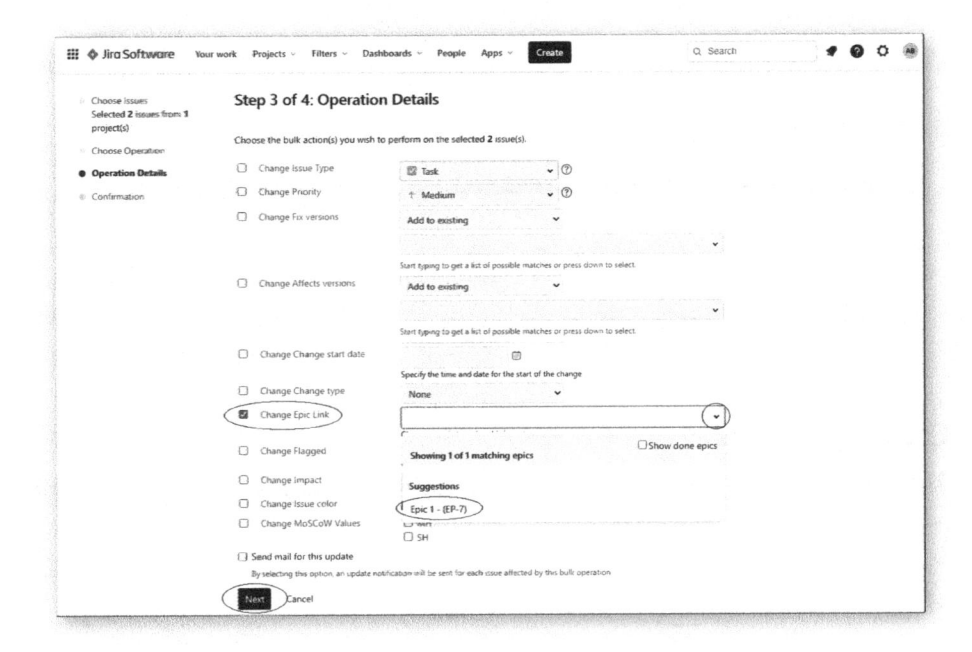

Step 4 of the Bulk Operation will appear. Select `Confirm` on the Confirmation screen.

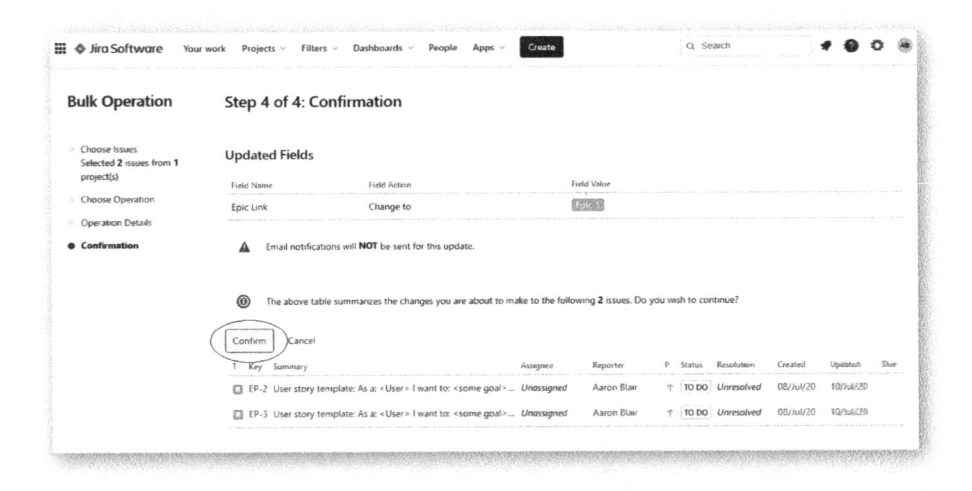

152   AGILE PROJECT DELIVERY

`Acknowledge` the change. User stories will now appear linked to the epic in the backlog.

Creating Sprints

To create sprints, select `Projects` from the navigation bar. Then select the appropriate project.

Select the `Backlog` menu item from the project sub-menu. Select the `Create sprint` button.

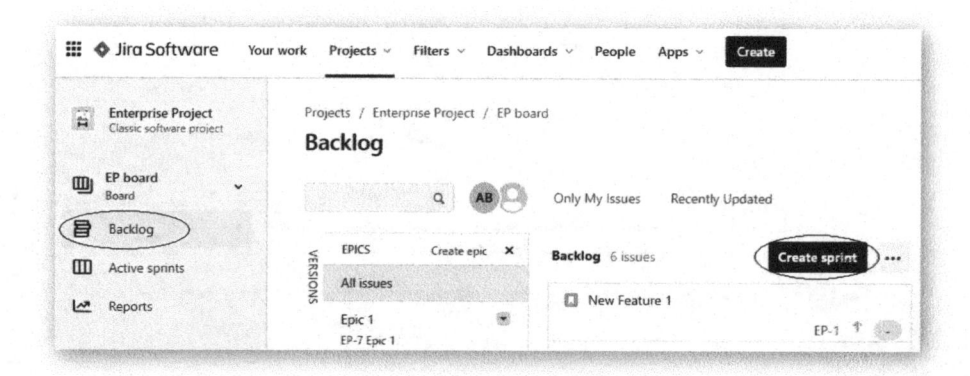

Stories can be dragged into the Plan your sprint area of the Backlog screen.

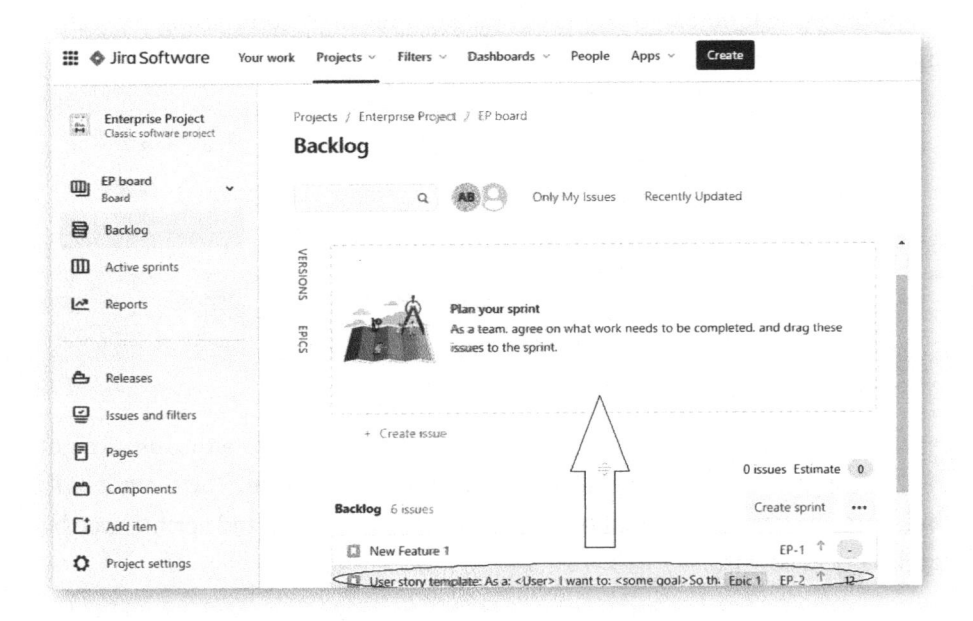

When user stories are added to the sprint, the story points will be aggregated along with the total number of issues. The `Start sprint` button will also become active.

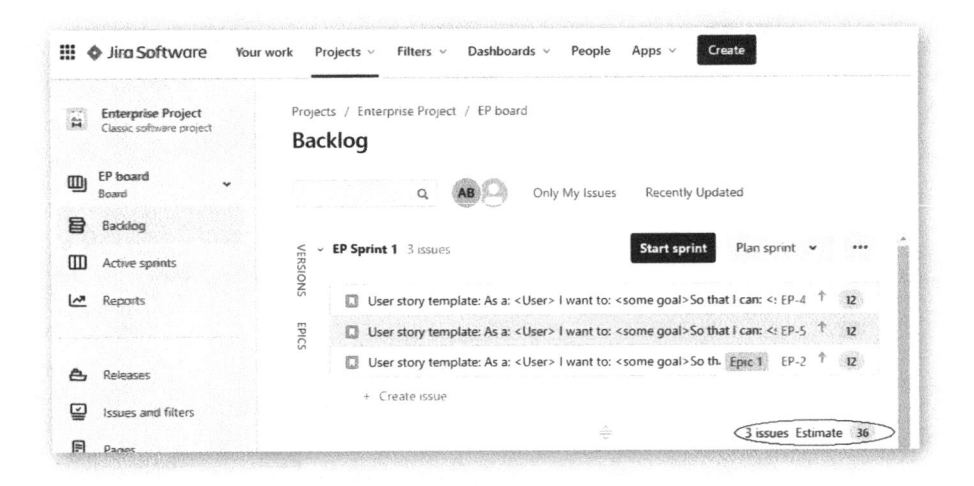

Creating Subtasks

From the navigation bar, select Filters. Find the user stories using pre-existing filters or create a new filter (chapter 6). Select the user story.

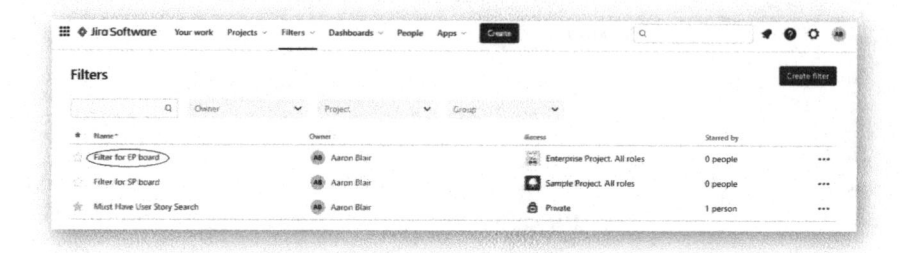

To create a subtask, open a user story and select Create subtask. An entry box will appear. Enter the task information and select Create. The subtask will be linked to the user story. Subtasks will follow the user story and sprints they have been associated with.

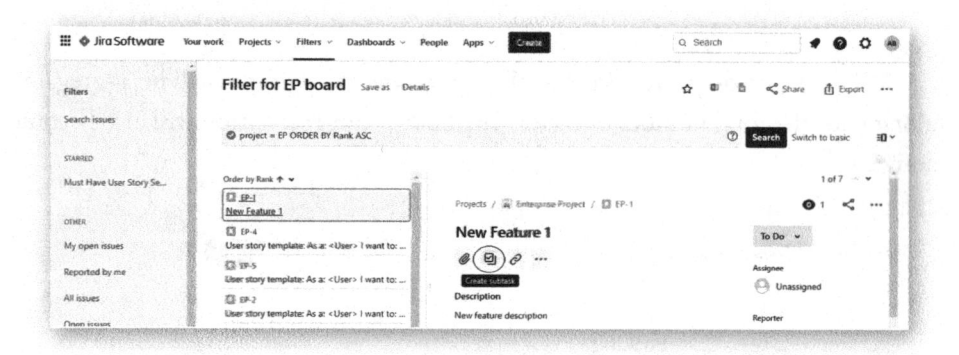

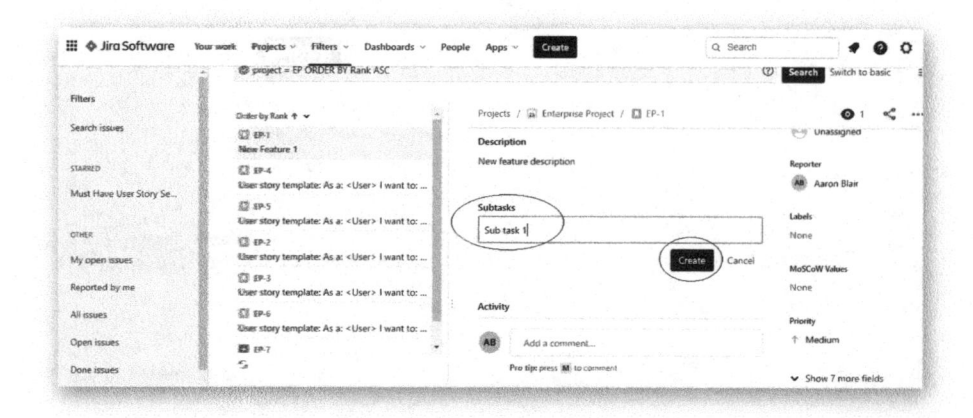

The subtask will appear in issue searches and screens along with the corresponding user story.

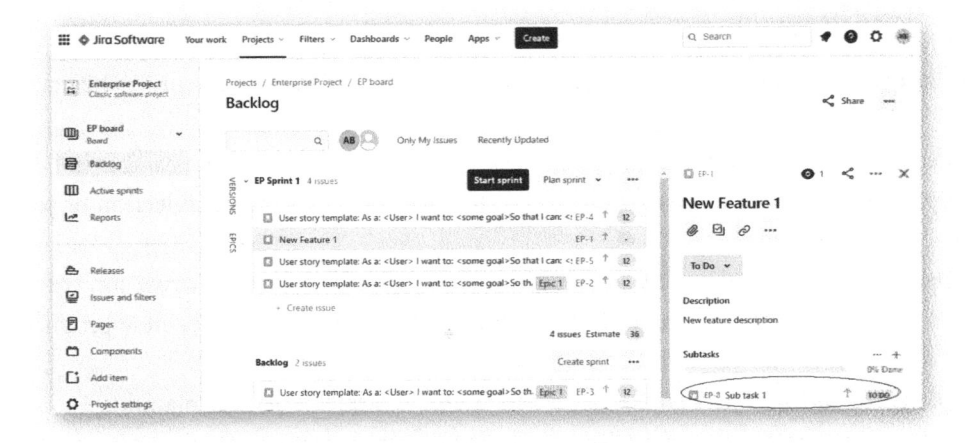

SUMMARY

- Sprint planning is done at the beginning of each sprint. By conducting the sprint planning event at the beginning of every sprint, product owners can reprioritize user stories to ensure the highest-priority stories are completed first.
- Sprint planning is a timeboxed activity. Sprint planning duration is correlated to the duration of a sprint. Sprint planning should take two hours per sprint week. Therefore, if a sprint duration is two weeks, a sprint planning session should be four hours.
- Goals are important to set at both the release and sprint levels. Release goals and dates are set to help prioritize user stories. Sprint goals are specific to each sprint. Sprint goals help prioritize user stories that correspond to the amount of work a team can commit to.
- A definition of done is created to help teams create user story tasks. The definition of done also helps achieve consistency amongst team members and across teams and helps establish expectations with stakeholders.
- A sprint backlog is created based on the prioritized list of product or project backlog items. Once the sprint backlog is created, it should not be modified. New user stories that arise during the sprint are added to the product or project backlog for future consideration.
- The sprint planning meeting is broken into two parts: the first part involves goal-setting—the release and sprint goals are set, along with sprint durations and release dates—and the second part is dedicated to decomposing user stories into tasks that are managed throughout the sprint.

KEY TERMS

definition of done: the set of criteria that must be met for a user story to be considered complete

dependency: a condition that must be satisfied before the next step can begin

epic: large body of work that can be broken down into a smaller collection of activities or stories

initiative: a collection of epics and/or stories that help a team drive toward a common goal. Initiatives can be synonymous with a project or new product introduction.

planning onion: refers to the layers associated to strategic project planning

release: represents functionality being made for broader use. This could refer to customer use or to making functionality readily available to other projects or members of a project team.

release date: a defined point in time when functionality is made readily available

release goal: the conditions a release must fulfill to achieve its business objective

sprint goal: the goal of the specific iteration. The sprint goal helps a team create a sprint backlog.

tasks: the items that need to be completed for the user story to meet the definition of done criteria

theme: large focus area that spans the organization. A theme can focus on process improvement or innovation. Projects that fit within these categories are listed under the appropriate theme.

timebox: a fixed unit of time that cannot be exceeded

velocity: the amount of work a team can complete within a given sprint. Velocity can be measured in hours or story points and should be based on empirical or historical data.

DISCUSSION QUESTIONS

1. Why are there two types of goals: release and sprint? Explain the differences between them and the importance of each.
2. Describe what it means to decompose a user story. Why is this important? What could happen if this activity does not occur?
3. Describe the importance of the statement "Once a sprint begins no user stories will be added to the sprint backlog." Does this align with Agile values and principles? Explain your answer.

4. What is a planning onion? Why is it referred to as an onion? Explain your answer.
5. Describe the concept of a dependency. How can this be managed in an Agile project?

NOTES

1. M. Cohn, *Agile Estimating and Planning* (Upper Saddle River, NJ: Prentice Hall, 2007).
2. www.atlassian.com
3. K. Rubin, *Essential Scrum: A Practical Guide to the Most Popular Agile Process* (Boston, MA: Addison-Wesley Professional, 2012).
4. Ibid.
5. Ibid.
6. Ibid.
7. Ibid.
8. Ibid.
9. Ibid.

PART IV

EXECUTING AGILE PROJECTS

In part IV of the text we focus on executing projects using Agile frameworks. During the execution stage, the scrum master takes on a more central role in the project's day-to-day activities. Readers will learn about the scrum process, what it means to be a self-organizing team, and how multiple project-team activities converge in large corporations that are managing enterprise projects using Agile techniques.

A key component of project execution is collecting performance data and sharing this information with project stakeholders. We will review how information is collected and shared in Agile frameworks as well as how tools can be used to aid the sharing of information.

By the end of part IV, readers will have an appreciation of how scrum approaches can be scaled to meet the challenges of large corporations, the use of information radiators, and how earned value can be modified to track projects using Agile frameworks. In addition, readers will be familiar with how Agile tools can be used to support the execution phase of an Agile project.

8 Scrum

CHAPTER OVERVIEW

Managing sprints is central to the execution stage of a project using Agile frameworks. Scrum is one of the more common frameworks used to manage an iteration cycle. Chapter 8 will focus on how to conduct successful scrums and will review how Scrum approaches can be applied to enterprise projects.

Agile promotes autonomous management techniques. This includes empowering teams to self-organize, practise effective communication techniques, and develop skilled generalist capabilities.

By the end of the chapter, readers will be familiar with how to apply Scrum, how scrums can be scaled to meet the needs of an enterprise project, and how autonomous teams can be built in distributed and virtual teams. Readers will also learn how to use Agile tools to help facilitate the execution stages of an Agile project.

USING SCRUM IN AGILE

Scrum is a term that originates from the sport of rugby. A scrum is a structured team of players who perform specific roles and is used to start or restart a play in rugby. Team members lock arms together with their heads down in order to gain possession of the ball and move forward.

Although *scrum* is a sports term, it aligns well with Agile project management. An Agile team is a structured group of professionals who use a scrum at the beginning of each day to stay in unison and make incremental progress forward towards achieving their sprint goal. The terms *daily stand-up* or *huddle* are often interchangeable with *scrum*. A scrum is one of the four Scrum events.

The scrum meeting is held daily and is timeboxed at 15 minutes. Because of its short duration, the scrum must focus on the following updates:

- Yesterday I completed [state task(s)].
- Today I plan to work on [state task(s)].
- The areas where I am blocked are [state impediments that are preventing task completion].

Because scrums are only 15 minutes in duration, it is important for the scrum master to ensure they do not become either platforms for problem-solving or status reports.[1]

Problems will arise, and projects using Agile techniques *do* have to devote time to problem-solving. However, it is not appropriate in a scrum setting. Consider the Lean principles: is sharing a personal status or attempting to problem-solve an individual's impediments helping the entire team complete their tasks? Likely not. Therefore, problem-solving and status-sharing do not create value for the entire team.

Although updating individual status and problem-solving do not serve the entire team, they should not be minimized. However, a more appropriate setting should be utilized and only the key stakeholders affected should be involved, so updating individual status and problem-solving should be conducted outside of the scrum. This **breakout session** is where affected team members discuss how to resolve problems.

Large corporations that are delivering enterprise projects may need to create targeted meetings to resolve problems. A vendor product owner may have **office hours**, or dedicated times to answer team member questions.

However, it is important to encourage team members to work together throughout the day to complete work and resolve issues. This is the essence of collaboration and the value of osmotic communication. If too many meetings are established, the team could lose some of its agility. The above approaches are only meant to complement Agile execution.

Other steps can be taken to ensure the 15-minute timebox is adhered to:

- Although anyone can attend a scrum, only the development team, scrum master, and product owners should speak.
- Have the team focus on coordination, not problem-solving. For example, if there's an impediment that is flagged, have team members commit to meeting rather than discussing the impediment in the scrum.
- Have team members stand up to answer the three daily questions: this isn't comfortable, so people want to finish quickly.
- Start the scrum on time.

- Focus on the priorities: do not get distracted by tasks that are not in the sprint backlog or are of low priority.[2]

Virtual, or distributed, teams can pose additional challenges to effective scrums. For virtual and distributed teams, the scrum master may have to take a stronger facilitator role. This is especially true if team members stray into providing a status report or begin problem-solving and are unable to take physical cues from the scrum master. Virtual teams can also be a challenge for scrum masters to facilitate because they may not be able to determine whether a non-core team member is speaking. In the early stages of a project, a scrum master may need to coach the team on the function of a scrum and reinforce the scrum ground rules. Tools such as video conferencing can help the scrum master manage virtual teams by monitoring the speaker and providing visual cues to team members if they stray from the scrum's purpose.

THE SELF-ORGANIZING TEAM

Agile principle 11:

11. The best architectures, requirements, and designs emerge from self-organizing teams.

What is a self-organizing team? Unlike traditional command and control leadership models, self-organizing teams are expected not to wait to be told what to do. The backlog is established, teams know what needs to be completed and can identify tasks they will complete, and teams are expected to have all the necessary resources at their disposal to complete their task. In addition, unlike waterfall projects, Agile frameworks are not prescriptive. The expectation is that experts are in the best position to determine how to solve a customer problem or achieve value. Therefore, team resources are not waiting for direction; they are driving the solution.

Part of what enables teams to be self-organizing is the concept of participatory decision-making. As covered in chapter 6, planning poker and a modified wideband Delphi approach produce better estimates. This is referred to as the **wisdom of the crowd** and relies on the collective input of a group of individuals rather than a single expert. A number of factors can negatively impact individual decisions, including bias, influence, or general "noise." During planning poker, individuals could provide drastically different estimates that are smoothed out through the process. The same is true during execution; rather than an individual determining the best approach to complete a user story, the group is expected to discuss and collaborate to determine the best solutions.[3]

The wisdom of the crowd is not unique to Agile projects; it should be fairly familiar to many. Democracy and the North American judicial system are based on the wisdom of the crowd.

Agile principle 4:

4. Business people and developers must work together daily throughout the project.

Business people and developers working together daily supports the concept of participatory or cooperative design, often referred to as **co-design**. Co-design is the approach of actively involving stakeholders in the design process to help ensure the design outcome is usable. Co-design supports Agile principle 1:

1. Our highest priority is to satisfy the customer through early and continuous delivery of valuable software.

In Agile, it is not enough to complete software development. Software must be valuable to the customer, or usable. Co-design enables teams to harness the wisdom of the crowd and leverage their knowledge in participatory design to produce the best possible outcomes. This is also why user stories are not definitive specifications but conversation starters to promote team collaboration.[4]

Agile principle 5:

5. Build projects around motivated individuals. Give them the environment and support they need, and trust them to get the job done.

Agile principle 5 is the essence of a self-organizing team. Agile provides the framework for motivated individuals to be self-organizing to complete their work. Motivated individuals do the following:

- Commit to the sprint goals and the user stories they will complete.
- Decompose user stories into tasks and provide estimates to complete their work.
- Focus on communication and collaborate across functions.
- Drive to decisions based on consensus and active participation.[5]

The scrum or daily stand-up is limited to 15 minutes to enable the team to make commitments and coordinate their day. The expectation is that the team will determine the best way to work together to meet their daily commitments, which is the essence of the self-organizing team. Self-organization also supports the Lean principles of valuing people and their input and creating customer value.

A final aspect of the self-organizing team is its **cross-functional** nature. A cross-functional team comprises a number of skill sets and business backgrounds. This helps create skilled generalists as well as embedding co-design principles within the team. The following are indications that teams are truly cross-functional:

- They are not constrained by their job-description boundaries and embrace the opportunity to expand their skills.
- They are flexible and open to input.
- They are helpful and look to support other team members who may be blocked.[6]

Case Study 8.1 • Daily Business Support in a Large Corporation

During his daily scrums, Imran found that there were a number of tasks that remained or were moved into the blocked category due to lack of access to business experts. Team members identified that it was difficult to pull their business contacts away from their day-to-day responsibilities.

The vendor product owner identified sprint periods as being four weeks in length, based on previous implementations. During the scrum, the vendor product owner suggested that the team proceed as best as it could, based on the knowledge the team members had acquired during value stream mapping activities.

Imran was concerned that without regular business interaction, his team might produce outputs that did not align with the business's expectations. This could put the project at risk and could result in leaving out highly desirable requirements.

Imran decided to establish a weekly user-group committee where business stakeholders would attend and answer questions and provide feedback on work in progress. Imran decided to break user groups into modules to ensure that participants felt their time was being valued.

After the initial meeting, Imran recognized the need for committees to have terms of reference to guide the discussion and meeting logistics. Within two weeks of the introduction of committee meetings, the number of items in a blocked state was reduced, and the team members were feeling more confident about their work and interactions with business.

A residual benefit to setting up committees was that business stakeholders became more open to ad-hoc conversations with the development team.

A self-organizing team enables team members to self-manage their time, which includes the following:

- *Allowing others to lead*—Different people bring different skills to the table. This means there will be times when each team member should be given the opportunity to lead.
- *Reporting progress transparently*—Setbacks are natural occurrences in projects. Being open and transparent gives the team the best opportunity to succeed.
- *Resolving conflict internally*—Conflict will arise, and this can be productive. Different perspectives help teams determine the best approach to a problem. Trusting the wisdom of the crowd and making decisions through consensus can help the team resolve conflict far more quickly than escalating outside of the team. Resolving conflict internally helps foster a sense of team and continued collaboration.
- *Adaptation*—The need to adapt will always be present in an Agile project. When requirements are uncertain, outcomes can be a journey of discovery. Keeping an open mind and being receptive to change enables teams to effectively navigate uncertainty.[7]

The acronym **C-FORC** is often used to describe desired behaviours associated with self-organizing teams:

Commitment to success
Focus on excellent work
Openness about concerns
Respect by sharing success and failures
Courage to undertake great challenges[8]

Because Agile teams are self-organizing, scrum masters play a different role than a traditional project manager. As captured in chapter 5, scrum masters are servant leaders. Servant leaders managing self-organizing teams should possess the following attributes:

- They take responsibility for creating the conditions to maximize team throughput.
- They put *we* before *me* and allow the team to earn the accolades for a job well done.

- They are responsible for creating a culture of collaboration.
- They are experts in Agile methods and act as a process coach for the team.
- They can influence without formal power.
- They demonstrate commitment to the team.[9]

EXECUTING AGILE PROJECTS AND COMMUNICATION

Effective communication is key to any project success. However, Agile places a high degree of importance on team interaction, as evidenced in Agile principle 6:

6. The most efficient and effective method of conveying information to and within a development team is face-to-face conversation.

Face-to-face conversation and team co-location support the principle of osmotic communication, which was covered in chapter 5. However, in large, complex organizations, face-to-face interaction is not always feasible. When working in distributed Agile teams, the different methods of communication available to project team members must be considered. Not all methods are equal when it comes to effective communication.

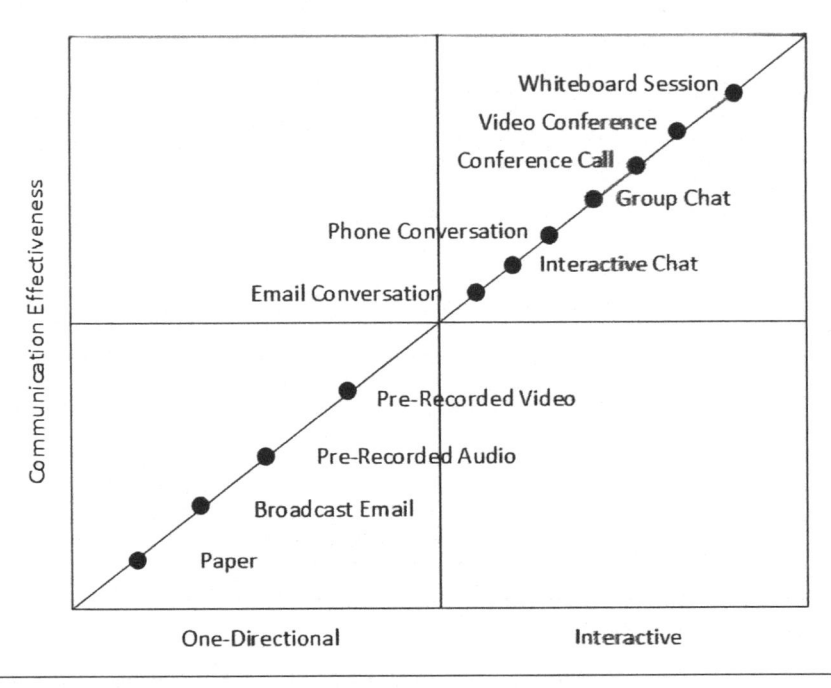

Figure 8.1 • Types of Communication and Their Effectiveness

Figure 8.1 illustrates different types of communication and their effectiveness at ensuring the desired message is received. There are times when one-directional communication is appropriate, such as an organizational announcement or team update. However, considering Agile principle 6 and the value of face-to-face interaction, distributed Agile teams should rely on more interactive methods of communication.[10]

The Crystal approach to Agile projects uses the concept of scaling. Crystal uses different approaches depending on the size and complexity of a project. The larger and more critical a project, the greater the need for control.

When projects are highly critical and complex, they receive a heightened rating. By categorizing projects by their size and complexity, Crystal recognizes that project methodologies may need to be tailored accordingly. A C6 Crystal Clear project will not require the same type of coordination and communication as an L200 Crystal Maroon project. Crystal uses a colour approach to quickly identify the size and scale of a project, as this helps leaders understand the staffing levels needed to achieve project success.[11]

		Crystal Method to Use				
		Clear	Yellow	Orange	Red	Maroon
Criticality of the Project	Life	L6	L20	L40	L80	L200
	Essential	E6	E20	E40	E80	E200
	Discretionary	D6	D20	D40	D80	D200
	Comfort	C6	C20	C40	C80	C200
		1–6	7–20	21–40	41–80	81–200
		Number of People on the Project				

Figure 8.2 • Crystal Methods Based on Scale

Source: Adapted from A. Cockburn, *Agile Software Development: The Cooperative Game*, 2nd ed. (Boston, MA: Addison-Wesley Professional, 2006).

Although large projects using Agile frameworks can involve hundreds of team members, Agile frameworks recommend that teams are limited in size. As covered in chapter 5, Scrum teams are size-limited to six, plus or minus three, members. By size-limiting teams, the following Agile values are fostered:

- Communication
- Development of skills
- Ownership
- Cross-functionality

Most enterprise projects would have teams in the red or maroon categories due to their size. Therefore, multiple teams would be required to execute an Agile project.

SCRUM OF SCRUMS

When multiple Agile teams are used for a project, coordinating across teams can become a challenge. Agile teams are size-limited and relatively self-contained. However, in enterprise projects, there can be dependencies across Agile teams.

To manage cross-team activities, a **scrum of scrums** approach can be used. The scrum of scrums is a session where multiple Agile teams review their team progress. A scrum of scrums should have representation from each team and is attended by the scrum master and a technical team member who supports the scrum master should technical questions arise.

A scrum of scrums occurs less frequently than a scrum; it should be conducted within the sprint duration. For example, a two-week sprint should have a monthly scrum of scrums, a four-week sprint should have a bi-monthly one, and so on. However, as a project approaches significant milestones, a more frequent scrum of scrums may be necessary.[12]

The scrum of scrums should cover several topics:

- Dependencies
- Issues that impact multiple teams
- Scheduling

A typical agenda could include these items:

- Changes since last meeting
- Plan until the next meeting

- Identifying where assistance is required
- Issues that impact the product backlog

Highlighting cross-dependency items in the project backlog may result in a once low-priority user story rising in priority because of the dependency it resolves. For example, if an interface team is dependent on a low-priority user story from a module team, the scrum of scrums output could raise the priority of the user story to ensure the interface team is not delayed in starting its activities.

Scrum of scrums can also assist with identifying risk or defects that affect interdependent user stories. This can help prioritize defects and generate new user stories that mitigate risk. Due to the broad nature of a scrum of scrums, it is not limited to the fifteen-minute timebox associated with a scrum.

BUILDING SKILLED GENERALISTS IN VIRTUAL TEAMS

The XP Agile methodology utilizes an approach to delivery called **pair programming**, which partners two development team members together during user story execution. Pair programming helps team members build their skill set while providing regular peer feedback. This approach supports the concept of *jidoka* and the Lean value of completing an activity correctly the first time.[13]

For distributed Agile teams, partnering two development team members separated by geography can contribute to osmotic communication as well as building team members into skilled generalists. Team members can interact using screen-sharing and conferencing technologies to ask questions, perform reviews, and share progress. When paired team members perform peer reviews, it can help prepare them for sprint reviews where completed work is showcased to stakeholders. Peer reviews can also help identify issues prior to testing activities, further supporting the concept of *jidoka*.

Having regularly scheduled office hours helps ensure that team members commit to interacting. Office hours, as discussed in relation to the vendor product owner, are a commitment of blocks of time when team members make themselves available to each other. Meetings during office hours do not need to follow a structured agenda. However, this time is a commitment and should not be given lower priority than other activities. Even if there is not as much content to cover, knowledge can be acquired through interaction.

CONTINUOUS INTEGRATION

Like paired programming, **continuous integration** is an XP Agile development concept. In software development, this involves developers checking in their code at regular intervals. An engine then integrates code into a single update; this form of automation supports the concept of *jidoka*. Integration engines often include quality scripts that identify where code is incomplete or conflicts with other checked-in code. This can also be referred to as unit testing.[14]

In the software-quality testing pyramid, the majority of tests should be automated and resolve the majority of issues.

Continuous integration is not exclusive to software development projects. It simply involves ensuring that work is shared across teams in a common repository, which minimizes duplication of work and conflicting submissions. All projects benefit from sharing knowledge and information. Continuous integration supports transparency across teams and geographies in the case of distributed and virtual teams.

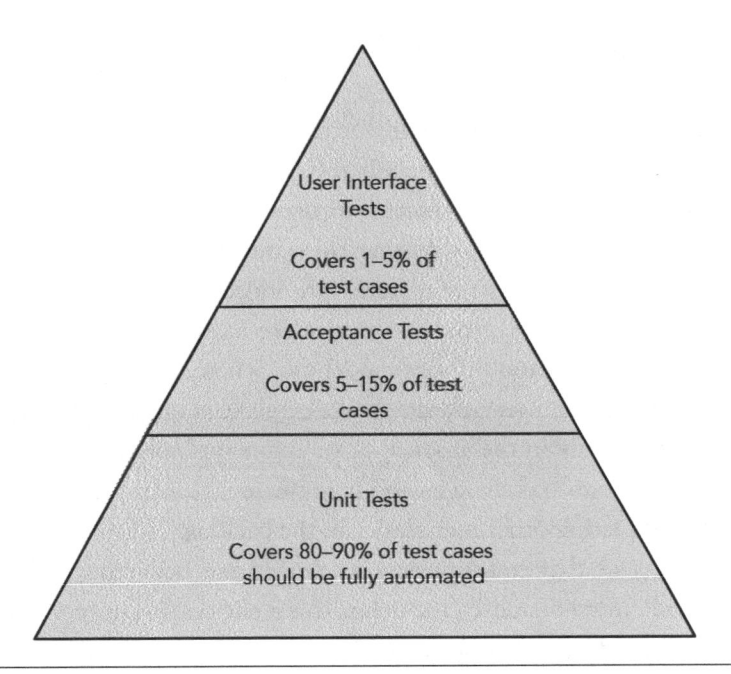

Figure 8.3 • Testing Pyramid

Source: Adapted from R. Black and G. Coleman, *Agile Testing Foundations: An ISTQB Foundation Level Agile Tester Guide* (London, UK: BCS, The Chartered Institute for IT, 2017).

INTEGRATION TESTING

Integration testing often occurs when a development team has completed its work. This step is necessary for enterprise projects because it is when work across teams is consolidated and available for use. Integration testing should only represent 1 to 5 percent of the test case volume; however, it is an integral step. Because enterprise

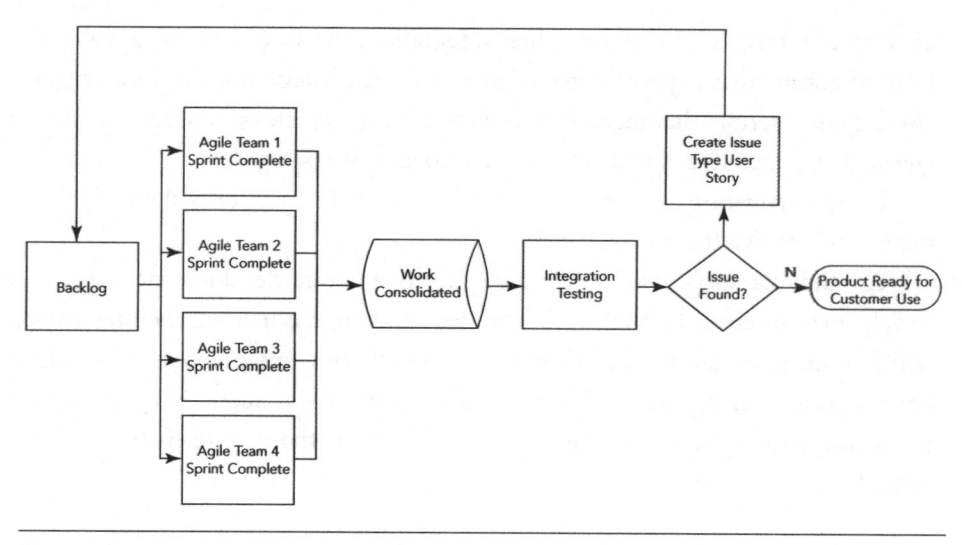

Figure 8.4 • Integration Testing Issue Identification and Assignment Flow

projects have numerous Agile teams contributing to a final product, a separate integration testing team is often required to validate cross-module workflows.

If issues or bugs are found, **issue type user stories** are created. Issue type user stories are specific actions the development team needs to take to resolve the identified issue or bug. Issue type user stories are added to the backlog and prioritized for a sprint. Not all issue type user stories are high priority. Priority should be driven based on the Kano priority model and whether there are available **workarounds** to minimize user impact. A workaround is an ad-hoc process that can be used operationally in the absence of an automated solution. It is not ideal but may be acceptable to stakeholders and help the team understand the issue priority relative to completing other user stories in the backlog.

Critical issues that could prevent a release from occurring should be prioritized and fixed immediately by the team. This is the one instance where something "new" could be added to the sprint.

USE OF COMMITTEES IN MATRIX-MANAGED ENVIRONMENTS

Agile principle 4 can be difficult to achieve in a matrixed environment.

4. Business people and developers must work together daily throughout the project.

Business leads may not be available daily to the development team. Operational work may interfere with business leads' ability to be readily available to answer questions and collaborate.

For large, complex organizations, the use of **committees** may be necessary to help facilitate regular business participation. Similarly to office hours, committees are scheduled, timeboxed commitments involving the necessary stakeholders who can answer development team questions, make decisions, and provide feedback. Committee stakeholders will be leveraged for the sprint review processes; however, finding issues at the sprint review stage of the process could be too late. As per the principle of *jidoka*, building regular business participation can help resolve issues at their source.

Committees should be small in number and focused to ensure that participants' time is being utilized efficiently. This means stakeholders should not be idle, listening to questions that are not relevant to their area. Committee participants should actively participate throughout the meeting. For example, a finance committee may be too broad to maximize stakeholder value. A more focused committee, such as payroll, may be more appropriate. This could mean that the development team attends many committee meetings; however, stakeholders should not.

Committees should be guided by a terms of reference. A **terms of reference**, or **ToR**, helps to guide committee purpose, establishes ground rules for interaction,

Table 8.1 • Sample Terms of Reference

Sample Terms of Reference
The X committee will meet at X frequency. The goal of the X committee is to: Membership shall include: • Chair: • Vice chair: • X voting members Meetings will: • Have an agenda distributed a minimum of 48 hours prior to the meeting Members commit to: • Come to the meeting prepared • Actively participate in discussion • Make timely decisions • Be supportive and open to negotiation Decisions will be prioritized by: • Legal and regulatory requirements • Organizational policy • Industry best practices • Customer value • Vendor recommendation   If a vote is required, there must be quorum, which would require X voting members to be present.

and could contain decision-making criteria. Terms of reference should include meeting frequency, composition, and voting logistics. Committees should meet during the sprint cycle to ensure that any questions that arise can be resolved without jeopardizing the sprint goal.

Use of committees supports the wisdom of the crowd and co-design principles of decision-making.

AGILE TOOLS: LAUNCHING A SPRINT AND MODIFYING TASKS/STORIES

Configuring a Sprint Board

From the navigation bar, select `Projects`. Then select the appropriate project.

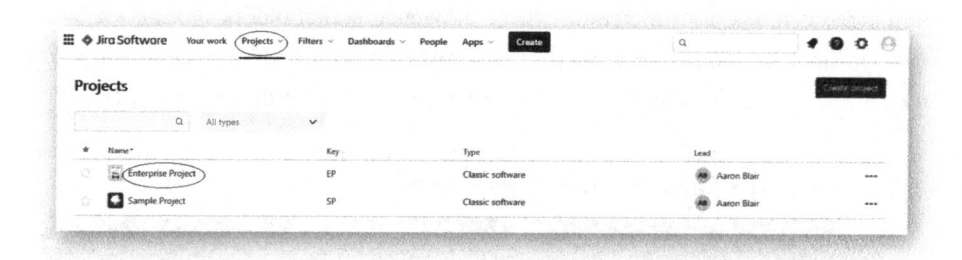

Select the `Backlog` menu. In the Backlog screen, select the `ellipsis` at the top right and then select `Board settings`.

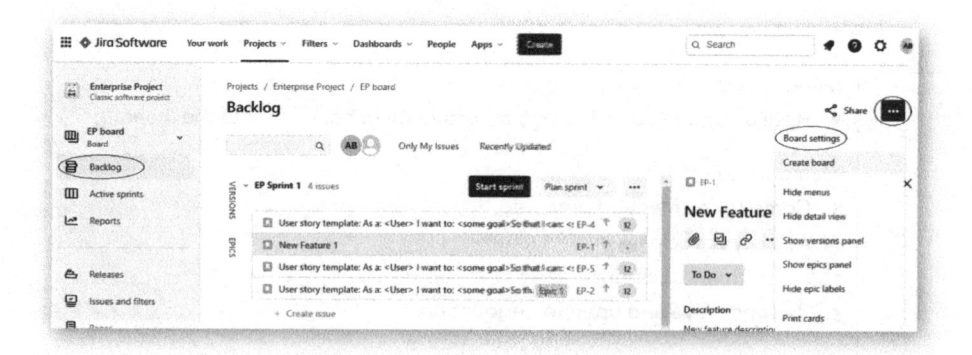

From the board settings screen, both task statuses and board columns can be created by selecting the appropriate button.

To add a new status, select the `Add status` button.

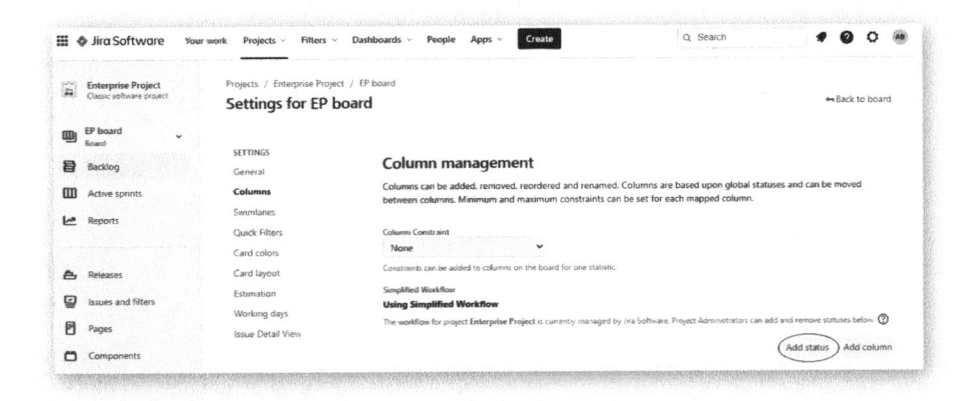

The Add status window will appear. Enter the new status name and which category it should appear within. Select `Add`.

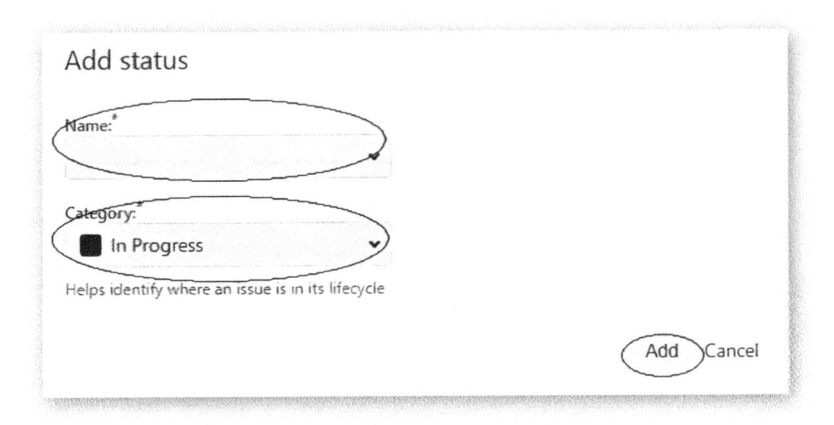

Columns can also be added to the board. From the same board settings option accessed earlier, select `Add column`.

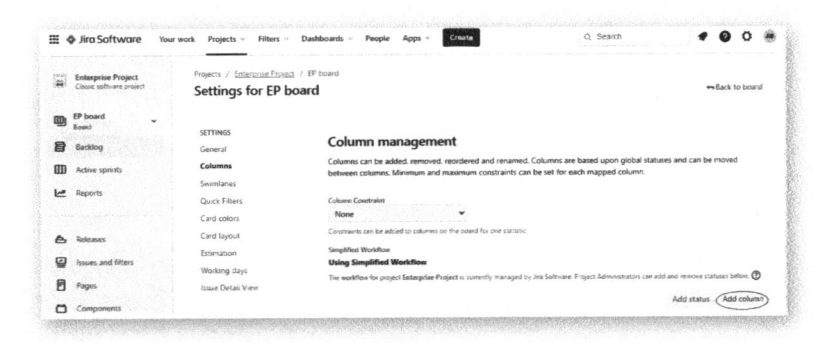

AGILE PROJECT DELIVERY

The Add column window will appear. Enter the new column name and which category it should appear within. Select Add.

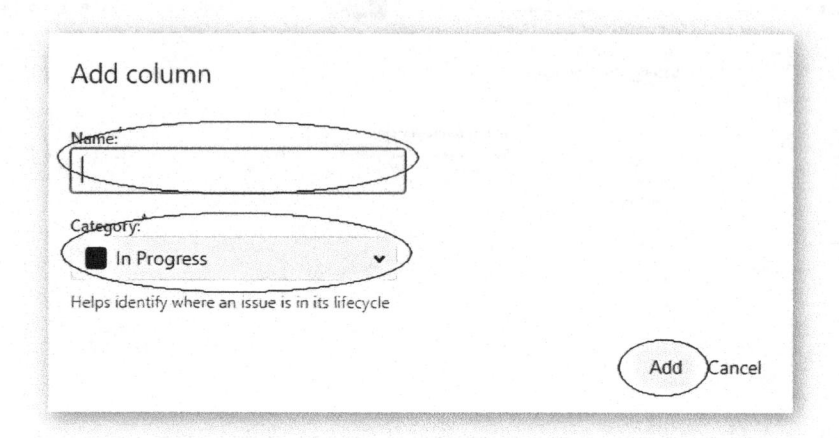

When complete, the custom board will be visible.

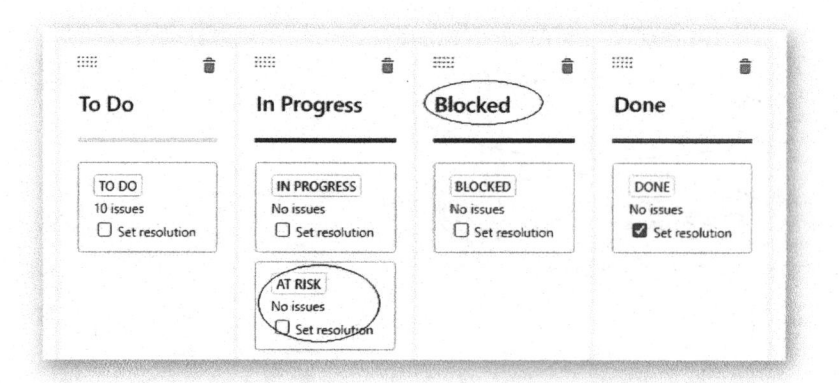

Activating a Sprint

Navigate to the project screen by selecting Projects from the navigation menu and selecting the appropriate project.

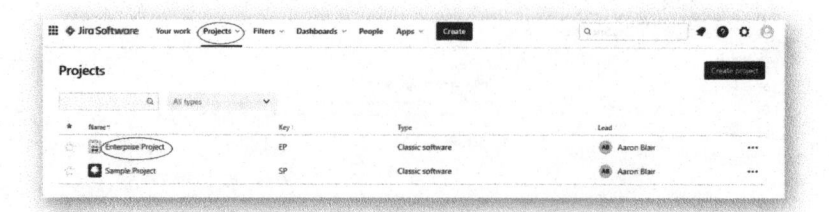

Select the appropriate project. Select `Backlog` from the project menu and select `Start sprint`.

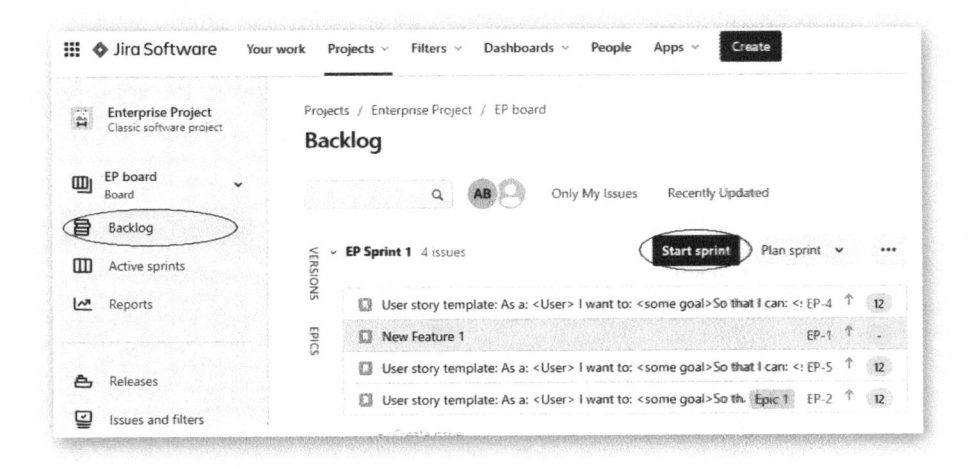

The Start sprint window will appear. Enter the sprint name, its duration, the sprint start and end dates, and the sprint goal. Select `Start`.

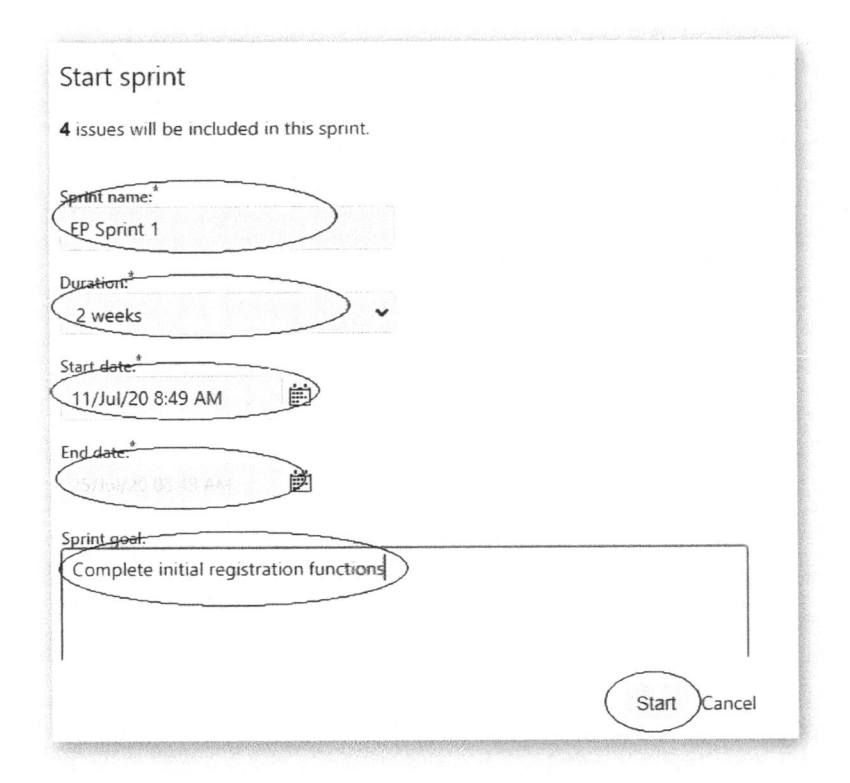

Modifying Tasks/Stories on the Scrum Board

Once a sprint has been started, users will be taken to the Active sprints screen. Stories will appear under the TO DO column by default. Stories can be moved to different columns to track progress.

To update the user story status, select the story and drag it to the appropriate column.

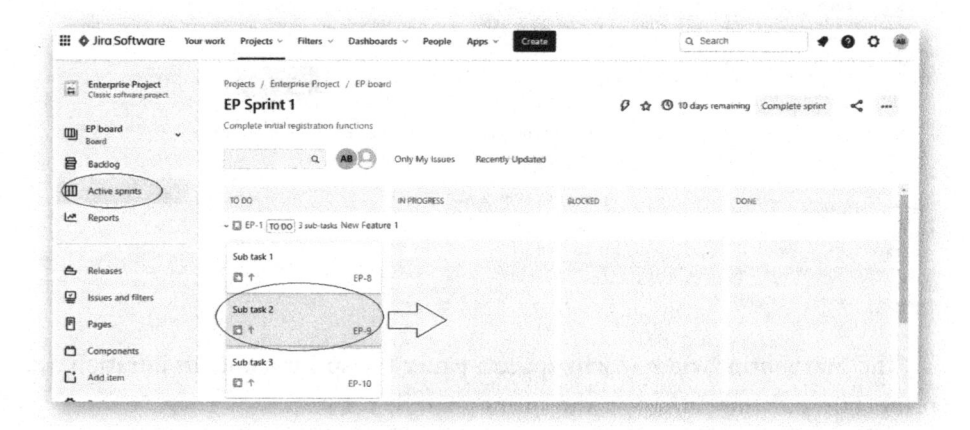

When subtasks are moved to the DONE column, once all of a user story's subtasks are completed, a notification will appear confirming whether the parent user story should be marked as done. Select Update to confirm.

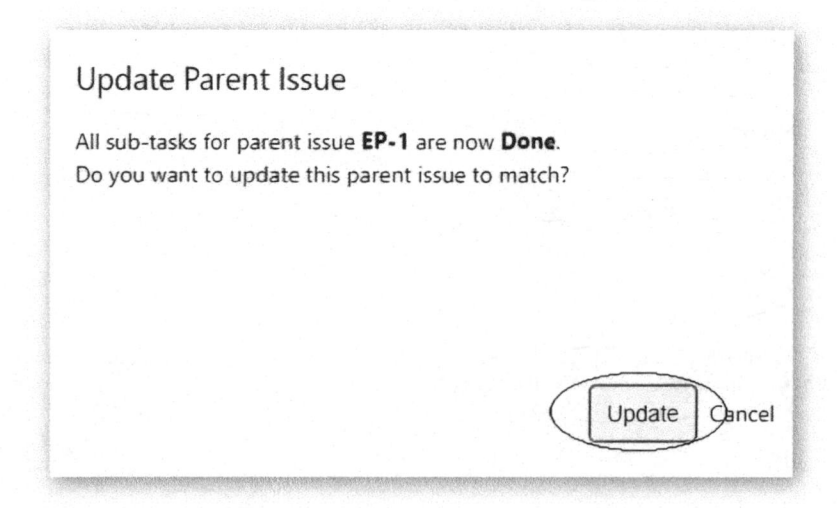

Creating an Issue Type User Story

Issue type user stories can be created in numerous locations within Jira. Wherever an issue can be created, an issue type user story can be created as well.

Select the Create button from the navigation bar. Select the appropriate project from the Project pull-down menu. From the Issue Type menu, select Bug. Enter the issue details and select Create.

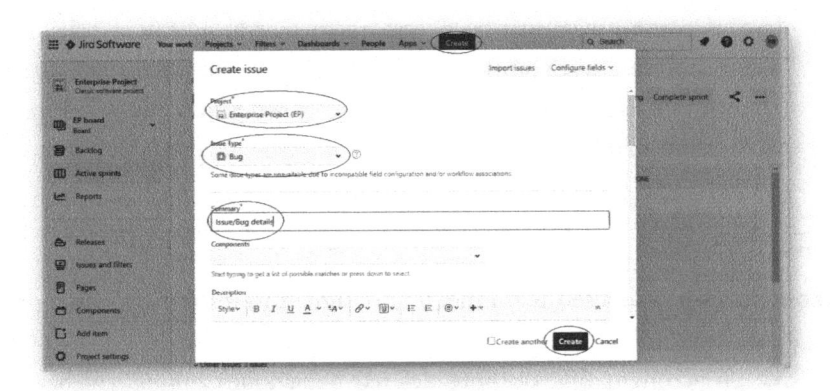

Issue type stories are added to the backlog and can be assigned as per any user story covered in chapter 6.

SUMMARY

- Scrum is a timeboxed Scrum event that lasts only 15 minutes and focuses on three questions.
- Scrum masters facilitate scrum sessions and act as process coaches to ensure development team members do not use the scrum to provide status updates or initiate problem-solving.
- Breakout sessions and office hours are structured time for problem-solving and feature elaboration.
- Development teams are treated as autonomous and self-organizing. They are responsible for proactively managing their time, completing their tasks, and communicating with necessary team members or stakeholders to complete their work.
- Agile teams depend on the wisdom of the crowd, or decision by consensus.
- Communication is central to successful Agile teams. Communication is most effective face-to-face, but for distributed or virtual teams selecting highly interactive communication approaches is integral.

- For enterprise projects that have numerous Agile teams working in parallel, a scrum of scrums approach may be required to facilitate cross-team dependencies and issues.
- Pair programming approaches to work help build skilled generalists and encourage osmotic communication amongst distributed Agile teams.
- Continuous integration is a key feature of Agile methodologies. Continuous integration encourages regular sharing of work in a shared repository.
- Use of committees may be necessary in matrix-managed organizations where business leads are not readily available due to operational work. Committee use supports wisdom of the crowd and co-design approaches to decision-making.

KEY TERMS

breakout session: a focused team meeting designed to resolve a specific problem or issue

C-FORC: an acronym that outlines desired behaviours among self-organizing teams: Commitment to success, Focus on excellent work, Openness about concerns, Respect by sharing success and failures, Courage to undertake great challenges

co-design: the approach of actively involving all stakeholders in the design process to help ensure the design outcome is usable

committee: a collection of stakeholders that provides direction and decision-making for development teams

continuous integration: the XP concept of regular code check-ins. For non-software development projects, this may refer to regular upload or sharing of work deliverables on a shared repository.

cross-functional: refers to a team that is composed of a number of skill sets and business backgrounds

issue type user stories: user stories that are specific actions the development team needs to take to resolve the identified issue or bug

office hours: dedicated timeboxes set up to answer development team questions

pair programming: the XP concept that partners two development team members together during user story execution

scrum of scrums: a scrum where designates from multiple Agile teams review their collective team progress and review shared issues and dependencies

terms of reference: a document that helps guide committee purpose, ground rules for interaction, and decision-making criteria

ToR: an acronym for terms of reference

wisdom of the crowd: a decision-making approach that leverages the collective input of a group of individuals rather than a single expert

workaround: an ad-hoc process that can be used operationally in the absence of an automated solution

DISCUSSION QUESTIONS

1. Agile values interactive communication to deliver projects. Can you think of an example where one-directional communication is preferred? Explain your answer.
2. If Agile teams are self-organizing and autonomous, why is there a daily scrum?
3. How can software development terms such as *continuous integration* and *pair programming* be applied to non-software development projects?
4. If a project is Crystal Maroon level, can it still be managed as an Agile project? Explain your answer.
5. A scrum of scrums identifies issues that may impact multiple Agile teams. Can you think of an example of an issue that meets this criterion? Explain your answer.

NOTES

1. K. Rubin, *Essential Scrum: A Practical Guide to the Most Popular Agile Process* (Boston, MA: Addison-Wesley Professional, 2012).
2. Ibid.
3. W. D. Eggers and S. K. Singh, *The Public Innovator's Playbook: Nurturing Bold Ideas in Government* (Deloitte Development LLC, 2009).
4. C. Bason, *Leading Public Sector Innovation: Co-Creating for a Better Society* (Bristol, UK; Portland, OR: Policy Press at the University of Bristol, 2010).
5. Rubin, *Essential Scrum*.
6. Ibid.
7. Ibid.
8. K. Schwaber and J. Sutherland, *The Scrum Guide* (2017), www.scrumguides.org.
9. Rubin, *Essential Scrum*.
10. R. L. Daftand and R. H. Lengel, "Organizational Information Requirements, Media Richness and Structural Design," *Management Science* 32, no. 5 (1986): 554–571.

11. A. Cockburn, *Agile Software Development: The Cooperative Game*, 2nd ed. (Boston, MA: Addison-Wesley Professional, 2006).
12. C. Larman and B. Vodde, *Large-Scale Scrum: More with LeSS* (Boston, MA: Addison-Wesley Professional, 2016).
13. H. Baumeister and B. Weber, *Agile Processes in Software Engineering and Extreme Programming: 14th International Conference, XP 2013, Vienna, Austria, June 3–7, 2013, Proceedings*. Heidelberg, Germany: Springer, 2013.
14. Ibid.

9 Information Radiators

CHAPTER OVERVIEW

Chapter 9 focuses on tracking and communicating project progress. Agile frameworks often incorporate empiricism when collecting and communicating team performance data. By capturing empirical data, Agile teams are able to better understand team velocity and how to plan for future iterations.

Similarly to Lean, many Agile frameworks value visual management approaches. These visual representations of progress are known as information radiators. Information radiators enable stakeholders to quickly understand project progress without having to be experts in Agile.

By the end of chapter 9, readers will be able to identify different types of information radiators, how they are used, and how to generate information radiators from Agile tools.

THE THREE PILLARS OF SCRUM

There are three pillars central to the scrum methodology, based on empirical process control theory:

- Transparency refers to providing visibility of the overall process to those responsible for the outcome.
- Inspection refers to timely checks on the progress towards a sprint goal to detect variance.
- Adaptation refers to adjusting process to correct for variance.[1]

The three pillars of Scrum align with both Agile and Lean principles:

- Use techniques for reducing variation and eliminating waste.
- Keep things moving—in a value-added and effective manner.

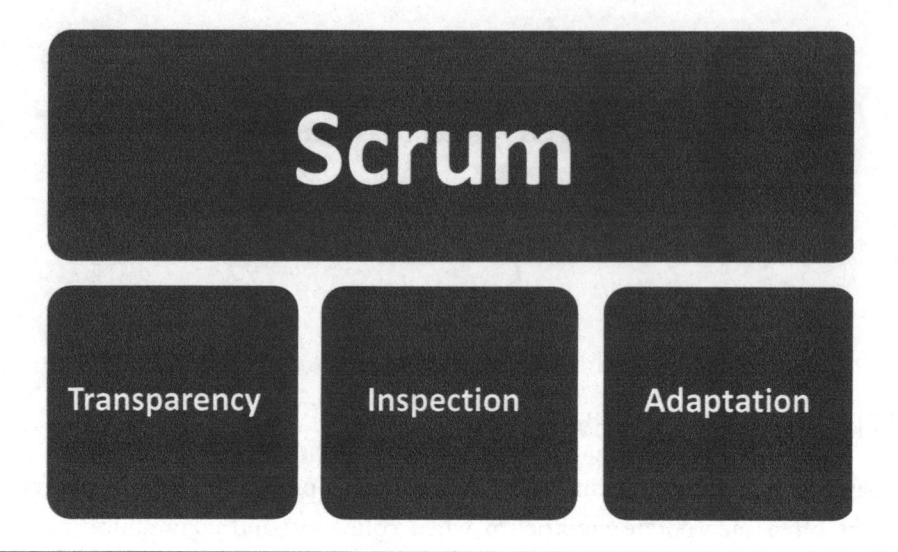

Figure 9.1 • The Three Pillars of Scrum

8. Agile processes promote sustainable development. The sponsors, developers, and users should be able to maintain a constant pace indefinitely.

To support the transparency pillar of scrum, Agile teams use **information radiators**. An information radiator is a visual display of critical team information that helps track project progress. Information radiators are updated regularly and are strategically placed so a team can easily refer to them. An information radiator is a **visual management** technique. Visual management displays expectations, performance, standards, or warnings in a way that requires little or no training to understand the information that the display is conveying.[2]

Information radiators are not just for the project team. Therefore, they should be prominent and located in areas where both stakeholders and team members will pass by them frequently. If information radiators are located in spaces where they are not, or cannot be, seen, they do not serve their purpose. They should also be simple enough that any stakeholder who passes by is able to quickly understand the information being displayed. If information radiators are too complex, they do not serve their purpose.[3]

In addition to conveying critical project information, information radiators can help gamify team performance. **Gamification** refers to the application of video game elements to non-game concepts to help drive engagement, performance, and behaviours. Displaying information that recognizes performance, such as the team member with the most story points completed in a day or week, can motivate competition amongst team members to perform.

KANBAN BOARD AND MANAGING WORK IN PROGRESS

Kanban boards or scrum boards are interactive information radiators used by projects leveraging Agile frameworks.

Kanban boards and scrum boards are simple to understand. One does not need specialized training to interpret them. Unlike most forms of information radiators, Kanban boards and scrum boards can be updated in real time by the development team by moving notes and stories into the appropriate column.

Kanban boards or scrum boards also help identify when there is a growing amount of work in progress, or WIP. Too many tasks in an "in-progress" state signifies that the team is experiencing a **bottleneck**, which interrupts the flow of work and could impact sustainable development.

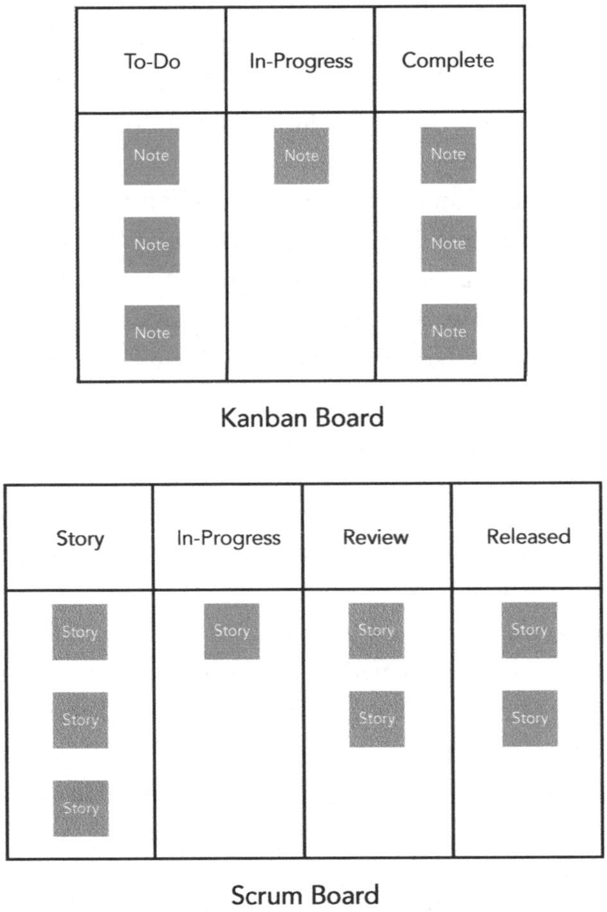

Kanban Board

Scrum Board

Figure 9.2 • Kanban Board and Scrum Board

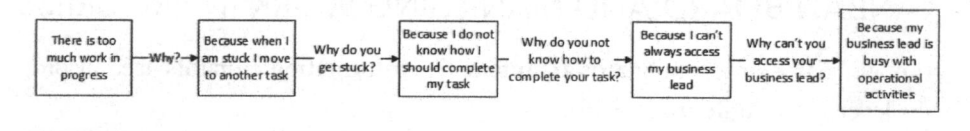

Figure 9.3 • Example of Five Whys

When bottlenecks occur, using tools such as the **five whys** technique can help teams understand the root cause that is impacting efficiency. The five whys is an iterative interrogative technique that explores cause-and-effect relationships of a particular problem. The term *interrogative* may seem punitive. However, the five whys should be used as a basis for exploration amongst the team to arrive at a collective conclusion and solution.[4]

In the text's case study, Imran proactively recognized the risk of not having regular access to business leads. However, figure 9.3 highlights how the five whys technique may be used if WIP became a bottleneck due to lack of business-lead access. Imran's solution of having dedicated committee time mitigated the risk prior to it becoming an issue.

Establishing **control limits** can help ensure WIP is monitored effectively. Control limits place a numerical limit on the quantity of WIP tasks. There can be an upper control limit but also a lower control limit. A lower control limit identifies when the team is idle and work is not occurring. By setting limits, project teams can receive alerts when WIP is outside of established control limits and can take action.[5]

BURNDOWN CHARTS AND BURNUP CHARTS

Burndown charts and burnup charts are static information radiators. They are not interactive like Kanban boards or scrum boards; therefore, they need to be refreshed regularly to ensure they are current.

A **burndown chart** shows the amount of work left to do versus the time remaining. The backlog is represented on the vertical axis, while time remaining is represented on the horizontal axis. Burndown charts can help predict whether the sprint goal will be achieved.[6]

A **burnup chart** captures work completed. It is essentially the same as a burndown chart; however, instead of depicting work remaining versus time, it depicts work completed versus scope goal.

The burnup chart also depicts a scope baseline. There should be no additions to scope once a sprint has started. However, if scope is added, a burnup chart will depict the change and help detect when **scope creep** occurs during a sprint.[7]

Burndown charts also help identify development team engagement.

Chapter 9 • Information Radiators 187

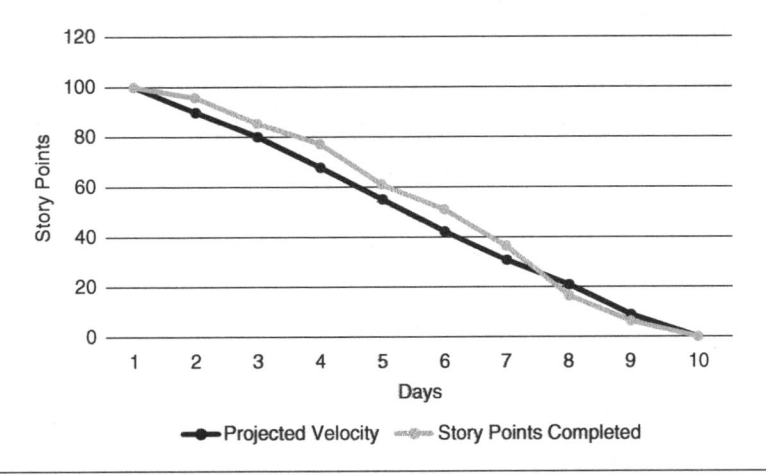

Figure 9.4 • Burndown Chart

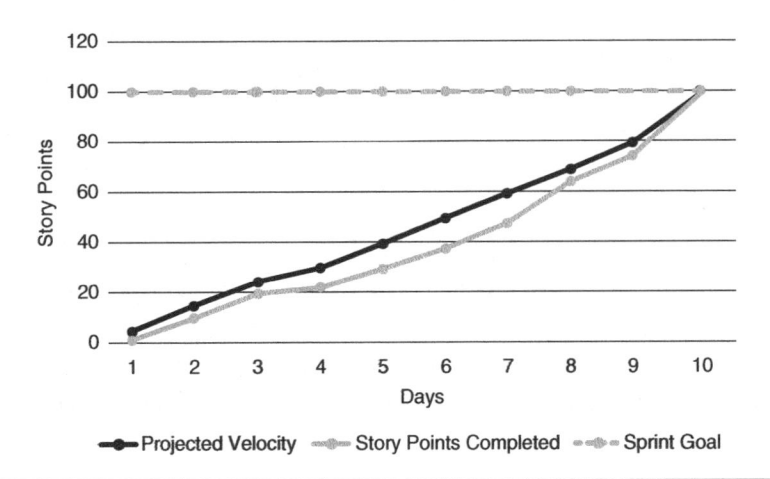

Figure 9.5 • Burnup Chart

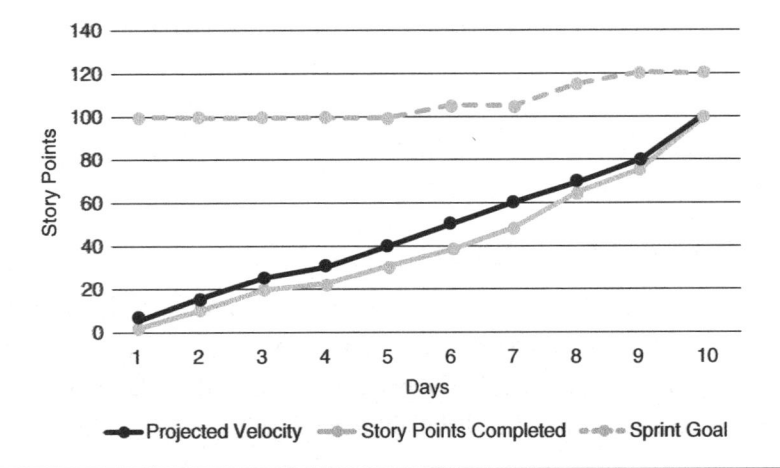

Figure 9.6 • Burnup Chart with Added Scope

Ideal Engagement

A burndown chart that shows that teams are effectively engaged will likely depict slower initial progress. This is typical as teams become familiar with the new user stories as well as each other. When teams spend time elaborating user stories, they are spending less time completing work. Once the team has become comfortable with their understanding, velocity will often pick up at a sustainable pace to the end of the sprint.[8]

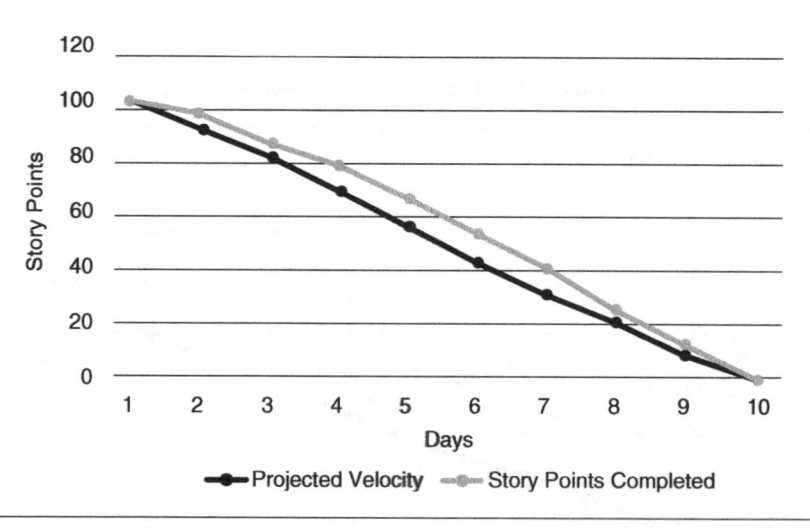

Figure 9.7 • Ideal Engagement Burndown Chart

Source: Adapted from M. Layton, *Agile Foundations LiveLessons* (Addison-Wesley Professional, 2016), video course.

Conforming

A burndown chart that shows a completion rate identical to the projected velocity is likely a sign that the team is conforming to expectation. This may mean that the team is entering progress based on the expected result rather than the actual rate of performance. When burndown charts depict a conforming pattern, it is important for scrum masters and the team to review work completed.[9]

Underestimated Complexity

When teams do not effectively estimate user story complexity, burndown charts will likely depict a rate of completion less than what was projected. Ideally, underestimation only occurs early in the project. Future sprint-planning session estimates are refactored with the additional knowledge.[10]

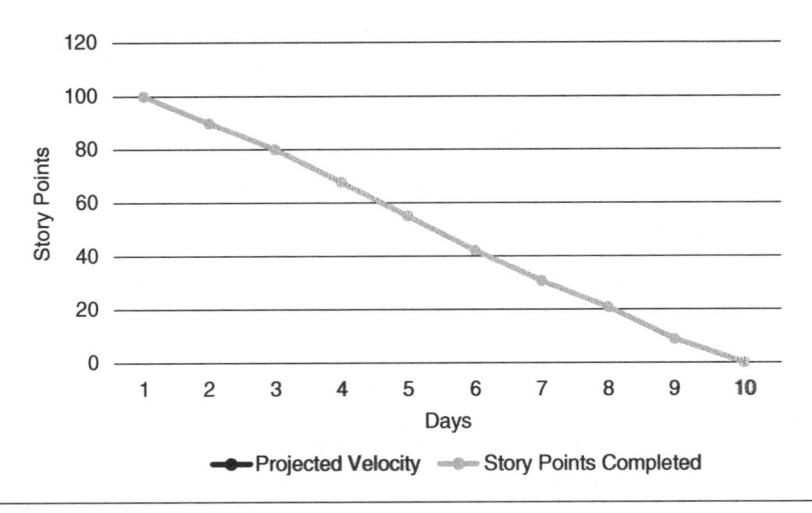

Figure 9.8 • Conforming Burndown Chart

Source: Adapted from M. Layton, *Agile Foundations LiveLessons* (Addison-Wesley Professional, 2016), video course.

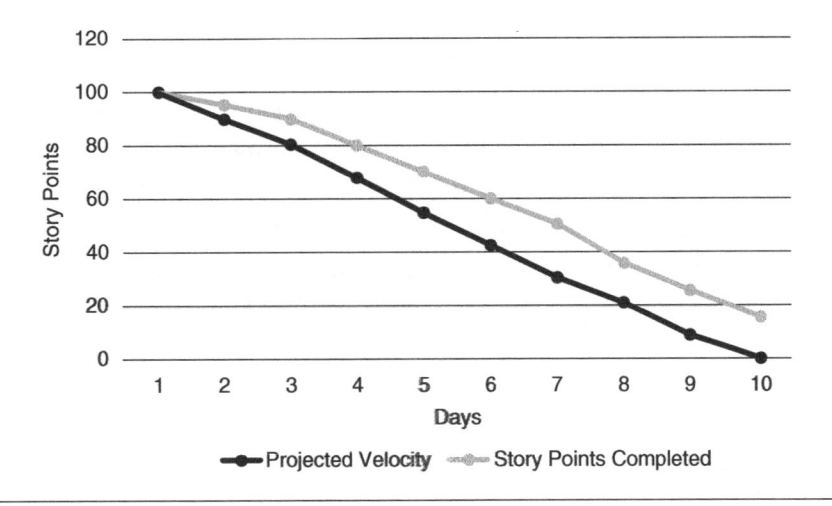

Figure 9.9 • Underestimated Burndown Chart

Source: Adapted from M. Layton, *Agile Foundations LiveLessons* (Addison-Wesley Professional, 2016), video course.

Overestimated Complexity

When teams overestimate user story complexity, they will initially exceed projected velocity. However, due to Parkinson's law (discussed in chapter 6) teams can collectively "relax" during the sprint, with the knowledge they are on target to achieve the sprint goal. When this occurs, resources are not being utilized to their maximum capabilities. Although it is not ideal to add user stories mid-sprint, this may be appropriate when teams have overestimated the user story complexity.[11]

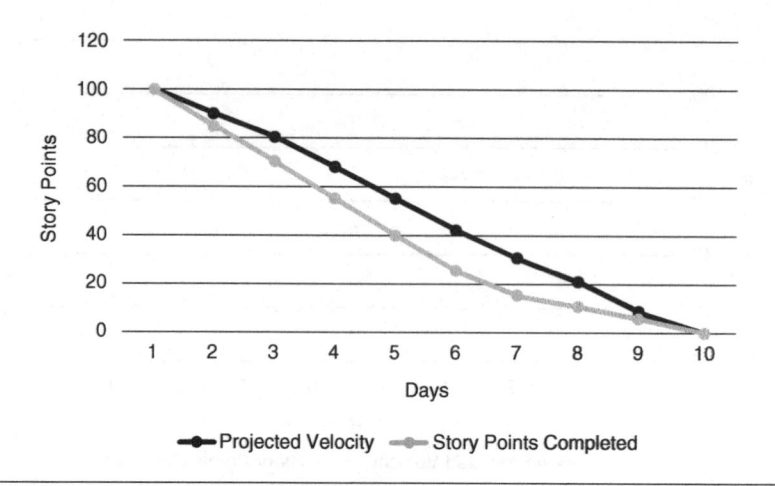

Figure 9.10 • Overestimated Burndown Chart

Source: Adapted from M. Layton, *Agile Foundations LiveLessons* (Addison-Wesley Professional, 2016), video course.

No Engagement

When teams are not engaged, progress is not updated regularly. This would look like no progress being made until the end of the sprint, when all tasks are completed. In this instance, not only do the development team members lack engagement, but so do the product owner and scrum master. The scrum master is a process expert and should be coaching the team to update its progress daily.[12]

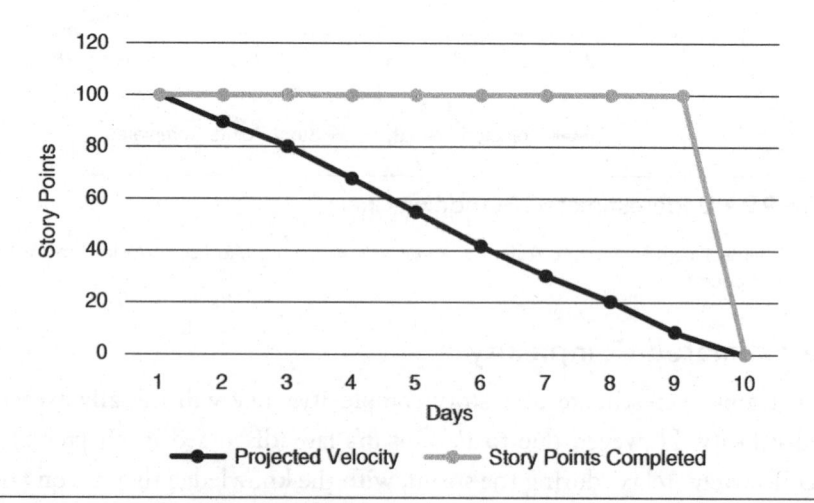

Figure 9.11 • No Engagement Burndown Chart

Source: Adapted from M. Layton, *Agile Foundations LiveLessons* (Addison-Wesley Professional, 2016), video course.

Cancelled Sprint

There are a number of reasons a sprint could be cancelled: a collection of user stories may no longer be required, or insufficient elaboration may have been completed, leaving the user stories too high-level to be completed. In these instances, it may make more sense to abandon a sprint rather than spend resource cycles on unnecessary work or work that is not ready to be started. Only a product owner should be able to authorize the cancellation of a sprint.[13]

Burndown charts are valuable information radiators that help projects track progress. They are also integral to establishing a team's velocity. Sprint planning should be based on empirical data. Information radiators help collect sprint performance in an empirical way that will enable **velocity-driven planning** for future sprints.

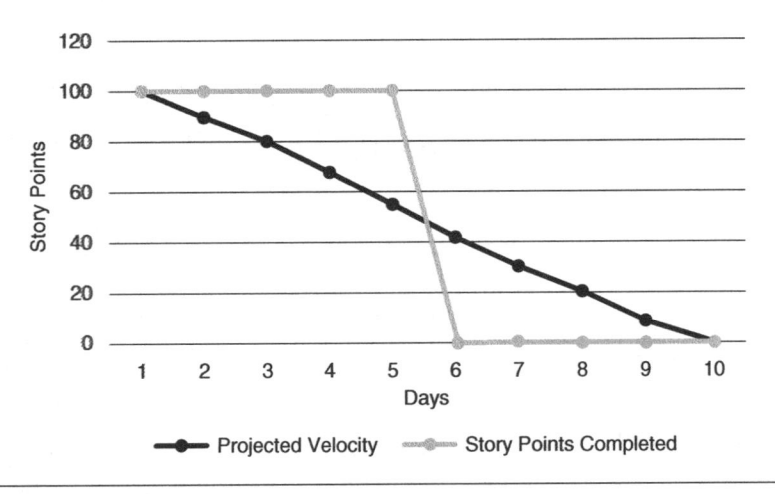

Figure 9.12 • Cancelled Sprint

Source: Adapted from M. Layton, *Agile Foundations LiveLessons* (Addison-Wesley Professional, 2016), video course.

Parking Lot Chart Information Radiator

Burndown charts and burnup charts often focus on the sprint-level progress. However, with larger, more complex projects, it is helpful to display progress at a higher level. The **parking lot chart** is a chart that displays the overall completion progress of the stories that are part of a theme or epic. Because these types of stories may span multiple sprints, a parking lot chart will display to key stakeholders the health of the collection of features that make up a theme or epic. If the completion of a theme or epic is required to meet the release goal, the parking lot chart can function as an early warning that will identify whether a particular collection of stories is not progressing as expected. This allows for additional support to the development team to clarify or prioritize the necessary user stories to achieve the release goal.[14]

Registration Parking Lot

Registration Stories	Scheduling Stories	Room Booking Stories
20/30	10/40	20/25

Health Information Parking Lot

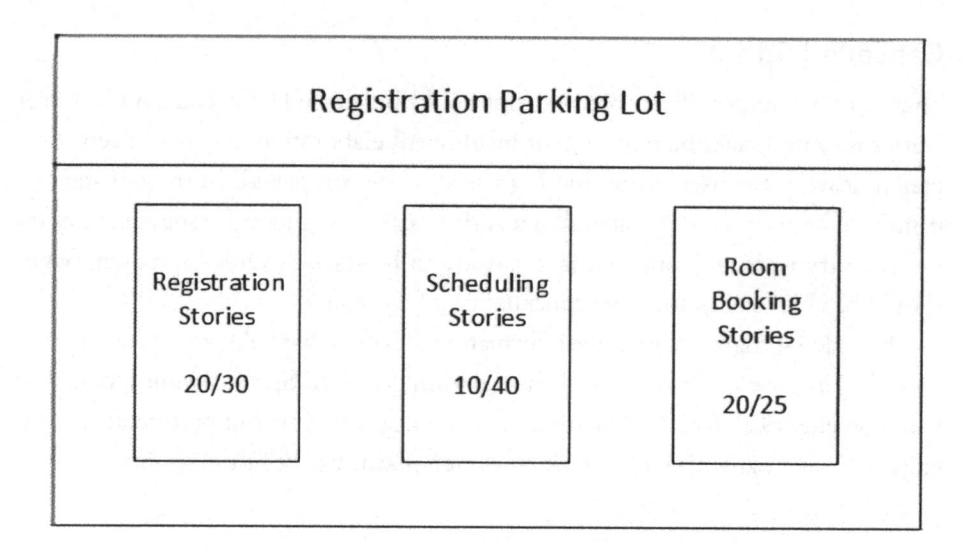

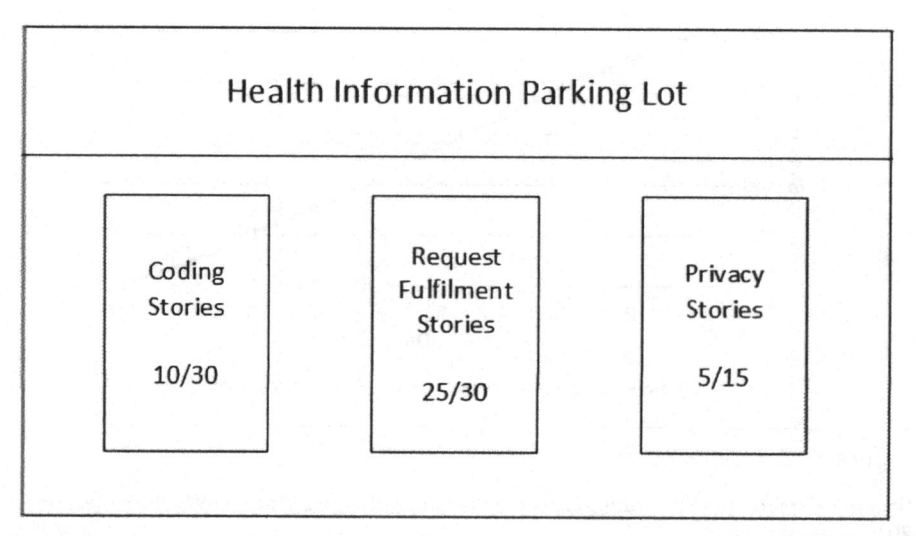

Coding Stories	Request Fulfilment Stories	Privacy Stories
10/30	25/30	5/15

Figure 9.13 • Parking Lot Chart

EARNED VALUE MANAGEMENT

Earned value management (EVM) is a traditional project management approach to both tracking and forecasting progress. Much of EVM utilizes Microsoft Project functions. This text will not cover EVM used for traditional project management. However, it will introduce some of the earned value techniques that can be used by Agile.

When managing an Agile project for a non-software development corporation, corporate finance departments may look to an Agile project to provide data that identifies the value achieved versus the actual cost, as compared with the original cost estimates. This, in essence, is earned value: tracking how much value a project has achieved based on its actual costs and progress compared to planned costs and progress.

Because Agile frameworks value empiricism, data collected by the project can often be converted into value data that corporate sponsors and stakeholders may expect.

EVM adapted for Agile frameworks requires some core metrics:

Product backlog in points—The total scope of the project contained within the backlog, presented as a number of points. This can be acquired either through planning poker or, more likely, by estimating the entire backlog based on affinity mapping.

Baseline velocity—The number of points the team is able to complete per sprint. If empirical data are not available, this can be applied after velocity data are captured from the first sprint, or based on a benchmark of previous team performance.

Cost per story point—The estimated cost per story point completed. This can often be calculated based on number of resources and hours committed per week. An hourly rate should be applied to resource time. The rate should be an organizational rate, usually loaded for direct and indirect resource costs, as covered in chapter 6. The total can be divided based on the number of points planned per sprint. Therefore, *(resource time × rate) / story points = cost per story point*. For example, two resources at 20 hours per week would equal 40 hours. If their rate was a loaded cost of $100 per hour, the weekly cost would be $4,000. If the number of story points the team committed to was 20, the cost per story point would be $200.[15]

Scope earned value formulas include the following values:

- *Planned story release points (PSRP)*—The sum of all story points that make up the project / product backlog
- *Expected percent complete (EPC)*—Current sprint / total planned sprints
- *Actual percent complete (APC)*—Story points completed / total planned story points

Budget earned value formulas include the following values:

- *Budget at completion (BAC)*—PSRP × cost per story point
- *Planned number of iterations*—Product backlog / baseline velocity[16]

Challenges with EVM for Agile Projects

Using EVM for Agile projects can pose a challenge, as it assumes a fixed scope. Recall Agile principle 2:

> 2. Welcome changing requirements, even late in development. Agile processes harness change for the customer's competitive advantage.

At the end of a sprint, additional items can be added to the product backlog. This means that the total number of story points for the project could grow per iteration. As a result, Agile EVM could depict a fluctuation in progress as story points are added. The relationship between adding must-have user stories and the time required to complete is important for project teams to convey to stakeholders. Must-have user story additions will likely impact the project cost and duration.

The **triple constraint**, or **iron triangle** concept, is a dynamic often associated with traditional project management; however, it is still applicable to projects leveraging Agile frameworks. Modification to one constraint will affect the other constraints. Therefore, if scope is added, more time and cost will be required to complete the entire scope.

When scope continues to grow, traditional project management often recommends creating phases, enabling the project to release completed work in stages. The concept of phases is inherent in Agile methodologies: the Agile equivalent of

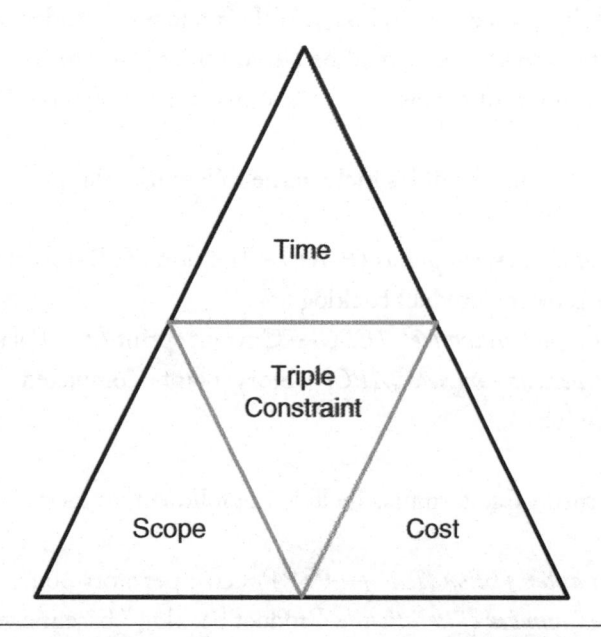

Figure 9.14 • The Triple Constraint or Iron Triangle of Project Management

phases are releases. By fixing scope at the release level, organizations ensure that additional user stories will not impact the short-term project goals.

When to Use EVM in Agile Projects

For many Agile projects, EVM is not required. Burndown and burnup charts typically provide enough insight into team and project performance. However, if enterprise projects have multiple sprint backlogs and even release or project backlogs, then aggregating the data and measuring performance can give a rolled-up view of overall health.

NIKO-NIKO CHART OR CALENDAR

A **niko-niko chart or calendar** is an information radiator that captures the mood of each team member at the end of each day. Moods are captured using emoticons and charts can be colour-coded.[17]

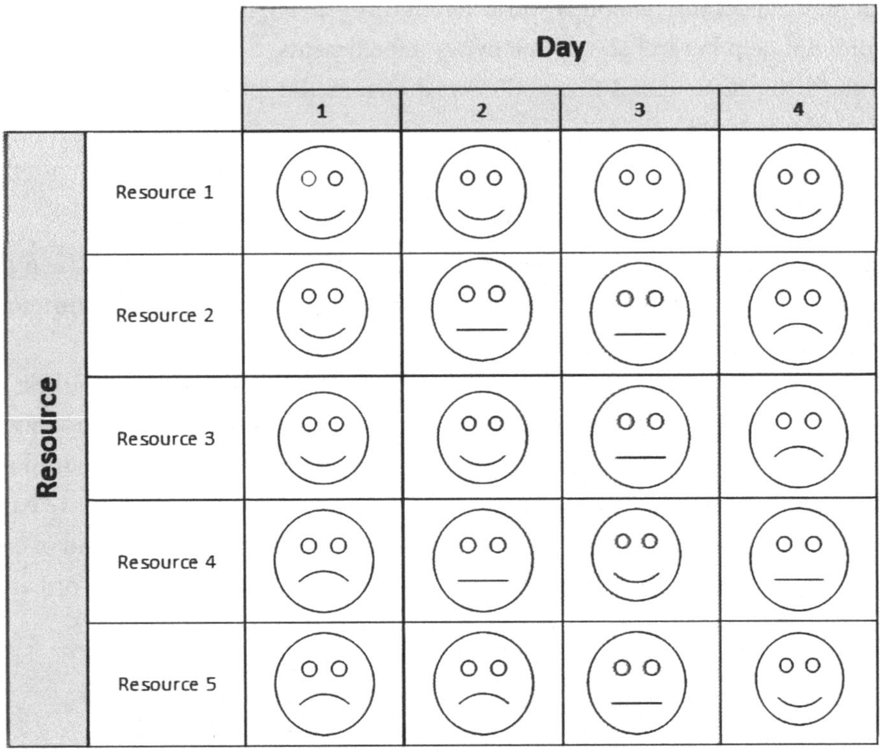

Figure 9.15 • Sample Niko-Niko Chart

Source: Adapted from R. Black and G. Coleman, *Agile Testing Foundations: An ISTQB Foundation Level Agile Tester Guide* (London, UK: BCS, The Chartered Institute for IT, 2017).

Niko-Niko Charts That Show Resources Neutral to Sad During Early Stages of the Sprint

This often shows that team members are uncertain or lack confidence in their ability to complete their work, and can happen when team members are new to Agile or are learning a new skill. Scrum masters will need to provide additional coaching and encouragement to these resources.

Niko-Niko Charts That Show Resource Mood Progressively Degrading

This phenomenon can be a product of team members finding more issues than expected or having difficulty getting support from teammates or business leads. Scrum masters will need to help remove these impediments for these resources.

Niko-Niko Charts That Show Drastic Fluctuation in Mood

This could be attributed to a resource finding unexpected issues or a personal issue that may impact their mood at work. Often this is a signal that the resource needs additional help beyond simply removing impediments. Scrum masters should be sensitive to drastic mood fluctuations and engage the resource immediately in a supportive manner.

Niko-Niko Charts That Show No Fluctuation in Mood

This may be a product of resources not utilizing the niko-niko chart. When this occurs, scrum masters should monitor and approach the resources with some open-ended follow-up questions.

Niko-niko charts or calendars rely on the notion that mood is the earliest indicator of how work is progressing. Moods beginning to shift negatively is a signal that work is not progressing as expected. Although burnup charts and burndown charts will capture performance data, this is reactive. Performance data are based on work being completed. Mood information will often be captured ahead of code check-ins and task completion. This makes niko-niko charts valuable information radiators that scrum masters can use to proactively support their team.

> **Case Study 9.1 • Leveraging Information Radiators to Trigger Corrective Action**
>
> Imran's sprints were underway. During the daily stand-ups, Imran was impressed with the progress his health information resource was making. However, looking at the niko-niko chart, he noticed that his health information resource was regularly choosing a negative emoticon to capture her mood. Imran attempted to be supportive by remarking how impressed he was with her rate of story point completion. He asked if she was experiencing any impediments he could help alleviate, worrying that maybe the resource was not comfortable expressing them in the stand-up meeting. She replied that there was nothing impeding her at that time.
>
> Imran noticed in the following days that his health information resource continued to have a negative mood rating captured on the niko-niko chart. Returning to his office, Imran found his project director waiting for him. She had performed an earned value calculation and found that Imran's collection of modules was lagging behind.
>
> Imran created an information radiator and confirmed that the health information module was lagging behind other modules, which was negatively impacting his overall collection of modules. Based on the burndown chart, it was unlikely health information would be able to achieve the sprint goal.
>
> Imran decided to use a burnup chart. The burnup chart showed that his health information team was completing work at a faster rate than the majority of the team. Using the empirical data, Imran presented the information to his project director and the vendor product owner. The risk Imran had flagged had become an issue that required corrective action.
>
> By capturing performance in a burnup chart, Imran was confident that the inability to achieve the sprint goal was not related to resource ability, but rather improper estimation of resources required.

USING INFORMATION RADIATORS TO DETECT TEAM MEMBER STRESS AND POTENTIAL BURNOUT

Information radiators can be utilized to track performance but also can provide insights to team stress and mood. The iterative nature of Agile frameworks can place continued stress on team members through repetitive work peaks.

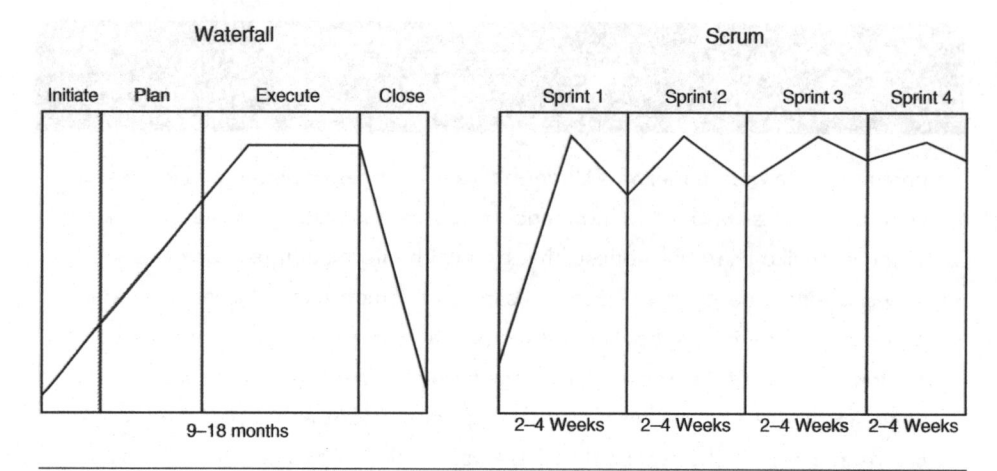

Figure 9.16 • Waterfall versus Agile Work Peak Cycles

Waterfall has a slower build towards a prolonged work peak. Agile iterations see peaks during every two- to four-week cycle. An enterprise project that extends for 9 to 18 months could result in 12 to 24 sprints, resulting in Agile team members spending more time in peak cycles over extended durations than their waterfall counterparts. This can lead to team-member burnout. It is important to apply Lean and Agile principles when considering team output:

- Value and respect people.
- Take the long-term view.

1. Agile processes promote sustainable development. The sponsors, developers, and users should be able to maintain a constant pace indefinitely.

When teams overcommit to the number of user stories they can complete, the team's focus can become completion of user stories, rather than the people working on the team. Although it is appealing to maximize productivity, this should not come at the expense of Lean and Agile principles. The goal of valuing people and taking a long-term view leads to sustainable development. If team members become burned out and the team loses them, the aforementioned principles have not been achieved.

Project leaders must review information radiators not only to look at progress but also to check on team health. Decreases in productivity or increases in negative mood indicators from niko-niko calendars can help identify when adjustments need to be made to enable development team sustainability.

AGILE TOOLS: INFORMATION RADIATORS

The following section will guide users in creating information radiators using Jira. Open the project workspace by selecting the `Projects` menu item from the navigation bar and select the appropriate project.

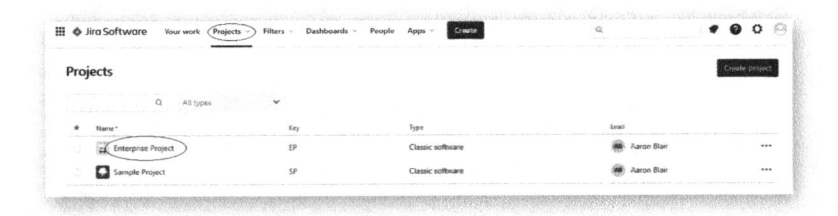

From the project workspace, select the `Reports` menu item. There are many reports to choose from. Select the desired report.

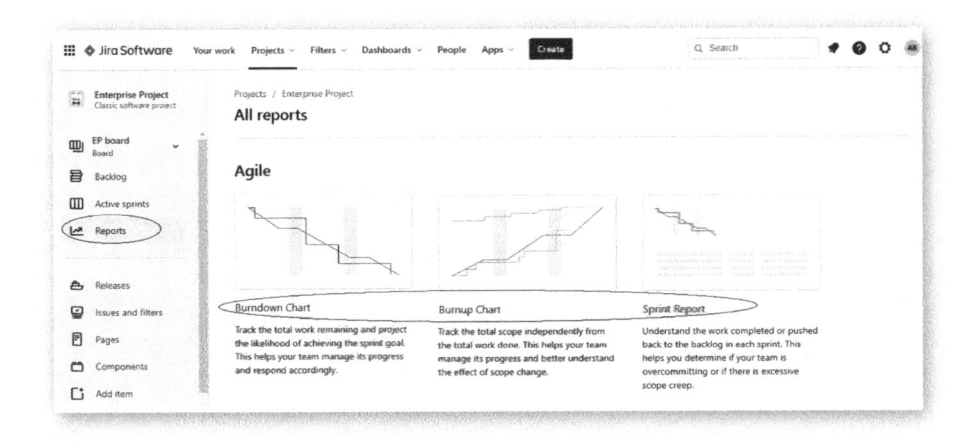

Jira will automatically generate charts based on the scrum board progress.

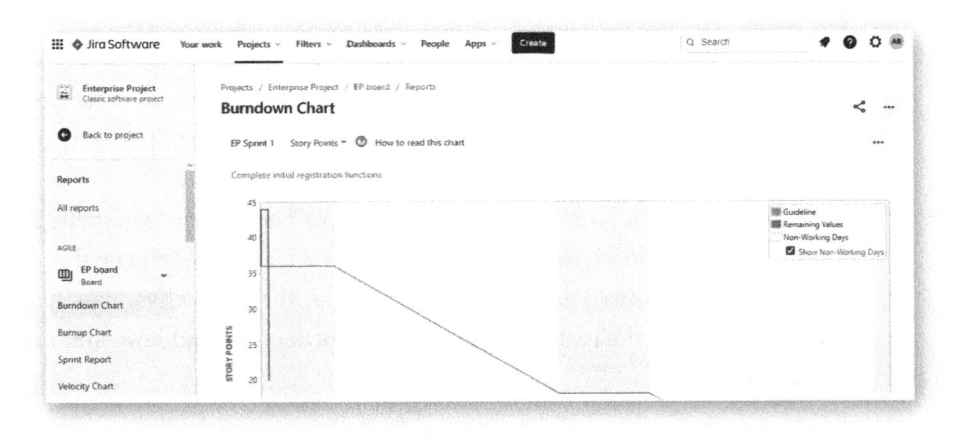

To share burndown charts, select the share icon at the top right of the report screen. A Share screen will appear. Enter the email, team name, or resource names to share the report with.

To change the view from Story Points to other criteria, select the pull-down menu.

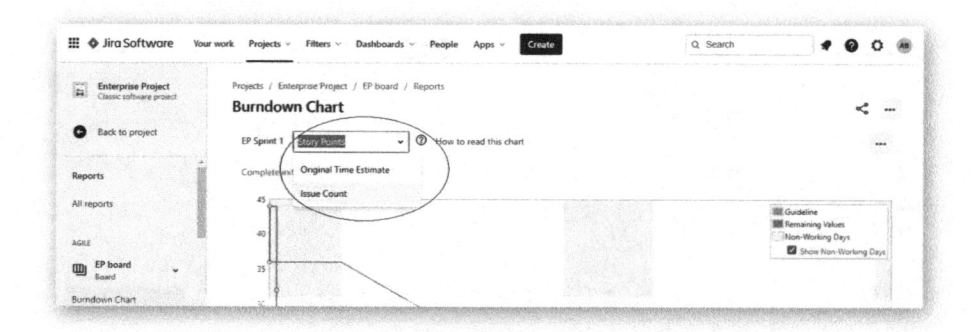

SUMMARY

- The three pillars of Scrum—transparency, inspection, and adaptation—support Lean and Agile principles.
- Information radiators are a form of visual management that enable passersby to understand project progress with minimal to no training.
- Scrum boards and Kanban boards are a form of gamification that promotes self-organization and autonomy amongst the team to perform at a high level.
- Establishing work in progress, or control, limits can help identify bottlenecks and issues that could impact the team's ability to achieve the sprint goal.
- Using root-cause analysis techniques, such as the five whys, can help teams understand the issues contributing to bottlenecks and how they can be resolved.

- Burndown charts and burnup charts are information radiators that can also help identify team engagement.
- Earned value management is a concept borrowed from traditional project management. EVM for Agile is effective for enterprise projects that need to aggregate multiple sprints' data where burndown charts may be too cumbersome to correlate.
- Niko-niko charts help gauge a team's mood and confidence level. Mood is an early indicator of performance and of a team's confidence level at completing the sprint backlog.

KEY TERMS

bottleneck: work accumulating without being completed in a timely manner. This can happen at the resource or team level.

burndown chart: a chart that shows the amount of work left to complete versus the time remaining

burnup chart: a chart that depicts work completed versus scope goal

control limit: a numerical limit on the quantity of work in progress (WIP) tasks. It can be applied at the resource or team level.

earned value management: a traditional project management technique that uses mathematical formulas to both track and forecast project performance

EVM: an acronym for earned value management

five whys: an iterative interrogative technique that explores the cause-and-effect relationships of a particular problem

gamification: the application of video game elements to non-game concepts to help drive team engagement, performance, and behaviours

information radiator: a visual display with critical team and project progress information that is updated regularly and strategically located so a team can regularly refer to it

iron triangle: the dynamic that causes modification to one of the three constraints (cost, scope, and time) to affect the other constraints. Also known as the triple constraint.

niko-niko chart or calendar: an information radiator that captures the mood of each team member at the end of each day

parking lot chart: a chart that displays the overall completion progress of the stories that are part of a theme or epic

scope creep: the unauthorized addition of user stories to a sprint or backlog

triple constraint: the dynamic that causes modification to one of the three constraints (cost, scope, and time) to affect the other constraints. Also known as the iron triangle.

velocity-driven planning: an empirical approach to using team velocity, or story points completed during a sprint, to inform sprint planning and the number of iterations that may be needed to achieve a release goal

visual management: a management technique that displays expectations, performance, standards, or warnings in a way that requires little or no training to understand what the display is conveying

DISCUSSION QUESTIONS

1. Are visual management techniques more or less effective than non-visual techniques? Explain your answer.
2. How do burndown charts and burnup charts enable management to draw insights into development team engagement levels? Explain your answer.
3. What is scope creep? How would it impact the triple constraint? Explain your answer.
4. Can you think of other examples of gamification, either from work or in your consumption of goods and services? Provide examples and explain.
5. Why is assessing a team's mood the fastest way to determine how a sprint is progressing? Explain your answer.

NOTES

1. K. Schwaber and J. Sutherland, *The Scrum Guide* (2017), www.scrumguides.org.
2. A. Cockburn, *Agile Software Development: The Cooperative Game,* 2nd ed. (Boston, MA: Addison-Wesley Professional, 2006).
3. Ibid.
4. C. Wright, *Fundamentals of Assurance for Lean Projects* (Cambridgeshire, UK: IT Governance, 2017).
5. C. Protzman, F. Whiton, and D. Protzman, *Implementing Lean* (Productivity Press, 2018).
6. P. Measey, *Agile Foundations: Principles, Practices and Frameworks* (London, UK: BCS, The Chartered Institute for IT, 2015).
7. Ibid.
8. M. Layton, *Agile Foundations LiveLessons* (Addison-Wesley Professional, 2016), video course.

9. Ibid.
10. Ibid.
11. Ibid.
12. Ibid.
13. Ibid.
14. M. Cohn, *Agile Estimating and Planning* (Upper Saddle River, NJ: Prentice Hall, 2007).
15. S. Jones, *Agile and Earned Value: A White Paper* (Association for Project Management, 2013), https://www.apm.org.uk/media/1190/agile-and-earned-value.pdf.
16. Ibid.
17. R. Black and G. Coleman, *Agile Testing Foundations: An ISTQB Foundation Level Agile Tester Guide* (London, UK: BCS, The Chartered Institute for IT, 2017).

PART V

CLOSING THE SPRINT AND PREPARING FOR RELEASE

In part V of the text, we focus on how Agile frameworks treat closure processes. Closure can be divided into two categories, the first of which is closure of an iteration or completion of a project. Because projects utilizing Agile frameworks are iterative, every iteration closes before the next iteration begins. Iteration closure includes presenting work to stakeholders, "grooming" the backlog, reflection and continuous improvement, and incorporating risk-management activities.

The second form of closure is preparing work for release and support. Large and complex organizations can often utilize service management frameworks such as ITIL. Part V will review how Agile projects can align with service management as they prepare to launch.

By the end of part V, readers will appreciate how iterative work finishes and restarts as well as the actions necessary to release a product into a controlled environment.

10 Reviewing Work

CHAPTER OVERVIEW

In chapter 10 we review one of the four Scrum events, the sprint review. During the sprint review, teams demonstrate their work to stakeholders. The goals of sprint reviews are to solicit from stakeholders feedback and input that will be used for future sprint planning.

By the end of chapter 10, readers will understand the goals of a sprint review meeting, the roles and responsibilities of different team members when conducting a sprint review, and how to prepare and conduct a successful sprint review. In addition, readers will understand how Agile tools are used to manage incomplete work.

THE SPRINT REVIEW

The sprint review is one of the four Scrum events. Sprint reviews occur at the end of every sprint, enabling stakeholders to provide immediate feedback on the completed work.

Similar to the layers of the planning onion, iterations have layers of feedback, known as **feedback cycles** or feedback loops.

Each layer enables teams to refine and improve their work to achieve customer value.

- Team members work collaboratively on a daily basis to refine work based on peer reviews and informal communication.
- Throughout the sprint, the product owner provides feedback on completed user stories.
- At the end of each sprint, project stakeholders provide feedback by reviewing completed work and providing approval.
- With each release, end-users or customers provide feedback about the solution.[1]

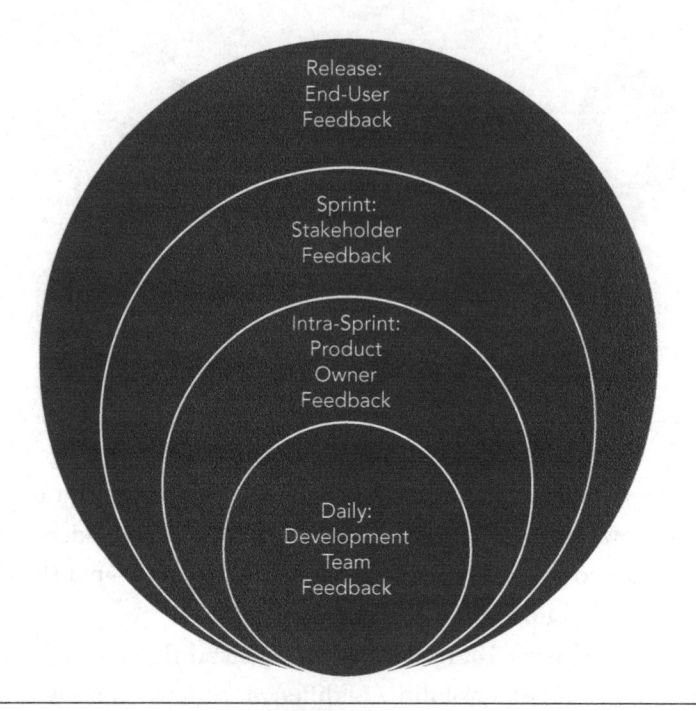

Figure 10.1 • Layered Feedback Example

(Concentric circles from outer to inner: Release: End-User Feedback; Sprint: Stakeholder Feedback; Intra-Sprint: Product Owner Feedback; Daily: Development Team Feedback)

Continuous feedback loops help ensure that the team is producing stakeholder value. The iterative approach also helps Agile teams to manage stakeholders. There are 10 principles to Agile stakeholder management:

1. Stakeholder interests need to align over time.
2. Success is achieved through intense conversation with stakeholders, even more so with those who resist.
3. Encourage a culture of volunteerism where regular interaction is encouraged and not hindered by governance.
4. Stakeholders are human; they are complex. They have personal lives and families. They are real and have a face and name. They should be treated with these realities in mind.
5. Solutions should be focused at solving problems for many, not just one, as much as possible. By considering how we work together, we both achieve greater respect for each other's value and will consider solutions that complement our shared goals and working relationships.
6. Benefit statements should be general and describe how the whole of the organization will benefit from a solution.

7. There should be no trade-offs between stakeholder needs. All stakeholders should be treated equally and decisions made by consensus.
8. There are multiple levels of stakeholders (primary, secondary, etc.). All should be engaged throughout the project.
9. Stakeholder value is the primary focus of the team and should be demonstrated in everything the project team does.
10. We regularly review and refine our processes to make them better serve the stakeholder community.[2]

Stakeholder management principles are aligned with both Lean and Agile values and principles: focusing on value, valuing people, placing stakeholders or customers at the centre of the process, and striving for continuous improvement.

The sprint review also supports **change management** concepts. Change management encompasses the activities necessary to ensure that the implementation of new capabilities, functions, processes, and tools is successful. **Prosci,** like PMI and the Agile Alliance, is an organization devoted to furthering individual and organizational change management capabilities. The Prosci change-management process includes the following key areas, known as **ADKAR**[3]:

Awareness—Ensuring the organization and the people within understand the need for change, the risk of not changing, and the internal and external drivers creating the organizational need for change

Desire—Creating the conditions for people to support and engage in change activities

Knowledge—Acquiring the skills and understanding required to know how to change

Ability—Transforms knowledge into action by applying newly acquired skills to practical scenarios. This often includes leads who mentor and coach those impacted by change to develop the new skills and abilities to support the change.

Reinforcement—Ensuring the change is sustainable and becomes part of the future operations of an organization without reverting to previous and less desirable states

The Agile framework helps support change management principles by doing the following:

- Focusing on creating value
- Interacting with stakeholders and business leads regularly

- Fostering an environment of co-design and, as a result, promoting co-ownership
- Maintaining regular feedback loops to ensure outcomes are aligned with stakeholder needs

The sprint review event is integral to managing change. Demonstration of completed stories enables business leads and stakeholders to confirm and approve the team's work.

By seeking validation, the sprint review event creates change leaders within the review team. Business leads have reviewed and approved the work to date and can be leveraged to help communicate upcoming changes to the rest of the organization as well as highlighting the need and benefits of the upcoming change.

> **Case Study 10.1 • Creating Business Owners through Sprint Reviews**
>
> During the initial phases of the project, a particular business lead raised numerous objections to changing the current state. Recognizing the significance of the business lead's position in the organization and her influence, Imran knew he needed to have her fully engaged in the design process.
>
> Imran went to great lengths to schedule reviews around the business lead's busy schedule and welcomed her to invite key people in her organization to participate. Although initial meetings were challenging, Imran was able to get the business lead to focus on what would create value for her team.
>
> As work was completed, Imran scheduled sprint reviews with the business lead and her team. Work progressed and refinements were made based on her team's input, and the tone of the meetings changed from resistant to receptive.
>
> When broader reviews were scheduled with user groups, the business lead's area voiced objections to the change. She heard her area's objections during the broader reviews, so she stood and spoke to her area, explaining the need for change, the decisions that were made, and how the changes would benefit the area in the long run.
>
> Once the business lead had finished speaking, the tone of the reviews changed from avoidance to acceptance. By following ADKAR principles, Imran was able to convert the challenging business lead into a champion who would be integral to helping the organization carry out change.

PREPARING FOR THE SPRINT REVIEW

The sprint review is a timeboxed activity. Sprint reviews require one hour per week of sprint duration. Therefore, a four-week sprint would plan a four-hour sprint review.[4]

Prior to performing the sprint review, the team completes its work. Only work that meets the definition of done criteria will be shared during the sprint review. Work that is not completed is carried over to the next sprint.

The sprint review is for showcasing completed work. Therefore, static meeting materials should be minimized. Attendees are present not to be told what was done, but to see what was done and offer feedback and approval.

The entire team should attend sprint reviews: the scrum master, product owner, and development team. Any stakeholder is welcome to attend.[5]

THE SPRINT REVIEW MEETING

The sprint review is introduced by the product owner. The meeting is handed over to the development team to showcase the work that each development team member has completed.

Demonstrations of completed work should be done using resources that reflect day-to-day operational use. Therefore, if the team is developing a mobile application, demonstrations should be done on a mobile device. At the end of each demonstration, stakeholders can ask questions and provide feedback.

Feedback should be collected throughout the meeting. Stakeholder feedback is valuable and could provide insights for new requirements and improvement opportunities.

The product owner facilitates a discussion about upcoming sprints and additions made to the backlog. Based on the sprint and sprint review, additions can be made to the backlog that go beyond functionality. Additions could include the following:

- Non-functional requirements such as performance feedback
- Risks that could impact change management activities
- Maintenance and operational considerations
- Additional resources or stakeholders that should be consulted
- New requirements that are derived from elaboration[6]

The team should welcome feedback and changes. This input helps the team achieve customer value and allows for **mid-course corrections**.

If we recall the cone of uncertainty from chapter 6, as the project progresses, greater elaboration occurs, leading to greater certainty about the work to be performed. This is integral to ensuring the work that is performed fulfills stakeholder needs. Elaboration occurs through feedback loops such as the sprint review meeting.

Through elaboration, Agile teams embrace input and adjust backlog priority. Mid-course corrections arise from direct input of the stakeholder community and may change priority of user stories, add new high-priority user stories, and so on. This process of elaboration and mid-course corrections often results in a path that might not reflect the original plan. By actively engaging stakeholders as part of the design process, variation from plan is a product of stakeholder input. Mid-course corrections should not be considered a lack of ability of the team.

Having a path that deviates from the original plan is not always negative. Changes that the team adopts should focus on customer value, and so deliverables should generate a greater level of satisfaction from project stakeholders. Other factors, such as time to market, may influence necessary mid-course corrections, such as sacrificing low-priority user stories to meet timeline requirements. It is important, however, to monitor the project's **zone of success**. The zone of success refers to the **minimum marketable product (MMP)**. The MMP is the minimum that the

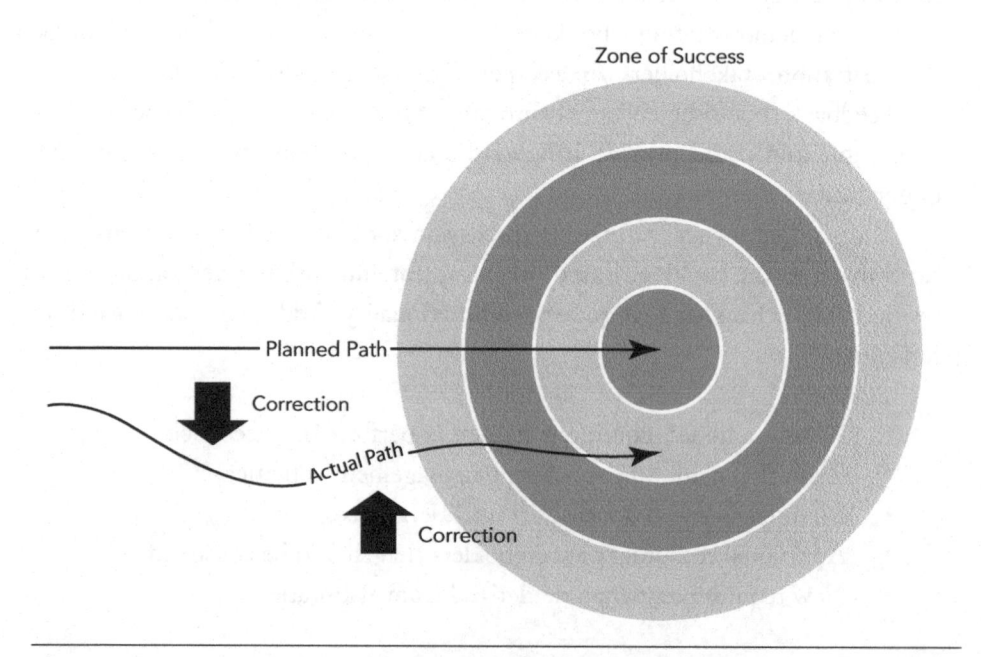

Figure 10.2 • Mid-Course Corrections and the Zone of Success

product must meet to achieve an organization's goals. If mid-course corrections take the project so far off of the zone of success such that the product won't meet the minimum requirements within the number of allocated sprints, then a deeper project review may be necessary.[7]

Resistance to Change

With any change comes resistance. Discovery Learning Inc. suggests there are three types of individual disposition to change: conservers, pragmatists, and originators.[8] The majority of individuals belong to the pragmatist group, with the remainder being spread evenly between conservers and originators.[9] The following outlines how each category reacts to change:

- Conservers prefer change that maintains the current structure, enjoy predictability, and honour tradition and established practice.
- Pragmatists prefer change that emphasizes workable outcomes, are more focused on results than structure, and are open to both sides of the argument.
- Originators prefer change that challenges the current structure, can challenge assumptions, and enjoy risk and uncertainty.[10]

Each category resists change in its own way. As a result, it important to modify change management approaches. Managing resistance should not be seen as one-size-fits-all. The following provides approaches to how resistance from each category can be managed:

- Conservers respect previous traditions and structure, share practical realities that drive change, and reinforce the organizational commitment to change.
- Pragmatists use past experiences to solve current problems, may participate in a pilot project, and encourage and foster cooperation.
- Originators encourage risk, provide the long-range vision, and demonstrate how change will reorganize the system.[11]

Importantly, all different types of change dispositions add value, and all dispositions should be engaged in the process early. This will help to ensure the best transition and adoption. When changes are managed effectively, this helps organizations realize the benefits of change earlier.

AGILE TOOLS: COMPLETING THE SPRINT

Open the desired project by selecting the `Projects` workspace from the navigation bar.

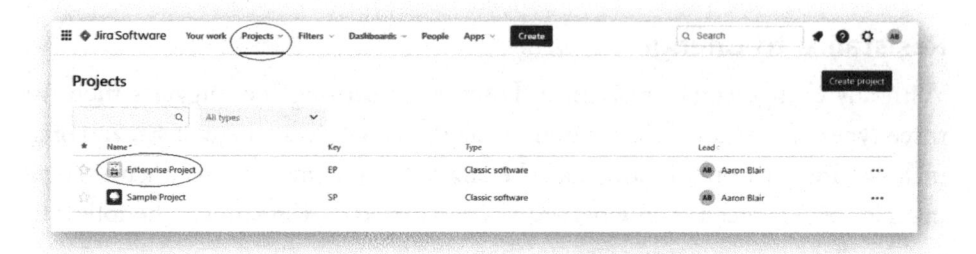

From the project menu, select `Active sprints`.

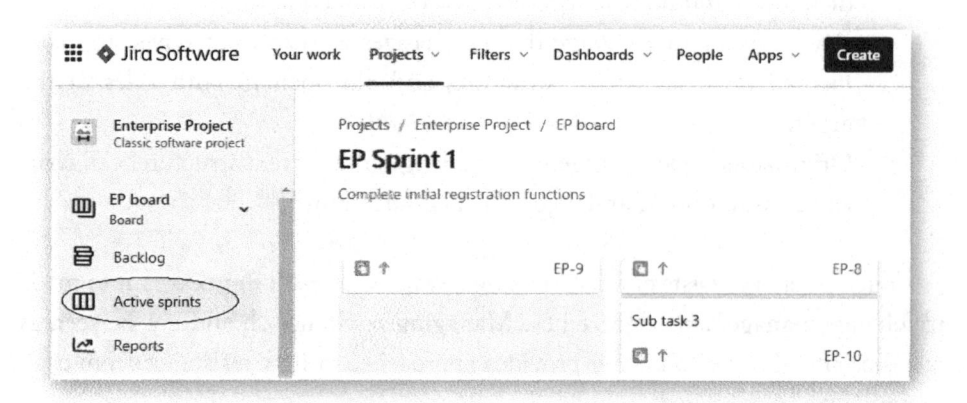

Ensure all tasks and stories are in the correct sprint buckets. Then select the `Complete sprint` button in the top right.

If there are open tasks or stories remaining on the board, a confirmation screen will appear. Choose what is to be done with the open stories: move into a New sprint or move to the Backlog. Select `Complete`.

Complete sprint: EP Sprint 1

3 issues were done
1 issue was incomplete

Select where all the incomplete issues should be moved:

Move to
[New sprint ▼]

Backlog   ...e and are always included in the same sprint as their parent

[**Complete**] Cancel

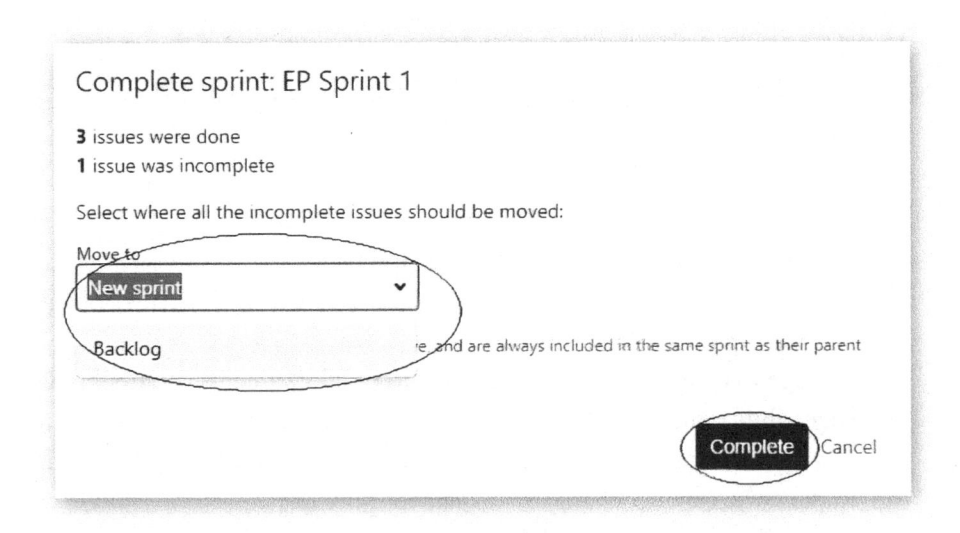

A Sprint Report will appear once the sprint is closed. The Sprint Report can be shared with stakeholders via the same process used for burnup and burndown information radiators, covered in chapter 9.

When returning to the Backlog in the project work space, the incomplete stories will be visible in the next planned sprint.

SUMMARY

- Feedback loops provide layered feedback as different stakeholders are engaged to provide input.
- Sprint reviews are timeboxed activities at the end of sprints. The goals of sprint reviews are to showcase the work completed by the development team and solicit stakeholder input and approval.
- There are 10 principles of stakeholder management that align with Agile and Lean principles and values.
- Change management approaches look to build awareness, desire, knowledge, ability, and reinforcement. Engaging stakeholders in the sprint review process creates stakeholder ownership and organizational change leaders who support change management principles.
- The Agile team must attend the sprint review. Any stakeholder is welcome to attend.
- Only completed work will be showcased. Work that does not meet the definition of done will be carried forward into a future sprint.
- Static material such as slides or documentation should be minimal. Work should be dynamically demonstrated under operational conditions and scenarios.
- Sprint reviews enable teams to apply mid-course corrections to work, based on stakeholder feedback. This may impact the original plan but allows a higher probability of creating customer satisfaction.
- Feedback may generate additional user stories but can also create new items for the backlog related to risk, new resource groups to be consulted, operational and maintenance items, and performance requirements.

KEY TERMS

ADKAR: a change management acronym representing change management milestones developed by Prosci. ADKAR stands for Awareness, Desire, Knowledge, Ability, and Reinforcement.

change management: the activities necessary to ensure the implementation of new capabilities, functions, processes, and tools is successful

feedback cycle: an iterative feedback approach that helps teams elaborate stakeholder needs and build change management capabilities in stakeholders

mid-course correction: the application of changes to the original plan to ensure the project still achieves customer value

minimum marketable product: the minimum set of requirements that a product must meet to achieve value

MMP: an acronym for minimum marketable product
Prosci: an organization like PMI and the Agile Alliance that specializes in furthering individual and organizational change management capabilities
zone of success: a threshold that identifies how much deviation from plan can be tolerated before a project will not achieve customer value

DISCUSSION QUESTIONS

1. Why are individuals resistant to change? What are some strategies you've seen or used based on the ADKAR model to overcome resistance?
2. Why do mid-course corrections contribute to project success? If an outcome deviates from plan, shouldn't it be considered a failure? Explain your answer.
3. Provide an example of a product you've been disappointed with that may not have met your personal MMP standards. Describe the product and how it did not meet your minimum needs.
4. Why do changes need to be managed? If a project is implementing a new function, shouldn't people just adopt it if it is part of their job?
5. Feedback cycles can provide additional information and requirements from project teams. List two and provide examples.

NOTES

1. K. Rubin, *Essential Scrum: A Practical Guide to the Most Popular Agile Process* (Boston, MA: Addison-Wesley Professional, 2012).
2. Ibid.
3. Prosci.com
4. Rubin, *Essential Scrum*.
5. Ibid.
6. Ibid.
7. A. Perttula and J. Kukkamäki, "Enabling Rapid Product Development through Improved Verification and Validation Processes," *Technology Innovation Management Review* 10, no. 3 (2020): 24–35.
8. C. Musselwhite, "In Focus/Dealing with Change—Knowing Change Preferences Is a Boon for Leaders," *Leadership in Action* 28, no. 3 (2008): 17–20.
9. Ibid.
10. Ibid.
11. Ibid.

11 Closing the Sprint

CHAPTER OVERVIEW

Chapter 11 focuses on sprint closure activities. Sprint closure activities do not imply that a project is complete. The iterative nature of Agile frameworks enables regular reflection on team performance and identifying areas of improvement.

Part of the process of reflection calls for a sprint retrospective, one of the four Scrum events. In addition to the sprint retrospective, Agile teams review the backlog. Backlog reviews enable teams to shift user story priorities, adjust the backlog for risk, and use empirical data such as **key performance indicators (KPIs)** to guide reflection. Agile tools can be leveraged to add risk-weighting and change user story priorities for future sprint planning activities.

By the end of the chapter, readers will understand how sprint retrospectives are conducted, the roles and responsibilities associated with conducting a sprint retrospective, and sprint retrospective outcomes.

THE SPRINT RETROSPECTIVE AND INCREMENTAL IMPROVEMENT

The sprint retrospective is one of the four Scrum events, which supports Agile principle number 12:

> 12. At regular intervals, the team reflects on how to become more effective, then tunes and adjusts its behaviour accordingly.

The sprint retrospective also supports key Lean concepts:

- Adopt a philosophy of continuous incremental improvement.
- Use techniques for reducing variation and eliminating waste.
- Value and respect people.
- Take the long-term view.

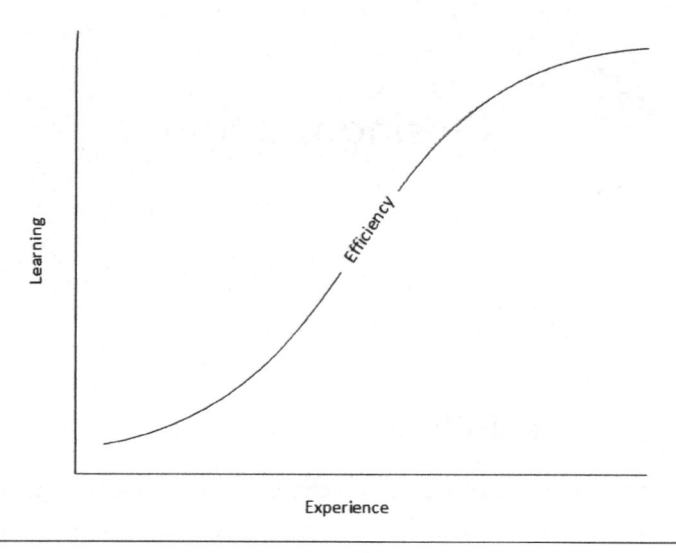

Figure 11.1 • Learning Curve

The goal of the sprint retrospective is to reflect on how the previous sprint went and what actions could be taken to improve future sprints.[1]

Typically, changes that are recommended should be incremental in nature: minor enhancements to improve efficiency. Radical change to team composition and processes would not build on previous success and would likely have a negative impact on the team's **learning curve**. A learning curve represents the growth in team efficiency through experience. The more experience a team acquires, the more efficient it becomes at performing similar tasks.[2]

The learning curve is why team velocity often improves over time. However, typically there is a plateau during the learning curve where a team becomes as efficient as it can be under the current operating paradigm.

The objective of incremental improvement is to implement a small, or incremental, change that will enable the team to rise above its efficiency plateau. This can also be called a *kaizen* activity, which was covered in chapter 2.

Figure 11.2 shows a minor dip in efficiency when a change is introduced. However, the decrease in efficiency should be short term as teams adjust to a minor change to their work routine. Once adjusted to the change, teams are able to move beyond their previous plateau.

Incremental improvements can be found through PDCA activities or value stream mapping. The sprint retrospective is a short PDCA activity at the end of each sprint.

Radical change can have deep impacts to team efficiency as teams must learn a new process.

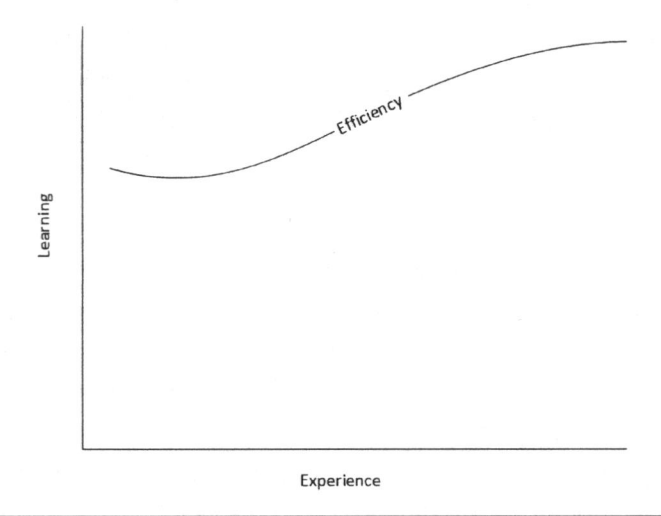

Figure 11.2 • Incremental Improvement Impact to the Learning Curve

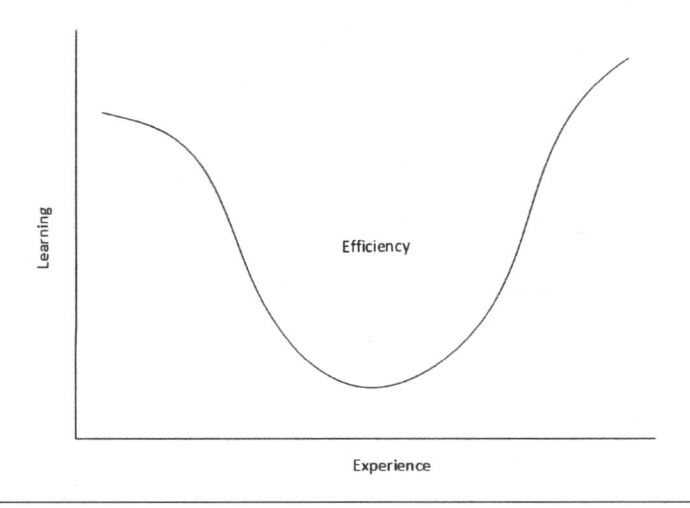

Figure 11.3 • Radical Change Impact to Efficiency

During a radical change, teams often experience a significant impact to efficiency as they learn new processes and/or tools. However, once mastery is once again achieved, teams may rise above their previous efficiency level. Radical change can occur at the process level or team composition level. If significant team turnover occurs, the new members will dip to early stages of performance as they learn to master processes and work as a team.

Reasons to implement radical change vary. Significant technology enhancements, regulatory mandates, or other factors may contribute to an organization's need to explore adopting a radical change. However, projects are often time-sensitive. Depending on the depth of the change and its impact to team efficiency, implementing radical change within a project duration could negatively impact a project delivery date.

THE SPRINT RETROSPECTIVE MEETING

The sprint retrospective is a timeboxed event. The sprint retrospective is scheduled to take 45 minutes for every week of sprint duration. Therefore, if a sprint is four weeks, the sprint retrospective will be 180 minutes, or three hours, in length.

The product owner, scrum master, and development team should all participate in the sprint retrospective.[3]

In Agile environments, the sprint retrospective is a closed activity. However, in a large corporation that has supplied resources in a matrix structure, there can be value in inviting additional stakeholders to the meeting. However, if outside stakeholders are invited, it should be very clear that attendees should be prepared to offer insights and input towards the goal of improving how sprints are performed. Stakeholders who are not regularly consulted likely won't have much to add. Stakeholders who are consulted regularly, on the other hand, could provide improvement ideas. The sprint retrospective organizer must ensure attendees understand the goals and expectations of the meeting.

Preparing for the Retrospective Meeting

Attendees should be prepared to answer the following questions in the meeting:

- What went well?
- What did not go well?
- What would you change?
- How would you change it?
- What is still unclear?[4]

Table 11.1 • Sprint Retrospective Pre-Meeting Template

What went well?	What did not go well?	What would you change?	How would you change it?	What is still unclear?

When teams are distributed, a template can be sent out prior to the meeting, and the scrum master can collect and aggregate responses. This approach is helpful to identify themes that the meeting should focus on. It also can help those who are less comfortable speaking in a group have a voice.

Agile relies on empirical data. Therefore, in preparation of the sprint retrospective, team members can review the sprint, project, program, and/or team key performance indicators (KPIs). KPIs are agreed-upon measures that indicate the health of a project. Metrics are often divided into thresholds that define when a project is healthy, at risk, or off target. KPIs can also be used as an information radiator. For corporations, KPIs can often be represented in a stoplight format. Therefore, it may be necessary to adapt Agile KPIs to a stoplight format to meet the needs of corporate stakeholders.

- A green KPI signifies the project is in a healthy state and is expected to achieve its goals.
- A yellow KPI signifies that the project is at risk and some goals may not be achieved.
- A red KPI signifies the project is off track and will not meet its objectives.

Often, when projects are yellow or red, intervention is required to keep the project healthy. Interventions usually impact the project triple constraints, covered in chapter 9, as shown in this example:

- If a project is at risk to achieve its scope, more time could be added for the team to complete all of its scope deliverables. Alternatively, more budget could be added to authorize overtime or add resources to help complete all of the project scope.
- If a project is at risk to achieve its timeline objective, scope could be reduced to enable the team to complete on time. Alternatively, more budget could be added to authorize overtime or add resources.
- If a project is at risk of going over budget, scope or time could be reduced, as long as the project is able to complete the minimum requirements required for launch.

Although KPIs are a form of information radiator, they are more aggregate and retrospective in nature. Therefore, they are not used to track daily or weekly progress but to capture team performance as a whole, so they can be useful as an input for the sprint retrospective meeting. The following are some common KPIs used for Agile projects:

Sprint goal success rate—How frequently the team achieves its sprint goal. This is often expressed as a percentage and is more valuable when tracked at the enterprise level, where many sprints are being conducted simultaneously. It can be used at the team level as well, but it becomes more meaningful once a number of sprints have been completed.

Escaped defects—If we recall the Lean concept of *jidoka*, defects that reach later stages of the process (or worse, the customer) are discovered too late. Quality should be built into the production process. Escaped defects are those that have occurred outside of the production process. This is an important metric to capture; it could point to a process problem that may require root-cause analysis tools, such as the five whys, covered in chapter 9.

Team output, such as burndown rate or velocity—This is an important trend to capture. The learning curve, discussed earlier in this chapter, should show a team's velocity improve over time as its members become more familiar with the project deliverables and complete their more complex and higher-risk user stories. If this metric performs below expectation, the team might be suffering from Parkinson's law, discussed in chapter 6, or there could be another problem requiring root-cause analysis.

Team or customer satisfaction—Team satisfaction is an important metric to capture. A negative team mood can be an early indicator of issues. Negative team moods can also indicate a lack of interaction or poor team space. Agile depends on an interactive team that thrives off of informal interaction. When a team has a negative mood, it may have an issue with team dynamics that needs correction.

Customer satisfaction is a more difficult metric to capture during a project. Usually, customer satisfaction requires a product or project to be launched for use. This can help product teams understand whether there are a number of escaped defects that may not have been reported. Poor customer satisfaction could be an indicator that the product teams aren't engaging stakeholders, or the right stakeholders, during the design stages of the product or project.

Customer satisfaction may also be used for measuring stakeholder engagement. Understanding whether stakeholders feel engaged and consulted throughout the project is important. Lack of engagement could result in solutions that do not meet stakeholder expectations, and poor engagement could result in change resistance. Poor customer satisfaction in this instance may point to a process deficiency that should be investigated.

Satisfaction metrics are often captured via surveys, which can pose additional challenges such as poor response rates or a propensity for responses to be weighted negatively since customers with positive or neutral experiences may not feel a need to respond.

Team member turnover—Team member turnover captures the rate at which team members leave the team, project, or organization, or are replaced mid-project by another team member. Losing people to either replacement or loss is one of Lean's seven forms of waste: movement waste. This chapter illustrates the negative impact that a significant change to a project or process has on the learning curve. The same is true for resource replacement. When team members are replaced or added, they will experience a dip in productivity as they become integrated within the team. This is also known as the **Tuckman stages of group development**, developed in 1965 by Bruce Tuckman. There are five stages of development:

- *Forming*—The team comes together and begins to build relationships and a team culture begins to form.
- *Storming*—The team begins to build trust and cohesiveness. The storming stage is where conflict arises most, as teams voice alternative views.
- *Norming*—Teams move to a spirit of cooperation as their conflicts and differences are resolved.
- *Performing*—Teams become increasingly efficient at their work.
- *Adjourning* (for projects)—Teams complete their work and ensure knowledge is transferred to operators.[5]

Agile teams depend on autonomy and self-organization. If a team is mired in the storming stage too long, this could impact its overall productivity. Adding or changing team members can move the group's development stage backwards. High rates of team member turnover could indicate that there are issues with team engagement, workload, unclear expectations, or poor working conditions.

Publishing KPIs in advance of the sprint retrospective gives teams empirical data to reflect upon. KPI data can be used to consider opportunities and methods to improve future sprints and KPI performance.

> **Case Study 11.1 • Adding Resources to Mitigate Underestimation**
>
> Imran monitored his health information resource performance. He had obtained authorization to use overtime pay to allow the health information resource work on completing user stories. Imran hoped the additional time would enable the team to achieve the sprint goal. However, he knew the model was not sustainable.
>
> The vendor product owner acknowledged that the estimates did not account for organizational and geographic differences from other implementations and recommended adding resources to the team to support the health information resource.
>
> Imran was concerned that adding resources would lead to a dip in team productivity as the new members became acclimatized to the project. Imran looked to find resources who had experience implementing the software previously and had extensive experience delivering non-functional requirements. This would enable the team member to work independently of the organization and geography while they became integrated with the team. Imran hoped that this approach would minimize the risk of a dip in productivity.
>
> The team hired a consultant based on a time and materials contract that would provide the team with flexibility from a sprint-to-sprint basis.

RISK MANAGEMENT

Risk refers to an uncertain event that could emerge as an issue that negatively impacts a project. The Agile methodology emerged as a risk-management response to waterfall project management approaches for software development projects, so it inherently has risk-management techniques incorporated into its methodology. The following are some ways Agile methodology manages risks commonly associated with traditional project management:

- *Changing requirements*—Accept changes throughout the sprint planning processes, prioritizing user stories based on the MoSCoW model
- *Customer satisfaction*—Regular face-to-face interaction with stakeholders where completed work is showcased and feedback is solicited
- *Schedule risk*—Fix schedule and have a releasable product at the end of every sprint
- *Scope risk*—Prioritize user stories, completing high-priority requirements early. Establish a definition of done and minimum marketable product user stories.

- *Budget risk*—Fix schedule based on budget requirements
- *Quality risk*—Have verification steps included in user stories
- *Communication risk*—Frequent face-to-face communication amongst team members
- *Support risks*—Include support documentation as part of definition of done and include support team member as one of the development team members
- *Interdependency risks*—Establish a scrum of scrums to identify interdependent user stories. User stories with dependencies have their priority escalated accordingly.

These are some examples of how the Agile methodology inherently manages risk. However, despite building risk management into the methodology, risk cannot be entirely eliminated. Projects will always have uncertainty. As a project progresses and user stories are elaborated, uncertainty is reduced.

Managing Uncertainty in Agile projects

To manage the risk of uncertainty, Agile can use the following measures:

Reduce the sprint durations to enable more frequent delivery—When there are greater levels of uncertainty, shortening sprints can help the team ensure it is on the right track and adapt accordingly. This approach supports the Lean concept of **failing fast**. Failing fast enables teams to identify quickly if they are off track, allowing them to cut their losses and adapt to a different mode, known as **pivoting**.

Create risk stories—When there is an actionable risk, a risk user story can be created and assigned to a resource. The risk user story will be treated like other user stories. However, risk user stories receive no story points. Therefore, team time spent on risk user stories does not help a team achieve its sprint goal, so such stories should be used sparingly or when absolutely necessary. Creating risk user stories ensures known risks are given time for discovery. A risk user story is the only user story type that can be assigned to a scrum master.

Plan spike stories—A **spike story** is a timeboxed period that enables teams to reduce uncertainty through elaboration. The focus of a spike can be better understanding of a feature, technology, or process. Spike stories do not produce a completed work, so they do not receive story points. They should be planned over a two-day period. Spike stories are added to the backlog and assigned to the participating team members.

Add uncertainty and dependency scores to stories—Adding uncertainty and dependency scores to user stories can help assign the appropriate priority to a user story. The additional scores can help identify stories with greater levels of risk. Moving these stories higher in the backlog enables further risk reduction. Completing high-risk stories early helps minimize schedule impact. If high-risk user stories are left too long and become an issue, teams may be unable to meet release dates. When issues arise, additional cycles are often required to resolve. By applying a **weighted factor model (WFM)**, a team can quickly identify when a user story is rising in priority due to risk and/or dependency. Planning poker or affinity mapping approaches (covered in chapter 6) can be used to assign scores; baseline points are established to align with a Fibonacci scale and are then totalled. In the example in table 11.2, points will be assigned on a 1 to 9 scale with 1 being the lowest and 9 being the highest.[6]

The above process can provide teams with another view when they are performing sprint planning. A weight is applied to each category, and then the weight is multiplied by the score to give a value. The value is totalled to provide a revised, or risk-weighted, score.

In table 11.2, user story priority is given the highest weight. When applying weights, story 4 has a medium level of priority and uncertainty. However, its high dependency score moves story 4 to a higher priority than story 3, which has low uncertainty and dependency scores. In this instance, the lower-priority item is moved up because of the relative risk and dependency it has compared to the high-priority story.

The high-priority item can be moved lower on the backlog because the team members are confident that they will be able to deliver the high-priority story, and it has little impact on other work streams, which means it can be included in a later sprint.

Table 11.2 • User Story Scoring Based on Uncertainty and Dependency

Story	Weight	Story 1	Story 2	Story 3	Story 4	Story 5
Priority	50%	9	3	9	6	1
Uncertainty	25%	9	9	1	3	9
Dependency	25%	9	3	1	9	1
Risk score	100%	9	4.5	5	6	3

Applying additional risk-management strategies can help the team unearth issues early and adapt. In addition, spikes and risk-adjusted scores can inform the backlog review process.

GROOMING THE BACKLOG

Grooming the backlog is a process where the team reviews the product backlog and makes adjustments to user stories and their priority based on knowledge acquired through sprint completion and sprint reviews.

The following actions occur during grooming:

- Adding new user stories based on product owner and stakeholder feedback
- Removing user stories that are no longer relevant
- Estimating new user stories
- Re-estimating user stories based on acquired knowledge
- Reprioritizing user stories based on risk scores
- Breaking epics into user stories and breaking user stories into tasks

The team should be spending approximately 20 percent of the sprint retrospective time grooming the backlog. Therefore, for each 45 minutes of sprint retrospective, approximately 9 minutes will be spent grooming the backlog. Grooming is not limited to the sprint retrospective; it can be done throughout a project. However, establishing a dedicated time during a sprint will ensure that grooming activities are not overlooked and that team members are focused on relevant and high-priority activities.

The outcome of a "groomed" backlog are user stories with a risk-adjusted priority as well as more refined estimation values, which will support future sprint planning.[7]

AGILE TOOLS: ADDING NEW ISSUE TYPES TO THE BACKLOG

From the navigation bar, select the cog icon menu option. Select Issues.

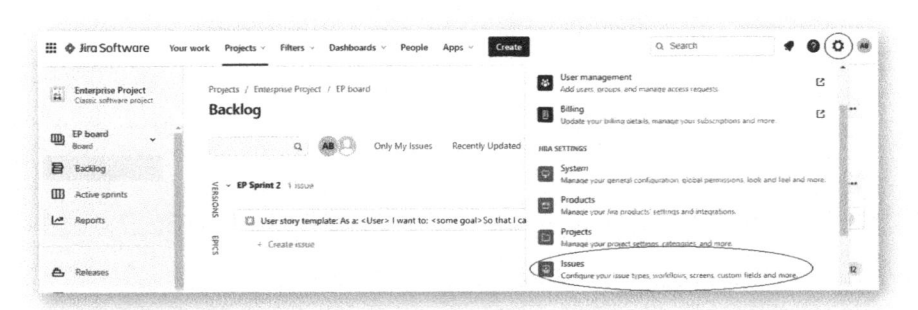

In the Jira settings Issues sub-menu, ensure `Issue types` is selected. Select the `Add issue type` button in the top right of the screen.

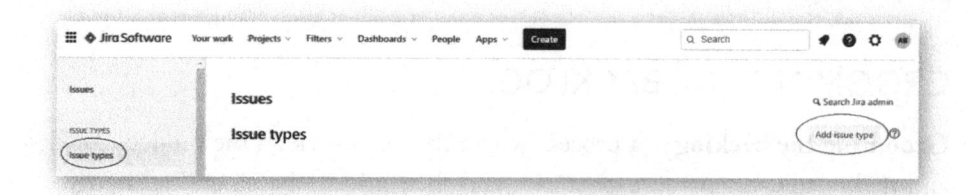

The Add Issue Type window will appear. Add the new issue type name and description, and select the `Add` button.

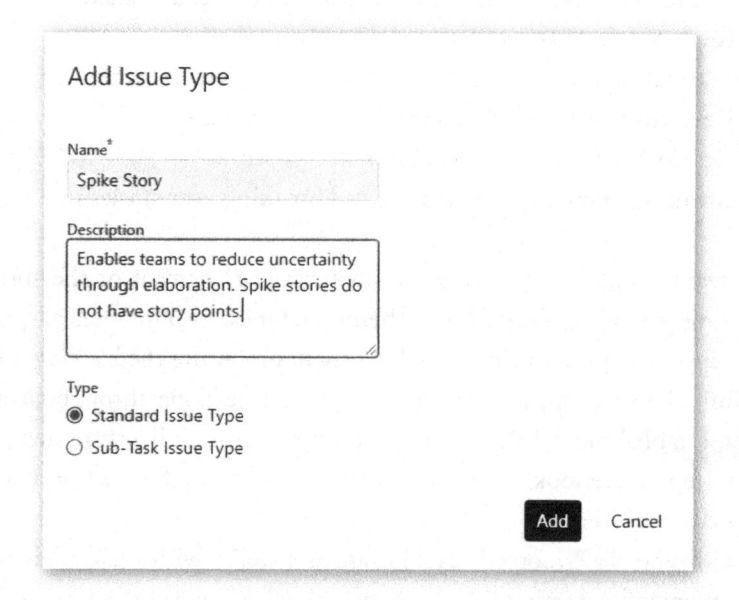

Select the `Issue type schemes` menu item to associate the new issue type with your project.

Select the `Edit` button for the appropriate project.

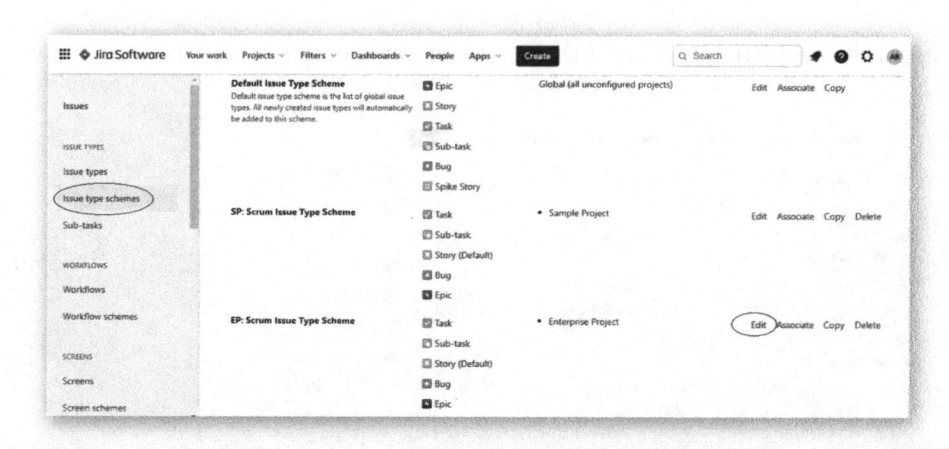

Drag and drop the new issue into the Issue Types for Current Scheme box.

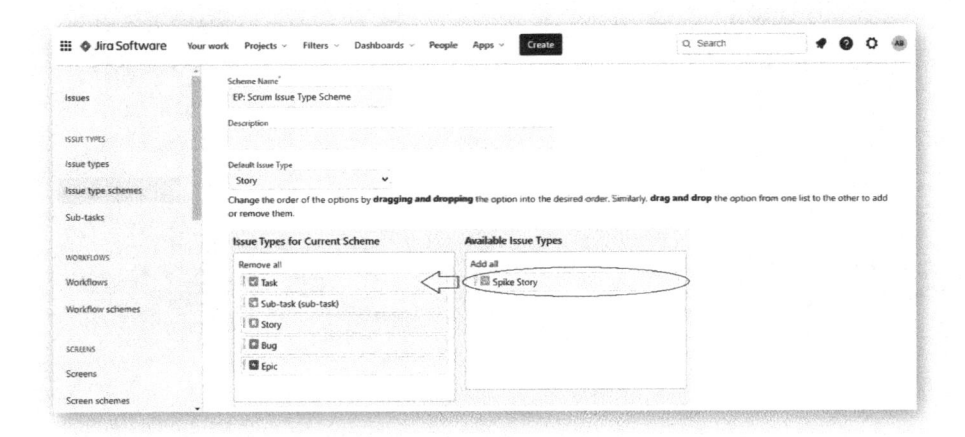

Then select Save.

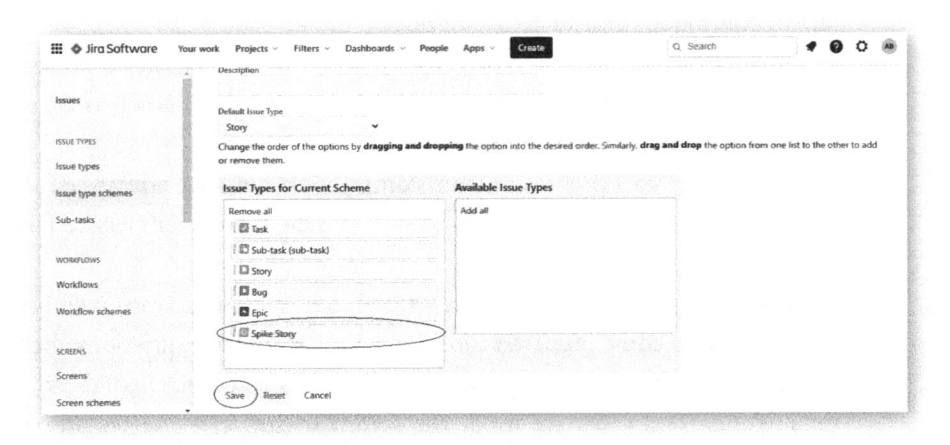

The issue type will now appear in the scheme.

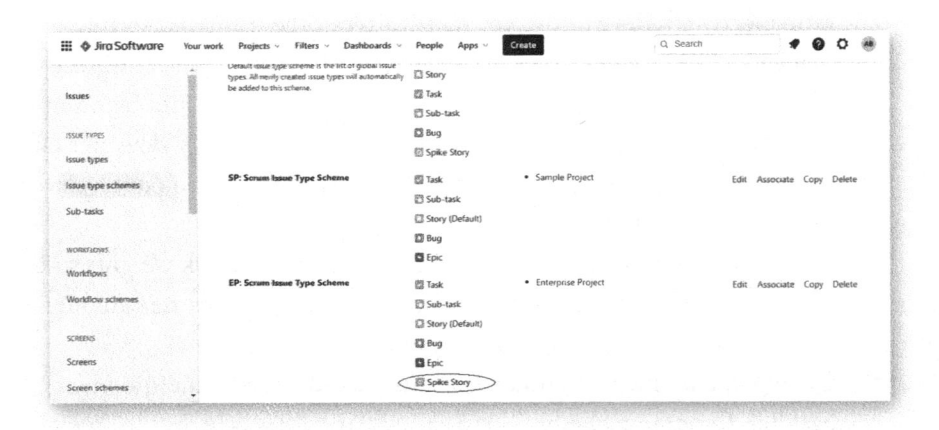

When creating new issues, the new issue type will now appear in the pull-down menu.

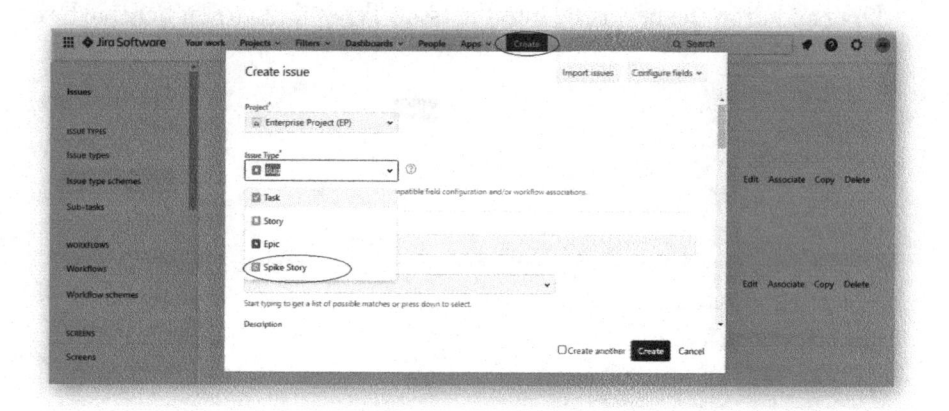

SUMMARY

- The sprint retrospective supports both Agile and Lean values and principles of continuous and sustainable improvement.
- Teams go through learning curve cycles. When teams master a process, they plateau. By introducing incremental improvements, known as *kaizen* activities in Lean, teams can move beyond their plateau.
- Radical change to a process or team composition can have adverse effects on the learning curve, as new processes or new team members require time to achieve efficiency.
- The sprint retrospective meeting is a timeboxed meeting. Team members are expected to come prepared to answer three to five key questions about the success of the previous sprint. Templates can be distributed ahead of time. When templates are used, the scrum master can consolidate the results and present common themes during the meeting.
- Key performance indicators (KPIs) can be used to help inform the sprint retrospective. KPIs capture key metrics about the team and sprint performance and can provide areas to focus on during the sprint retrospective.
- The Agile methodology is a risk response to common issues found in the waterfall methodology. However, the Agile methodology does not eliminate risk from a project. Additional risk measures can be put in place to help a team manage risk.
- Weighted factor models (WFM) can be used to add risk weights to user stories. WFMs can help identify which stories have greater amounts of risk and can be reprioritized accordingly.
- During the sprint retrospective, teams should spend time grooming the backlog. Grooming the backlog is a regular review where team members

look at user stories, re-estimate based on acquired knowledge, reprioritize based on other factors such as risk and dependencies, or remove user stories that are no longer relevant. Grooming helps ensure the team is focused on the most important and current list of stories during each sprint.

KEY TERMS

failing fast: teams quickly identifying if they are off track. Failing fast enables teams to cut their losses and adapt.

grooming the backlog: a process where the team reviews the product backlog and makes adjustments to user stories and their priority based on knowledge acquired through sprint completion and sprint reviews

key performance indicator: a measure that indicates the health of a project and team performance

KPI: an acronym for key performance indicator

learning curve: a representation of the growth in team efficiency as a result of experience

pivoting: the act of a team adapting and selecting a new approach based on failing fast

risk: an uncertain event that could emerge as an issue that impacts a project. Risks that become issues usually affect the project's triple constraint.

spike story: a timeboxed period that enables teams to reduce uncertainty through elaboration. Spike stories do not have story points.

Tuckman stages of group development: the five stages of development—forming, storming, norming, performing, and adjourning—developed by Bruce Tuckman in 1965

weighted factor model: the approach of applying weights to different categories such as risk, priority, and dependency to adjust the overall score of a user story. This helps teams prioritize user stories based on a variety of factors for future sprints.

WFM: an acronym for weighted factor model

DISCUSSION QUESTIONS

1. Apply a weighted factor model to buying a car. Choose four types of vehicles and apply weights for price, style, safety, and fuel efficiency. Present your results.
2. What is the difference between a risk and an issue? Provide an example and explain your answer.

3. Why are KPIs not an effective information radiator for tracking progress at the sprint level? Explain your answer.
4. How do retrospectives support Agile and Lean values and principles? Explain your answer.
5. Why do teams go through the five stages of development? Describe each phase and its importance.

NOTES

1. K. Rubin, *Essential Scrum: A Practical Guide to the Most Popular Agile Process* (Boston, MA: Addison-Wesley Professional, 2012).
2. S. Howick and C. Eden, "Learning in Disrupted Projects: On the Nature of Corporate and Personal Learning," *International Journal of Production Research* 45, no. 12 (2007): 2775–2797.
3. Rubin, *Essential Scrum*.
4. Ibid.
5. J. W. Marion, *Project Management: A Common-Sense Guide to the PMBOK Program*, part 2, *Plan and Execution* (New York, NY: Momentum Press, 2019).
6. Ibid.
7. Rubin, *Essential Scrum*.

12 Preparing for Release

CHAPTER OVERVIEW

In chapter 12, we cover the release process, which extends beyond promoting code to production. In large corporate environments, launching a product or service can have significant operational workforce and workflow implications. Many large corporations are controlled environments. Service management frameworks such as ITIL are common amongst large organizations, so Agile release processes must align with service management best practices.

By the end of the chapter, readers will be familiar with the concepts of service management and controlled environments and how releases affect operational environments and strategies that can be employed to integrate Agile with service management frameworks.

THE CONTROLLED ENVIRONMENT

Many large and complex organizations are **controlled environments**, or organizations that manage **change** through governance. For large and complex organizations, a disruption to operations as a result of uncontrolled change can have significant implications. Retail stores that are unable to process sales, manufacturing and supply-chain organizations that have non-functional production lines, healthcare organizations that cannot register patients or order medications, and call centres that are unable to receive calls are all examples of controlled environments that have little tolerance for disruption.[1]

To ensure continuous operations, many organizations utilize a **service management** framework. **ITIL** (formerly the **Information Technology Infrastructure Library**), which was originally a publication of the United Kingdom government, is a framework that has become one of the leading standards for technology service management. Service management frameworks look to align services with business needs; they form the processes, procedures, tasks, and checklists that ensure business continuity and service stability. A service management framework should not be technology-specific but generic enough to be applied to numerous business contexts. Service management shares Lean values through the following:

- Ensuring services align with value
- Investing in people and ensuring role competency
- Forming a baseline to plan, implement, and measure
- Using empirical data to measure compliance and improvement[2]

When Agile is employed within large and complex organizations, releases intersect with service management. Agile projects cannot release to production without complying with service management requirements.

THE SERVICE MANAGEMENT FRAMEWORK

Although there are many service management frameworks that span numerous sectors, this text will focus on the aforementioned ITIL framework, which has two key components:

- ITIL service value system (SVS)
- Four-dimensional model

ITIL SVS follows a cycle similar to change management, project management, and Lean frameworks:

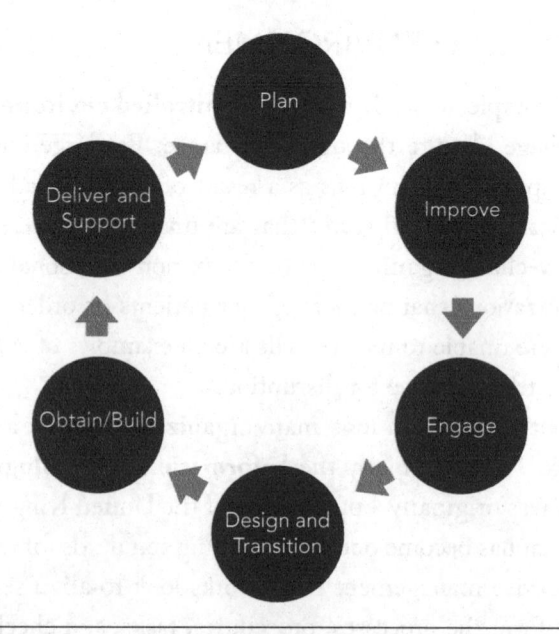

Figure 12.1 • ITIL Service Value System Cycle

Source: Adapted from C. Agutter, *ITIL 4 Essentials: Your Essential Guide for the ITIL 4 Foundation Exam and Beyond,* 2nd ed. (Cambridgeshire, UK: IT Governance, 2020).

To support the SVS cycle, ITIL has values that are also closely aligned with Lean and Agile philosophies:

- Focus on generating value directly or indirectly
- Maintain the good and improve where needed
- Progress through iterative incremental improvement with feedback
- Collaborate and be transparent
- Think and work holistically; take the long-range view
- Ensure solutions are practical and right-sized in their use of processes, tools, and resources
- Optimize and automate. Value people and use human intervention when absolutely necessary.[3]

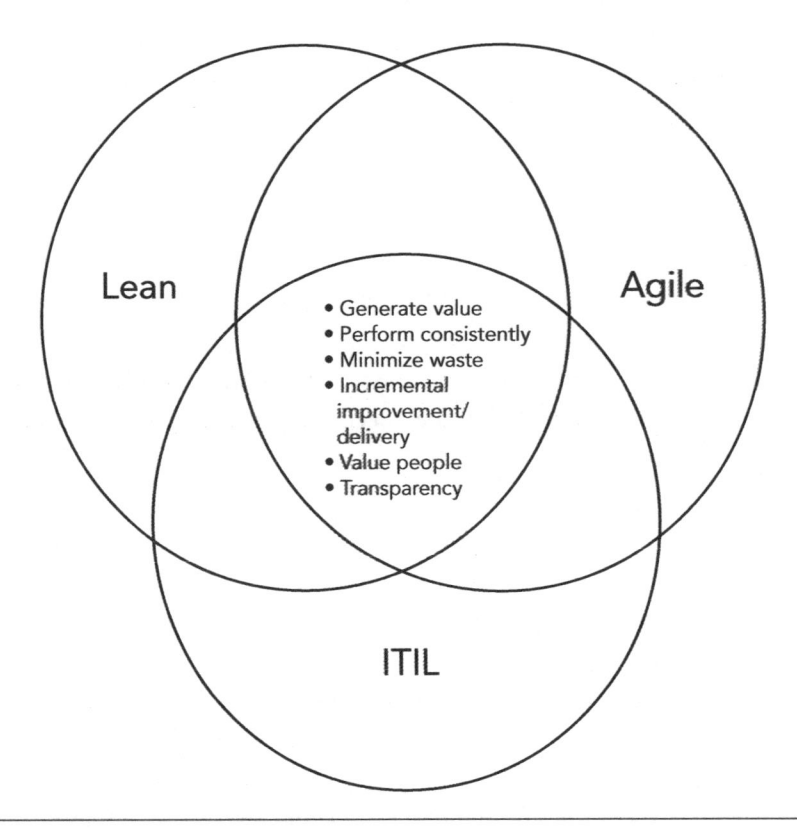

Figure 12.2 • Agile, Lean, ITIL Venn Diagram

To support the service management cycle and philosophies, ITIL uses a four-dimensional model called 4P.

People | Product
4Ps
Partners | Process

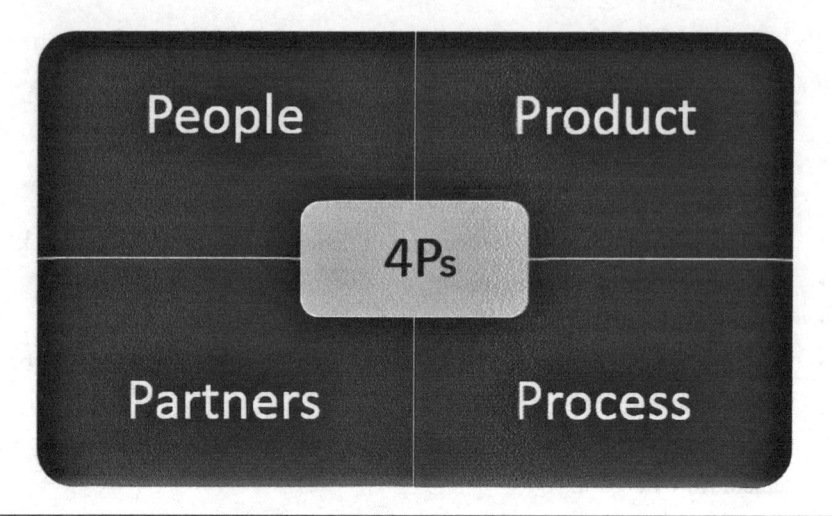

Figure 12.3 • ITIL Four-Dimensional Model

Source: Adapted from C. Agutter, *ITIL 4 Essentials: Your Essential Guide for the ITIL 4 Foundation Exam and Beyond*, 2nd ed. (Cambridgeshire, UK: IT Governance, 2020).

The 4Ps are the components that make up any service:

- The people who support the service
- The product(s) that make up the service.
- The processes that ensure service stability
- The partners that supply the service, whether as a whole or in part. This could include any one of the service components: product, people, or process.[4]

Overlaying the ITIL service value system and the 4Ps is **governance**, which is a framework or process that directs and controls an organization.

The role of governance in a large and complex environment is to ensure operations are not disrupted. Changes to a controlled environment are the largest contributor of **incidents,** which are events that disrupt operations, either affecting an organization's ability to perform a capability, or causing a decrease in service performance or a service interruption. Agile projects always deliver some form of change to an organization. Therefore, Agile teams in a large, complex environment likely need to create user stories, or user story subtasks, that align with the organizational governance standards.[5]

ITIL service management is built upon the IT service management (ITSM) framework, which is depicted in figure 12.4.

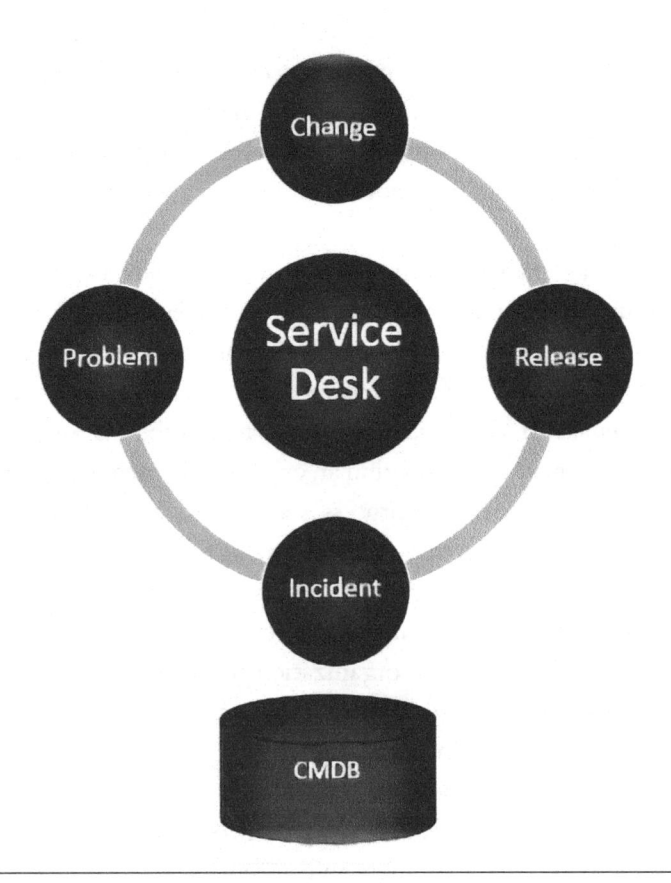

Figure 12.4 • IT Service Management Foundational Framework

Source: C. Agutter, *ITIL 4 Essentials: Your Essential Guide for the ITIL 4 Foundation Exam and Beyond*, 2nd ed. (Cambridgeshire, UK: IT Governance, 2020).

Service management frameworks focus on maintaining the stability of a system. There are common knowledge areas that help structure process groups to maintain system stability:

Change management—The processes that control changes being introduced to a controlled environment. Change management can also be referred to as change control. Change is usually overseen by a governing body such as a **change advisory board**, or **CAB**. CABs meet at regular intervals to review requested changes, ensure there are no change conflicts, and verify that the change requirements have been fulfilled so that the change can be approved to move to production.

Release management—The standards and processes associated with releasing a change into production. Release management includes ensuring the requisite planning and documentation has been completed. Completion of release activities is reviewed by a CAB prior to the board approving any release to production. Release management controls the release calendar, or list of approved changes that will move to production, the timing of each, and the teams responsible.

Incident management—The processes associated with identifying, recording, communicating, and resolving an issue or incident. This includes identifying criticality of a service and its components, communication standards, frequencies, and audiences when incidents occur. Escalation paths for resolution need to be established, and incident managers to lead the triage of major incidents that span numerous areas within an organization need to be identified.

Problem management—The processes associated with identifying recurring disturbances to a production environment that may not be attributable to a single incident or where root cause is unclear. Problem review boards (PRBs) meet at regular intervals to review recurring problems and work collaboratively across the organization to determine how best to investigate and determine root cause. Problems differ from incidents in that service usually remains available or was restored outside of standard incident-resolution processes.

Service desk—A central role in SVM frameworks. The service desk is the initial contact and triage for users and customers. The service desk intakes requests, logs them, and routes them to be completed by the appropriate team.

Configuration management database (CMDB)—A central repository that contains all information about an organization's services. This can include service description, documentation about the service such as training, troubleshooting, build books, vendor service-level agreements (SLAs), and contact information. In addition, the CMDB can include assets associated with the service, network information, and key customer and developer contacts, as well as internal operating-level agreements (OLAs).[6]

ITIL practices are divided into three categories:

- General management
- Service management
- Technical management[7]

In total, there are 34 ITIL practices or processes. Seventeen of the practices are related to service management. The service management practices can be categorized into three functions: proactive, reactive, and maintenance.

Chapter 12 • Preparing for Release

Table 12.1 • ITIL Service Management Processes Based on Categories

Proactive	Reactive	Maintenance
• Business analysis • Service design • Availability management • Capacity and performance management • Service continuity management • Monitoring and event management • Release management • Change control • Service validation and testing	• Service desk • Incident management • Service request management • Problem management	• Service catalogue management • Service-level management • Service configuration management • IT asset management

When considering releasing to production, Agile teams must be able to answer three core service questions, as detailed in figure 12.5. Each question has service management considerations. Agile teams must plan or prepare to address the questions and provide the artifacts that demonstrate the appropriate due diligence has been performed. Artifacts or deliverables related to the three service questions should be included in the definition of done and have dedicated subtasks or user stories that are completed as part of the sprint.

Can the service be requested/fulfilled?	Will disruptions be detected before the customer/user experiences it?	Can the service be fixed/rebuilt if it fails?
Service desk	Service design	Release management
Service request management	Availability management	Change control
Service catalogue management	Capacity and performance management	Incident management
Service-level management	Service continuity management	Service request management
Service validation and testing	Monitoring and event management	Problem management
Business analysis		
Service design		

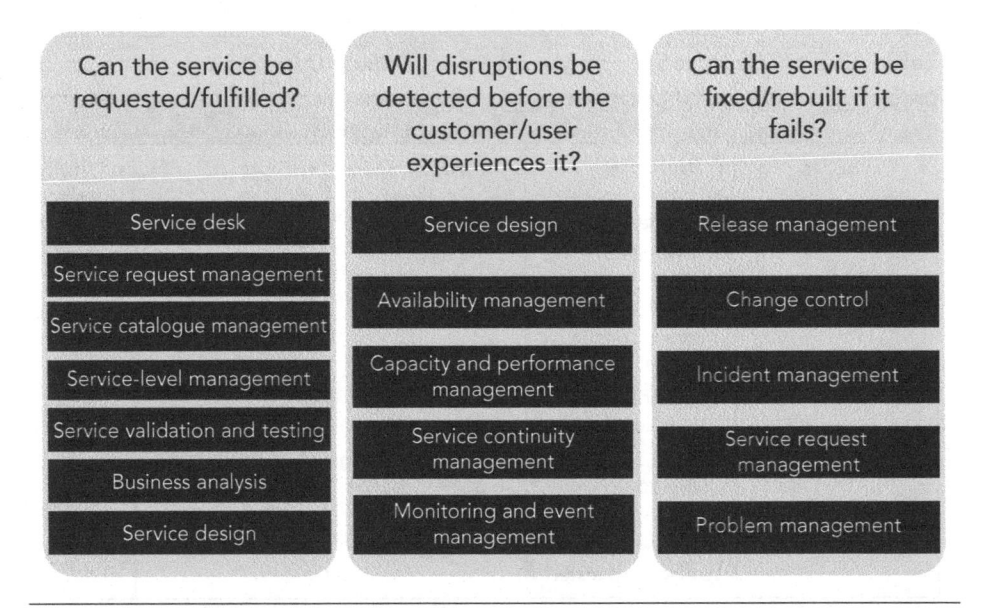

Figure 12.5 • Service Management Processes Aligned to Service Questions

Some of the ITIL practices span across questions and therefore appear multiple times. Projects that are unable to answer the questions may not be able to proceed to production.

Many of ITIL's proactive processes align with Agile methodologies. Service design, validation, and business analysis are all part of building user stories. Because Agile began in software development, its focus is often on coding. However, new processes, systems, and solutions often reside on infrastructure either in an organizational **data centre** or a **cloud environment**. Data centres and cloud environments provide the necessary technology infrastructure for solutions to operate. Data centres are often organizationally owned, while cloud environments are hosted by an external vendor. Proactive elements such as service capacity, availability, and monitoring and event management are often performed by infrastructure components of a solution.

Enterprise projects may have a dedicated infrastructure work stream or team members. Otherwise, these team members may be required as part of the development team to ensure the appropriate deliverables are created during sprints.

Deliverables to consider for key ITSM modules are outlined in table 12.2.

Because controlled environments may require a considerable number of deliverables, Agile teams can create dedicated release sprints. Release sprints are timeboxed sprints that ensure all service management requirements are fulfilled prior to release to production.

Table 12.2 • Common Service Management Deliverables for Release to Production

Release	Incident	Change	CMDB	Service Desk
• Run books • Release notes • Communications • Training • Troubleshooting guides	• Attributes created in incident management tools • Service monitoring in place • Service alerting in place • High availability tested • Business continuity plan in place and tested	• Change request completed • Change plan created • Change script created with roles, responsibilities, and contact information • Rollback plan in place if change fails	• SLAs • OLAs • Service description • Service asset information • Contact information • Service documentation • Networking information	• Attributes created to create request • Team queues created for request assignment • Troubleshooting guides • Communications • Support scripts • Contact information • Training

PRODUCTION SUPPORT

Once a product or service has been launched into production, a project team may be required to remain in place for a period of time—often called **a warranty period**—to support the release. During this time, a team remains co-located. However, instead of delivering new user stories for a sprint, development activities are paused to enable teams to resolve any escaped defects that have entered into production. Escaped defects are triaged through the service management framework and, once confirmed as a bug or defect, they are added to the backlog. Agile teams typically employ shorter cycles to resolve escaped defects to stabilize production as quickly as possible. Table 12.3 consolidates the various time-boxed activities covered throughout the text.

Issue Management

Prior to an issue being added to the development team's backlog, it must be confirmed by following an issue management process. Issue management frameworks are important because a number of factors can contribute to a user or customer experiencing challenges, only one of which is an actual defect.

Table 12.3 • Summary of Scrum Events and Activities

Activity	Duration	Frequency
Sprint	2 to 4 weeks	Variable, depending on how many sprints are required to fulfill a project backlog
Sprint planning	2 hours for each week of a sprint	Prior to the beginning of a sprint
Scrum or stand-up	15 minutes	Daily
Sprint review	1 hour for each week of a sprint	At the end of a sprint
Sprint retrospective	45 minutes for each week of a sprint	After the sprint review, prior to sprint planning
Committee review	30 minutes for each week of a sprint	At the mid-point of a sprint. Needed in matrix-managed environment where business lead time is scarce.
Spike stories	2 days	As needed
Release sprint	2 to 4 weeks	Prior to release, to ensure all release inputs have been completed
Warranty period	2 to 4 weeks	After launch
Grooming the backlog	20 percent of the sprint retrospective time	During sprint retrospective

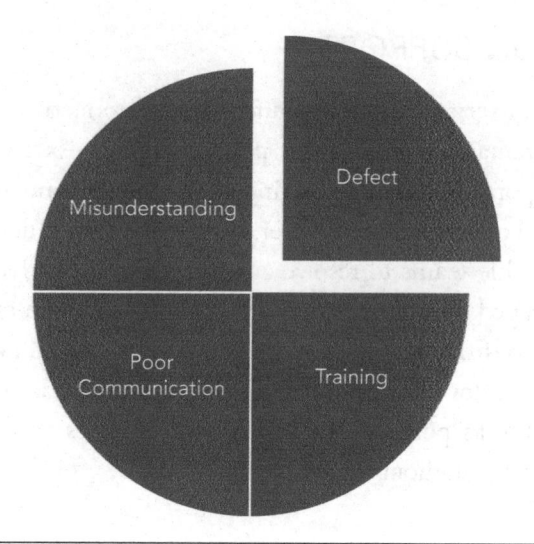

Figure 12.6 • Defect Share of Incidents

Development team time should not be spent on resolving training or communication issues with users or customers. The team's time should instead be focused on developing fixes for confirmed issues.

To confirm an issue, issue validation follows the cycle shown in figure 12.7.

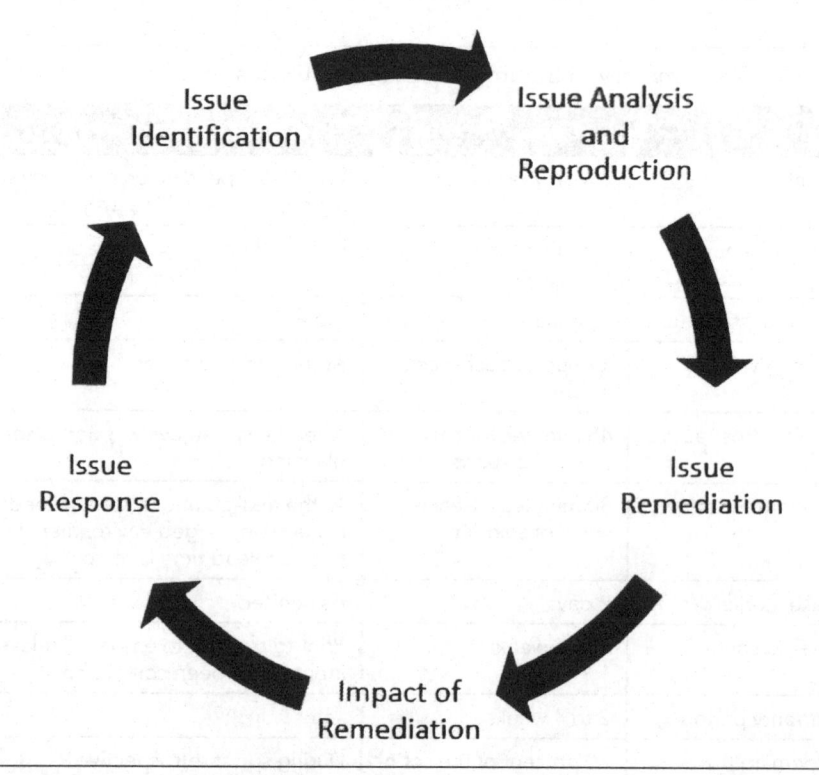

Figure 12.7 • Issue Management Cycle

Issues need to be reproduced so they can be isolated. Once issues are isolated, the root cause can be found and remediation strategies can commence. After issue remediation is complete, plans to promote fixes to production follow standard service management practices.

> **Case Study 12.1 • Planning for Live Support**
>
> Imran knew that support would be a challenge. The healthcare organization Imran was working for employed more than seven thousand employees, and these employees were not accustomed to using technology as part of their workflow. Compounding the challenge, the organization operated on a 24/7 schedule and needed to be supported during all times of the day.
>
> Leading up to go-live, Imran engaged his sponsor to use temporary support workers. Workers could be used to test the team's work as well as pilot the training program. Once familiarized with the tool, the workers could be deployed strategically to provide "at the elbow" support for users. Providing this level of support would help eliminate training issues and isolate escaped defects.
>
> Temporary workers would also be used to staff the service desk and triage support calls. The service desk would deploy "at the elbow" support to triage the issue at the point where it was occurring. This was to be done prior to escalating to the development team. The sponsor agreed and more than two hundred temporary workers were hired for the warranty period of launch.
>
> During the first 72 hours of launch, more than a thousand issues were logged. However, 95 percent of the issues were attributed to training, and only 5 percent were assigned to the development team.

The Role of DevOps in Agile Projects

DevOps is a growing function that helps organizations bridge between development and operations functions. In Agile frameworks, DevOps teams can often be a hand-off point from development teams to operations. Development teams create functioning code or products through Agile methodologies. DevOps teams validate the development team's output to ensure it can be safely deployed to a production technology ecosystem.

DevOps functions can include the following:

- Packaging the product into an automated installer that can be deployed to users and customers
- Validating installation
- Automating deployment and removal technologies
- Validating product compatibility on a variety of platforms
- Validating that product does not conflict with other applications currently deployed
- Load-testing to ensure production environments can support additional traffic, network or otherwise, that will be generated by the new product[8]

DevOps teams also ensure segregation of duties. In a controlled environment, development teams may not have access to production. This can help ensure that escaped defects do not accidentally get promoted to production. Having a DevOps function affords production environments an additional layer of security from an independent group charged with ensuring service stability.

DevOps teams support service management frameworks and, in some cases, can be leveraged to help create release deliverables to meet change control requirements. They are often an escalation point prior to assigning incidents to the development team. This is because DevOps teams often have automated diagnostic and validation tools that can help isolate issues.

Due to their experience with platform and infrastructure, DevOps teams are often engaged to assist with the technology management aspects of the service management framework. They can be leveraged to interface between the infrastructure teams, the development team, and service management teams.

In non-Agile environments, DevOps can function similarly to a development team, as they can be characterized by the following:

- Rapid development and deployment
- The leveraging of automated tools for verification
- Continual integration for code

Figure 12.8 illustrates the DevOps cycle and where DevOps teams complement Agile methods.

This chapter is only a summary of service management and controlled environments. The goal of introducing service management in this text is to create awareness of service management frameworks and their potential impact to Agile teams. Additional detail about service management can be found in numerous resources that specialize on the topic.

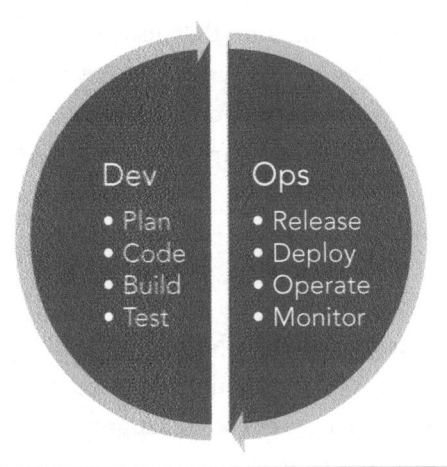

Figure 12.8 • DevOps Cycle

SUMMARY

- Many large and complex environments utilize service management frameworks to ensure service stability.
- Large, complex environments are often controlled environments, where there is a layer of governance that ensures no changes are made to a production environment until they have been reviewed and approved.
- Service management frameworks, such as ITIL, often have cycles that overlap with Agile and Lean, making them complementary.
- Service management frameworks often have standard deliverables and functions that need to be satisfied prior to a project launching into a controlled environment.
- Service management frameworks often have proactive functions—which align with Agile project deliverables—and reactive functions—which identify production issues. Production issues can result in new user stories that development teams will add to future releases.
- Because service management deliverables must be completed prior to launch, Agile teams can dedicate a release sprint to ensure all service management deliverables have been completed prior to launch.
- Issue management practices follow a cycle of reproduction, isolation, and resolution. The first two of these steps are completed by service management functions. Once an issue has been reproduced and isolated, it can be assigned to a development team. This process helps ensure development teams are working on known defects, rather than triaging other issues contributing to incidents, such as training.

- DevOps is a growing function that acts as a bridge between Agile teams and production. DevOps performs a variety of functions to ensure new products and services do not conflict with a production environment. DevOps teams often have a variety of tools that help ensure production stability.

KEY TERMS

CAB: an acronym for change advisory board

change: a new feature, fix, or product being introduced to a controlled environment

change advisory board: a change review and approval governance committee that meets at regular intervals to review requested changes and provides approval before changes are introduced to a controlled environment

cloud environment: technology infrastructure that is owned and operated by an external vendor that hosts a product or service

CMDB: an acronym for configuration management database

configuration management database: a central repository that contains all information about an organization's services

controlled environment: an organization that manages change through governance

data centre: technology infrastructure, often organizationally owned, that hosts a product or service

DevOps: a growing function that helps organizations bridge between development and operations functions

governance: a framework or process that directs and controls an organization

incident: an event that disrupts operations, either affecting an organization's ability to perform a capability, or causing a decrease in service performance or a service interruption

incident management: the processes associated with identifying, recording, communicating, and resolving an issue or incident

Information Technology Infrastructure Library: originally a publication of the United Kingdom government, this has become one of the leading standards for technology service management.

ITIL: an acronym for Information Technology Infrastructure Library

problem management: the processes associated with identifying recurring disturbances to a production environment that may not be attributable to a single incident, or where root cause is unclear

release management: the standards and processes associated with releasing a change into production

service desk: a central role in service management frameworks. The service desk is the initial contact and triage for users and customers. The service desk intakes requests, logs them, and routes them to be completed by the appropriate team.

service management: the processes, procedures, tasks, and checklists to ensure business continuity and service stability. Service management aligns services with business needs.

warranty period: a time after product launch when a project team remains co-located. Instead of delivering new user stories for a sprint, development activities are paused to enable teams to resolve any escaped defects that have entered into production.

DISCUSSION QUESTIONS

1. What is the difference between a problem and an incident? Explain your answer.
2. Explain the challenges Agile teams have building release deliverables into their sprints and why a release sprint could be required.
3. Do processes that govern change contribute to customer value? Explain your answer.
4. What is the difference between a release and a change? Explain your answer.
5. Describe a warranty period. Why is it important? What is its function?

NOTES

1. C. Agutter, *ITIL 4 Essentials: Your Essential Guide for the ITIL 4 Foundation Exam and Beyond*, 2nd ed. (Cambridgeshire, UK: IT Governance, 2020).
2. Ibid.
3. Ibid.
4. Ibid.
5. Ibid.
6. Ibid.
7. Ibid.
8. S. Vadapalli, *DevOps: Continuous Delivery, Integration, and Deployment with DevOps* (Birmingham, UK: Packt, 2018).

Appendix • A Summary of Tools and Techniques

AGILE PROJECT CHARTER TEMPLATE (SEE P. 49)

Project Name	Name of the Project
Project Vision	Describes why the project exists Example for a healthcare organization: • To improve the delivery of care services by harnessing the power of technology
Project Mission	Describes what will be done to achieve the project's mission Example for a healthcare organization: • To leverage best practices from similar organizations to guide decision-making and implementation
Project Success Criteria	Describes the factors that will contribute to project success Example for a healthcare organization: • A reduction in medication errors • A reduction in wait times • Improved bed turnaround when unoccupied

STAKEHOLDER LOG TEMPLATE (SEE P. 52)

Project Name	Name of the Project			
Stakeholder Name	Stakeholder Department	Processes Supported	Processes Owned
John Accounting	Finance	Payroll	Reporting

VALUE STREAM MAP TEMPLATE (SEE P. 67)

	Department - Process - Date of Validation
Department 1	
Department 2	
Department 3	

- Process
- Data Transmission
- Pre-Defined Process
- Decision Box
- Data Repository
- Start/End
- Manual Document
- Opportunity

ENTERPRISE USER STORY TEMPLATE (SEE P. 76)

User Story Template

Department	Process	Process Owner	User Story Name	Current System (System Name/ Manual/NA)	Type (Function, Validation, Reporting)	Description	Verification	Kano Scale	Priority (Must Have, Should Have, Could Have, Won't Have)	Transportation	Waiting	Overproduction	Defects	Inventory	Movement	Extra processing
Organizational department	Process the story supports	Process owner or customer to have follow-up discussions if needed	Name of story	How the requirement is being fulfilled in the current state	The goal of the story to fulfill a function, action, validation, or report	User story template: As a: <User> I want to: <some goal> So that I can: <some reason>	How the development team will know whether they fulfilled the story	Need Want Delighter	MH, SH, CH, WH							

RECOMMENDED FIELD MAPPINGS FOR USER STORY TEMPLATE (SEE P. 89)

Field Name	Mapping	Type
Department	Component	Create a component per department
Process	Custom field	Text value (single line)
Process owner	Custom field	Text value (single line)
User story name	Summary	Standard
Current system	Custom field	Text value (single line)
Type	Custom field	Select list (single choice): function, report, validation
Description	Description	Standard
Verification	Custom field	Text value (multi-line)
Kano scale	Custom field	Select list (single choice): need, want, delighter
MoSCoW	Custom field	Select list (single choice): MH, SH, CH, WH
Affinity mapping	Custom field	Select list (single choice): XS, S, M, L, XL

SAMPLE AGILE PROJECT BUDGET (SEE P. 126)

Resource	Loaded Rate	Hour Allocation	Weekly Cost	Sprint Cost
Resource 1	$80	20	$1,600	$6,400
Resource 2	$100	30	$3,000	$12,000
Resource 3	$120	40	$4,800	$19,200
Resource 4	$80	40	$3,200	$12,800
Resource 5	$80	20	$1,600	$6,400
Resource 6	$60	15	$900	$3,600
Total	$520	165	$15,100	$60,400

DEFINITION OF DONE CHECKLIST (SEE P. 144)

Definition of Done	
User story configured and loaded with no errors	
User story peer-reviewed	
User story tested	
User story support document created	
User story training material created	
User story reviewed and approved	

TERMS OF REFERENCE TEMPLATE (SEE P. 173)

Sample Terms of Reference
The X committee will meet at X frequency. The goal of the X committee is to: Membership shall include: • Chair: • Vice chair: • X voting members Meetings will: • Have an agenda distributed a minimum of 48 hours prior to the meeting Members commit to: • Come to the meeting prepared • Actively participate in discussion • Make timely decisions • Be supportive and open to negotiation Decisions will be prioritized by: • Legal and regulatory requirements • Organizational policy • Industry best practices • Customer value • Vendor recommendation   If a vote is required, there must be quorum, which would require X voting members to be present.

AGILE EARNED VALUE CONCEPTS AND FORMULAE (SEE P. 193)

Earned Value Concept	Formula
Product backlog in points	Sum of backlog story points
Baseline velocity	Sum of story points the team can complete per sprint
Cost per story point	(Resource time × rate) / story points
Planned story release points or PSRP	Sum of all story points that make up the project / product backlog
Expected percent complete or EPC	Current sprint / total planned sprints
Actual percent complete or APC	Story points completed / total planned story points
Budget at completion or BAC	PSRP × cost per story point
Planned number of iterations	Product backlog / baseline velocity

SPRINT RETROSPECTIVE PRE-MEETING TEMPLATE (SEE P. 222)

What went well?	What did not go well?	What would you change?	How would you change it?	What is still unclear?

USER STORY SCORING BASED ON UNCERTAINTY AND DEPENDENCY (SEE P. 228)

Story	Weight	Story 1	Story 2	Story 3	Story 4	Story 5
Priority	50%	9	3	9	6	1
Uncertainty	25%	9	9	1	3	9
Dependency	25%	9	3	1	9	1
Risk score	**100%**	9	4.5	5	6	3

Appendix • A Summary of Tools and Techniques

COMMON SERVICE MANAGEMENT DELIVERABLES FOR RELEASE TO PRODUCTION (SEE P. 242)

Release	Incident	Change	CMDB	Service Desk
• Run books • Release notes • Communications • Training • Troubleshooting guides	• Attributes created in incident management tools • Service monitoring in place • Service alerting in place • High availability tested • Business continuity plan in place and tested	• Change request completed • Change plan created • Change script created with roles, responsibilities, and contact information • Rollback plan in place if change fails	• SLAs • OLAs • Service description • Service asset information • Contact information • Service documentation • Networking information	• Attributes created to create requests • Team queues created for request assignment • Troubleshooting guides • Communications • Support scripts • Contact information • Training

SUMMARY OF SCRUM EVENTS AND ACTIVITIES (SEE P. 243)

Activity	Duration	Frequency
Sprint	2 to 4 weeks	Variable, depending on how many sprints are required to fulfill a project backlog
Sprint planning	2 hours for each week of a sprint	Prior to the beginning of a sprint
Scrum or stand-up	15 minutes	Daily
Sprint review	1 hour for each week of a sprint	At the end of a sprint
Sprint retrospective	45 minutes for each week of a sprint	After the sprint review, prior to sprint planning
Committee review	30 minutes for each week of a sprint	At the mid-point of a sprint. Needed in matrix-managed environment where business lead time is scarce.
Spike stories	2 days	As needed
Release sprint	2 to 4 weeks	Prior to release, to ensure all release inputs have been completed
Warranty period	2 to 4 weeks	After launch
Grooming the backlog	20 percent of the sprint retrospective time	During sprint retrospective

Glossary of Terms

accommodating negotiation approach: a negotiation approach that yields to the customer

adaptive project management: refers to using iterations to incrementally progress toward a project outcome

ADKAR: a change management acronym representing change management milestones developed by Prosci. ADKAR stands for Awareness, Desire, Knowledge, Ability, and Reinforcement.

affinity estimation: an estimation technique that quickly groups user stories into size categories; also known as T-shirt sizing or estimation

Agile contracting: the use of a time and materials procurement approach to acquiring Agile resources

Agile Manifesto: a document created by 17 developers in 2001 that forms the basis of the Agile methodology values and principles

Agile project charter: a document that authorizes an Agile project's existence, the work, and allocation of resources. An Agile project charter only provides high-level guidance to a project team, such as the project vision, mission, and success criteria. It helps focus the work and provides a shared purpose for the Agile project team.

asynchronous communication: team members see and contribute information at different times.

backlog: a prioritized list of user stories

backlog creation: a phase in the Agile project lifecycle where the Agile project team works on creating a backlog for the project

bottleneck: work accumulating without being completed in a timely manner. This can happen at the resource or team level.

breakout session: a focused team meeting designed to resolve a specific problem or issue

burndown chart: a chart that shows the amount of work left to complete versus the time remaining

burnup chart: a chart that depicts work completed versus scope goal

CAB: an acronym for change advisory board

C-FORC: an acronym that outlines desired behaviours among self-organizing teams: Commitment to success, Focus on excellent work, Openness about concerns, Respect by sharing success and failures, Courage to undertake great challenges

change: a new feature, fix, or product being introduced to a controlled environment

change advisory board: a change review and approval governance committee that meets at regular intervals to review requested changes and provides approval before changes are introduced to a controlled environment

change management: the activities necessary to ensure the implementation of new capabilities, functions, processes, and tools is successful

cloud environment: technology infrastructure that is owned and operated by an external vendor that hosts a product or service

CMDB: an acronym for configuration management database

co-design: the approach of actively involving all stakeholders in the design process to help ensure the design outcome is usable

collaborating negotiation approach: team members are free to negotiate a user story. The goal of this approach is to achieve a win-win outcome.

collaboration: a process mapping technique where project team members work with subject-matter experts to create a process map. The collaboration approach is used when observation is not viable.

co-located team: a team sharing a single space

committee: a collection of stakeholders that provides direction and decision-making for development teams

cone of uncertainty: the tendency for estimates to have less variability as a project progresses towards its goal

configuration management database: a central repository that contains all information about an organization's services

continuous improvement: an organization's ongoing effort to improve products, services, and/or processes. Continuous improvement can refer to incremental improvement over time as well as breakthrough improvement all at once.

continuous integration: the XP concept of regular code check-ins. For non-software development projects, this may refer to regular upload or sharing of work deliverables on a shared repository.

control limit: a numerical limit on the quantity of work in progress (WIP) tasks. It can be applied at the resource or team level.

controlled environment: an organization that manages change through governance

cross-functional: refers to a team that is composed of a number of skill sets and business backgrounds

Crystal: a software development methodology that is part of the Agile methodology family

current state process: captures how an organization performs an existing process

data centre: technology infrastructure, often organizationally owned, that hosts a product or service

dedicated/projectized teams: resources that are fully allocated to a project

definition of done: the set of criteria that must be met for a user story to be considered complete

dependency: a condition that must be satisfied before the next step can begin

development team: a project team member who directly contributes to the completion of deliverables

DevOps: a growing function that helps organizations bridge between development and operations functions

direct costs: costs that can be tied directly to the production of a product or service. In an Agile project, a direct cost is the resource labour but could include equipment such as the computers resources use to perform their work.

distributed team: team members are located in different geographies or different locations within a building.

DSDM: an acronym for Dynamic Systems Development Method

Dynamic Systems Development Method: an Agile framework that focuses on completing the minimum work required to move to subsequent steps and phases

earned value management: a traditional project management technique that uses mathematical formulas to both track and forecast project performance

elaborating: development team members learning more about user stories so they can validate their estimates and complete their work to meet customer expectations

epic: large body of work that can be broken down into a smaller collection of activities or stories

event: significant Scrum activity. There are four common Scrum events: sprint planning, scrum or the daily stand-up, sprint review, and sprint retrospective.

EVM: an acronym for earned value management

Extreme Programming: an Agile software methodology

failing fast: teams quickly identifying if they are off track. Failing fast enables teams to cut their losses and adapt.

feedback cycle: an iterative feedback approach that helps teams elaborate stakeholder needs and build change management capabilities in stakeholders

Fibonacci series: a series of numbers where each number in the series represents the sum of the previous two numbers

fields: a JQL search component. Fields available within Jira include Priority, Story Points, and Assigned To.

five whys: an iterative interrogative technique that explores the cause-and-effect relationships of a particular problem

flat organization: an organization with few or no levels of management between staff

functional manager: responsible for a collection of processes within an organization. In Agile, a functional manager supports the creation of the measurable success criteria and supplies resources for the project.

future state process: once a value stream is analyzed, the project team proposes an optimized process model referred to as the future state.

gamification: the application of video game elements to non-game concepts to help drive team engagement, performance, and behaviours

gemba walk: a process discovery technique where project team members go to where the process occurs and observe the process in action

genchi genbutsu: a Japanese term for "go and see (or confirm)"

governance: a framework or process that directs and controls an organization

grooming the backlog: a process where the team reviews the product backlog and makes adjustments to user stories and their priority based on knowledge acquired through sprint completion and sprint reviews

hierarchical organization: an organization with multiple layers of management. Workers are organized under each layer. Each layer usually specializes in performing a specific function for an organization such as finance, marketing, etc.

hybrid team: a team that has some dedicated resources and some resources supplied through matrix management

ideal time: an estimating technique that assigns an hour value based on the ideal time it would take to complete a user story. Ideal time is time that is uninterrupted and completely focused on work. It assumes that everything a resource needs to complete a user story is readily available.

incident: an event that disrupts operations, either affecting an organization's ability to perform a capability, or causing a decrease in service performance or a service interruption

incident management: the processes associated with identifying, recording, communicating, and resolving an issue or incident

indirect costs: costs that are not tied directly to project activity but are incurred by the project. This could include items such as insurance, utilities, or rent.

information radiator: a visual display with critical team and project progress information that is updated regularly and strategically located so a team can regularly refer to it

Information Technology Infrastructure Library: originally a publication of the United Kingdom government, this has become one of the leading standards for technology service management.

initiative: a collection of epics and/or stories that help a team drive towards a common goal. Initiatives can be synonymous with a project or new product introduction.

INVEST: an acronym that provides the attributes that define high-quality user stories: independent, negotiable, valuable, can be estimated, small, and testable

iron triangle: the dynamic that causes modification to one of the three constraints (cost, scope, and time) to affect the other constraints. Also known as the triple constraint.

issue type user stories: user stories that are specific actions the development team needs to take to resolve the identified issue or bug

iteration: a short cycle where work is performed

iterative methodology: usually characterized by a number of iteration cycles to produce an outcome. Agile is an iterative methodology.

ITIL: an acronym for Information Technology Infrastructure Library

jidoka: a Japanese term that strives to minimize defects from occurring by fixing the defect-causing behaviour at its source

Jira: a specialized software tool designed for managing Agile projects

JQL: a search language used in Jira to build custom filters. JQL comprises fields, operators, values, and keywords.

kaizen: a Japanese term meaning "to make good." Used in conjunction with a continuous improvement action.

Kanban: developed by Taiichi Ohno, *Kanban* is a Japanese term that means signal or "card you can see." Kanban is a visual management technique used to improve the flow of work and minimize work in progress.

Kano model: a product-development and customer-satisfaction approach that categorizes satisfaction into must-be or needs qualities, one-dimensional or wants qualities, and attractive or delighter qualities

key performance indicator: a measure that indicates the health of a project and team performance

keywords: specific words in JQL that help further refine searches by combining fields and values. Common examples are AND, OR, and IS.

KPI: an acronym for key performance indicator

Lean: a continuous improvement framework developed by Taiichi Ohno for the Toyota motor company

learning curve: a representation of the growth in team efficiency as a result of experience

loaded cost: the resource's hourly rate including an amount that represents the resource's impact on indirect costs

matrix management: organizational structures where resources report to multiple managers. This can also be referred to as dotted line reporting. This approach is common amongst large and complex organizations.

mid-course correction: the application of changes to the original plan to ensure the project still achieves customer value

minimum marketable product: the minimum set of requirements that a product must meet to achieve value

MMP: an acronym for minimum marketable product

MoSCoW: an acronym that breaks requirements into categories: must have, could have, should have, and won't have

muda: a Japanese term for waste. This form of waste refers to activities that do not directly contribute to customer value.

mura: a Japanese term for waste. This form of waste refers to unevenness or inconsistency in outcome or result.

muri: a Japanese term that refers to waste caused by overstressing people, equipment, and systems

niko-niko chart or calendar: an information radiator that captures the mood of each team member at the end of each day

observation: a process mapping technique where project teams observe a process in action. This can be done through job shadowing or by physically attending when the process occurs.

office hours: dedicated timeboxes set up to answer development team questions

operators: a JQL search component that provides direction to a query. Common operators include equals (=), does not equal (!=), and is less than or greater than (< >).

organizational decomposition: a process that facilitates breaking organizations into discrete functions and processes. Organizational decomposition enables a project to get closer to the end-user or customer as well as the service owner or process owner.

osmotic communication: knowledge being acquired by hearing team member conversations and informal team interaction

pair programming: the XP concept that partners two development team members together during user story execution

parking lot chart: a chart that displays the overall completion progress of the stories that are part of a theme or epic

Parkinson's law: stipulates that work expands to fill the time available for its completion

participatory decision-making: organizations identifying the degree to which employees will inform organizational decisions

PDM: an acronym for participatory decision-making

personal safety: the ability to speak about work without fear of ridicule. Part of the Crystal methodology values.

pivoting: the act of a team adapting and selecting a new approach based on failing fast

plan-do-check-act (PDCA)/plan-do-study-act (PDSA): an iterative process developed by Walter Shewhart to implement short projects quickly to help improve quality

planning onion: refers to the layers associated to strategic project planning

planning poker: an Agile estimation technique that uses cards arranged in a Fibonacci series. Participants use the cards to assign a value to a user story. The process is iterative until a consensus is reached.

PMI: an acronym for the Project Management Institute

predictive project management: the process of collecting information and building a plan, budget, and schedule based on known requirements and designs

problem management: the processes associated with identifying recurring disturbances to a production environment that may not be attributable to a single incident, or where root cause is unclear

process owner: an individual responsible for a specific process within an organization. In Agile, a process owner supports defining the measurable success criteria of a project and can be part of the development team.

product owner: an Agile team member that is responsible for defining user stories and prioritizing the team backlog. The product owner organizationally owns the product and outcome of the Agile project.

progressive elaboration: refers to uncertainty being reduced as a project progresses throughout its lifecycle

Project Management Institute: a non-profit organization that oversees a credentialling process for project management and publishes the *Project Management*

Body of Knowledge (*PMBOK*). It was established in the late 1960s to help improve project delivery consistency in physical engineering sectors.

Prosci: an organization like PMI and the Agile Alliance that specializes in furthering individual and organizational change management capabilities

release: represents functionality being made for broader use. This could refer to customer use or making functionality readily available to other projects or members of a project team.

release date: a defined point in time when functionality is made available

release goal: the conditions a release must fulfill to achieve its business objective

release management: the standards and processes associated with releasing a change into production

request for proposal: a formal purchase request to qualified vendors. It typically represents a commitment that an organization will be looking to purchase a solution or services to achieve a business need.

RFP: an acronym for request for proposal

risk: an uncertain event that could emerge as an issue that impacts a project. Risks that become issues usually affect the project's triple constraint.

scope creep: the unauthorized addition of user stories to a sprint or backlog

scrum: one of the four Scrum events, a timeboxed activity conducted at a set time when all team members meet to review sprint progress. The scrum is facilitated by the scrum master. It typically occurs daily and is meant to be short in duration.

scrum master: the facilitator of the Agile methodology. The scrum master does not directly perform or manage the work; they ensure that Agile principles are followed and coach and mentor the team to work in an Agile way.

scrum of scrums: a scrum where designates from multiple Agile teams review their collective team progress and review shared issues and dependencies

SDLC: an acronym for the software development lifecycle

seconded: resources that are supplied to the project from another function within the organization. A seconded resource is typically a dedicated project resource.

servant leader: a leader who puts employees at the centre of decision-making by sharing power and ensuring employees achieve their maximum potential

service desk: a central role in service management frameworks. The service desk is the initial contact and triage for users and customers. The service desk intakes request, logs them, and routes them to be completed by the appropriate team.

service management: the processes, procedures, tasks, and checklists to ensure business continuity and service stability. Service management aligns services with business needs.

service manager: a manager responsible for a collection of functions within an organization. The service manager supports the creation of the project vision and mission, facilitates the measurable success criteria of an Agile project, and can supply resources.

service owner: an executive responsible for a collection of functions within an organization. In Agile the service owner is responsible for the vision and mission of the project, and signs off on the project success criteria. The closest parallel to a service owner is an executive sponsor for a waterfall project.

seven forms of waste: Lean's waste categories: transportation waste, waiting waste, overproduction waste, defect waste, inventory waste, movement waste, extra processing waste

silo: a closed management system that does not interact or operate with other silos, or divisions, within an organization

skilled generalists: resources that are interchangeable and can "stand in" to perform multiple functions on a project.

software development lifecycle: a project management approach to deliver software projects. This process was commonly used prior to the Agile methodology and is still in use today. The software development lifecycle uses a waterfall approach.

spike story: a timeboxed period that enables teams to reduce uncertainty through elaboration. Spike stories do not have story points.

sprint: a pre-determined timebox where a number of working features are developed

sprint backlog: the backlog items to be completed specifically during a sprint.

sprint goal: the goal of the specific iteration. The sprint goal helps a team create a sprint backlog.

sprint planning: one of the four Scrum events, a phase of the Agile project lifecycle. It is a collaborative activity between Agile team members to determine the work to be completed during the upcoming sprint.

sprint retrospective: one of the four Scrum events, an activity where the team reflects on the previous sprint and discusses what can be done to improve future sprints.

sprint review: one of the four Scrum events, a meeting to review the user stories the development team has completed. The audience of a sprint review is typically the customer or stakeholders.

stakeholder: any person impacted by the project outcome. Stakeholders can be part of the project team, internal or external to an organization.

stakeholder log: a log used to capture and categorize internal stakeholders based on their department, process owners, and organizational processes they support but do not own

story points: a point system used for user stories. Points are assigned to a user story based on its complexity. The more time it will take to complete a user story, the more points it will receive.

swim lanes: a visual representation of cross-functional process interaction

synchronous communication: all team members meet and communicate in real time.

tasks: the items that need to be completed for the user story to meet the definition of done criteria

TDD: an acronym for test-driven development

terms of reference: a document that helps guide committee purpose, ground rules for interaction, and decision-making criteria

test-driven development: a process that requires the verification criteria to be created before the code

theme: large focus area that spans the organization. A theme can focus on process improvement or innovation. Projects that fit within these categories are listed under the appropriate theme.

time and materials contract: an agreement between customer and vendor where vendor resources charge a fixed hourly rate along with any material cost associated with work completion

timebox: a fixed unit of time that cannot be exceeded

ToR: an acronym for terms of reference

triple constraint: the dynamic that causes modification to one of the three constraints (cost, scope, and time) to affect the other constraints. Also known as the iron triangle.

Tuckman stages of group development: the five stages of development—forming, storming, norming, performing, and adjourning—developed by Bruce Tuckman in 1965

user: any person who will directly interact with the project outcome

user story: a short, simple description of a feature or requirement told from the perspective of the person who will benefit from the new capability. Also a phase of the Agile project lifecycle.

value stream mapping: a Lean management technique that is used to identify process waste

values: a JQL search component. Values are the actual data in the query, such as the search field must equal a certain value.

velocity: the amount of work a team can complete within a given sprint. Velocity can be measured in hours or story points and should be based on empirical or historical data.

velocity-driven planning: an empirical approach to using team velocity, or story points completed during a sprint, to inform sprint planning and number of iterations that may be needed to achieve a release goal

vendor product owner: a vendor designate in a purchased product or solution scenario. The vendor product owner is the most knowledgeable project resource about the product and/or services purchased. However, they may lack organizational context and will need to be partnered with a business representative.

visual management: a management technique that displays expectations, performance, standards, or warnings in a way that requires little or no training to understand what the display is conveying

warranty period: a time after product launch when a project team remains colocated. Instead of delivering new user stories for a sprint, development activities are paused to enable teams to resolve any escaped defects that have entered into production.

waterfall methodologies: project management approach that is more linear in nature than iterative approaches. Each step in the delivery process is dependent on the previous. If deliverables are not complete it could delay the start of the next phase.

weighted factor model: the approach of applying weights to different categories such as risk, priority, and dependency to adjust the overall score of a user story. This helps team prioritize user stories based on a variety of factors for future sprints.

WFM: an acronym for weighted factor model

wideband Delphi: an interactive approach to estimation whose goal is to achieve consensus amongst its participants. Planning poker is based on the wideband Delphi approach.

wisdom of the crowd: a decision-making approach that leverages the collective input of a group of individuals rather than a single expert

workaround: an ad-hoc process that can be used operationally in the absence of an automated solution

XP: an acronym for Extreme Programming

zone of success: a threshold that identifies how much deviation from plan can be tolerated before a project will not achieve customer value